Dorothy's Daughter
in the Land of Oz

Dorothy's Daughter
in the Land of Oz

Marlyn Butler Evers

ISBN: 0692892508
ISBN 13: 9780692892503
Library of Congress Control Number: 2017947276
Carissimi Opera Publishing, LLC
P. O. Box 368, McKinney, TX 75070

Dedication

I started writing just to record my memories for my children and grandchildren to read and know some history of their family. As I wrote, however, I started remembering more and more about Norton and the people I knew when growing up, and I began to realize that I became who I am because of growing up in Norton. Every person I knew affected me and helped me grow. This has become a letter of appreciation to the people and the town of Norton, Kansas.

I know that every person has memories and stories, and they may differ from my recollections, but all I can do is tell what I experienced, plus add some tales from my classmates. I apologize if I have forgotten anyone and if I have misspelled any names. I appreciate all my Norton classmates and friends who have given me so many memories and who have shared some of their memories and stories with me.

If the 'time line' of the book seems disjointed, I confess that I have always had a difficult time trying to file anything to a single location...there are so many possibilities: name, topic, situation, time. I write as I file. Thoughts seem to mushroom into other thoughts like fractals. In life, everything comes out of something else, and the weaving together of the fabric of our lives creates the whole of who we are.

I do thank my family for their patience and support in writing this book, as well as their encouragement to keep writing. I especially give credit to my daughter, Pamela, for her knowledge and help in editing, formatting text, and scanning photos.

Contents

KALEIDOSCOPE OF LIFE

By Marlyn Butler Evers

Hour by hour the days go by
Sometimes too many, often too few
Anticipation turns into remember
As perfection surrenders to "that's all I can do"

Play the song slower, I cry
What's the hurry?
New songs become old songs
High tide yields to low

Premieres wind toward final performances
Ingénues receive lifetime awards
Yesterday's tears dissolve into quiet acceptance
As each day becomes another yesterday

The wheel turns, we mark the years
Then sing Auld Lang Syne

DOROTHY'S DAUGHTER IN THE LAND OF OZ

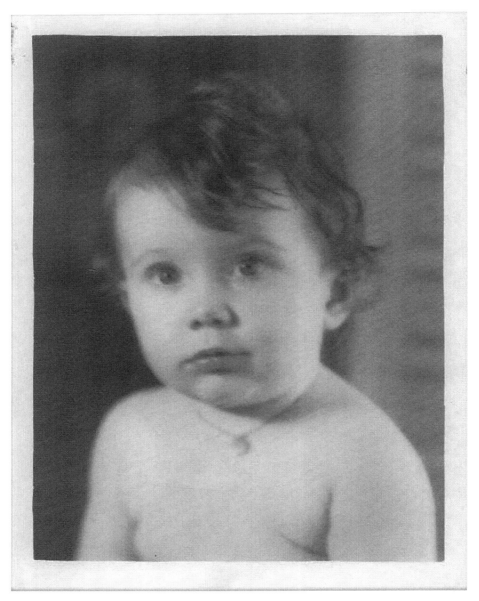

Marlyn Sue Butler

Forward

～

WHEN I WAS YOUNG, I was told often that I looked like someone else. When Margaret O'Brien was in "Meet Me in St. Louis", I was told I looked like her. When Natalie Wood was in "The Miracle on 34th Street", I was told I looked like her. When Elizabeth Taylor was in "Lassie Come Home" and "National Velvet", I was told I looked like her. When Audrey Hepburn was in anything, I was told I looked like her. I had dark brown hair and brown eyes and was shy and quiet...like all of them in those movies. I guess I looked like 'Every Girl'. When we are young, we are told many things by a lot of people, many of them being their judgments about who we are. "You're a good girl, you're a naughty girl, what's wrong with your hair?, don't do that, you're wrong, you're right, be nice, you're shy, don't laugh so loud, you don't sing very well, you have nice teeth, you have bad teeth, give me a big smile, don't smile so big, lower your voice, speak up," etc...etc...etc. I did not know WHO I was while growing up. Do I now? It takes a lifetime to become who YOU are.

I was the youngest of three children...and an accident. My mother was Dorothy Ruth Drummond Butler, born October 23, 1902 in Downs, Kansas, and my father was Howard Gustav Butler, born December 2, 1901, on a farm near Barada, Nebraska. My brother, Jerry, was born June 11, 1929 and my sister, Beverly, was born June 6, 1931, both at the Lathrop Hospital in Norton. Dr. Kennedy told Mother that she should not have more children, because she was anemic and not strong enough to care for three children. However, my father had gotten a new, fancy condom made out of snakeskin. It slipped off, and I was conceived. Mother laughingly told me this story, as part of the

Mother-Daughter 'sex talk' and as her clever and humorous way to warn me about how easy it is to get pregnant. So I was not a planned-for baby, but there I was, born on a Sunday afternoon, July 1, 1934, in the house at 209 North Wabash that my Great-Grandfather James Corfman built in Norton, Kansas. When Mother realized she was in labor, they asked the 'house girl', Katie Geary, to take Beverly and Jerry for a walk during my birth. I had a black curl right on top of my head when I was born; it did not last.

PART I

Families: The Crucible for Development

The family unit is where a person learns to become who they are. Each member with their different interests and personality traits have an influence either outwardly or subtly. These are the personalities who created my cradle of learning.

CHAPTER 1

My Roots in Norton Begin

MOTHER MAY NOT HAVE BEEN born in Norton, but she got there as soon as she could, as the saying goes, and she never wanted to live anywhere else. Her father, Abraham Lincoln Drummond, was born April 1, 1865 in Richland, Iowa and was the son of Isaac and Rebecca White Drummond. His father fought in the Civil War and came with his family in 1880 to Downs, Kansas, where he became publisher of the town newspaper. In 1884, A. L. Drummond boarded the Missouri Pacific train at Portis, Kansas and came further west. On arrival at Edmond, he arranged for an overland trip to Norton where he became an employee of G. W. Conway, editor of the "Champion" newspaper. He soon met my Grandmother, Minnie Corfman, who was called "The Belle of Bachelor Ridge", and who was the first woman to work downtown in Norton, as a milliner.

My Grandmother Minnie Drummond was born July 8, 1865, came to Norton from Iowa in 1879, traveling in a Prairie Schooner covered wagon, and lived in a 'soddy' near Lenora until moving to Norton as a young girl. Mother passed down the story of how the flame of a kerosene lamp flared a bit too high in the back of the wagon and set the fabric top of the wagon on fire. They tossed the lamp out the back of the wagon and managed to get the fire out, and then recovered the lamp. It was on display in the corner cupboard that sat in our dining room when I was growing up, and now I display it in my dining room in the same corner cupboard that my Great-Grandfather Corfman built. Minnie and Abraham Lincoln Drummond were married in 1887 and moved to Downs, Kansas where he worked with his father in the printing business. Three children were born there: John Drummond in 1889, Ruby Rebecca Drummond in 1891, and my mother, Dorothy Ruth Drummond in 1902.

Grandpa Drummond went to Colorado and wrote for a Cripple Creek newspaper during the gold mine boom in the 1890s. That is where he became interested in the Christian ministry. After the "Great Cripple Creek Fire" of 1896, he returned to Downs and studied to become a minister in the Christian Church, with his first assignment in Smith Center, Kansas. After my mother, Dorothy Drummond, was born, the family moved to Norton and Grandpa Drummond became the minister at the Christian Church.

A. L. Drummond was a kind of Renaissance man: he wore many hats. He worked in the printing business for the Norton Champion newspaper, was a Christian Church Minister, and owned a chicken hatchery in Norton on East Lincoln and raised Rhode Island Red chickens. He became interested in the law, studied for the law exam, was admitted to the Bar in 1916, and practiced law in Norton. He was elected to be the Mayor of Norton, was a Probate Judge, the County Attorney, and then he was elected to the Kansas House of Representatives. He was active in the Modern Woodmen, Lion's Club, Chamber of Commerce, Masonic Blue Lodge, a 32nd degree Mason and a member of The Knights Templar, active at the State level. He wrote and published many sermons, essays and books.

My grandmother's father, my Great-Grandfather Corfman, was a carpenter and built several houses in Norton, including the one at 209 North Wabash where I was born and the one next door, 211 North Wabash, where I lived till I was about six years old. My mother lived in those houses, too, till she was five when Great-Grandpa Corfman built the two story house at 519 East Lincoln; she lived there until she was married. All three of these houses are lived in still today. Mother writes about growing up and living there, her parents, and life in Norton in the early 1900s in her memoirs in the addendum of this book.

Sadly, I did not know my Drummond grandparents very long. After Grandpa Drummond died in 1936, we moved into the house at 211 North Wabash to take care of Grandma Drummond, who was in failing health, both mentally and physically. What I have been told, and what the photos of her show, is that she was a beautiful young woman. She was an excellent seamstress and milliner; Mother said she loved fabrics and had drawers full of silks, brocades, linens, and wools. I still have some of her fabrics that Mother saved.

In 1923 and 1924, Mother was going to college at Kansas State in Manhattan, Kansas. She became an Alpha Delta Pi, and was engaged to a Phi Delta Gamma. She loved being a Flapper and described the attitude of college students at that time as just wanting to laugh and have fun.

When she came home at the end of the fall semester in 1925, she planned to return to Manhattan. However, one evening in late December her sister, Ruby Drummond Dean, asked her to come to Ann and Ralph Butler's house for a party, wanting her to meet Ralph's brother, Howard, who was a new doctor in town. They hit it off. Mother said that he was handsome and could dance and swept her off her feet.

Handwritten on the back by Dad:

*This is the sweetest of all
and she is sweeter than that.
I love her so but she is too nice for me.
I would only be a blight to
her sparkling life but
I shall die with the memory of
each moment with her as a pearl
sealed up in my heart.*

Sweet thoughts like what Dad wrote on the back of the photo of Mother were certainly part of the 'sweeping'. She did not go back to Kansas State, ended the engagement without any letter of explanation, and started dating Dad. Mae and Les Mason, an optometrist, were going to vacation in Colorado in July of 1927, and asked Mother and Dad, "Why don't you get married and come on your honeymoon with us?" Why not?! They did! On July 23, 1927 Mother and Dad were married by Elder Stephen Epler, at the Christian Church parsonage on North State Street, across from the high school, and went with the Masons to Manitou, Colorado for a honeymoon. Mother's father had some doubts about Dad, telling Mother that he had heard Howard had a terrible temper (he did!), and Grandma Drummond refused to go to the wedding, either because she didn't like Dad or she simply didn't want Mother to get married.

Their first 'home' was an upstairs apartment looking out at the Norton County Courthouse across the street on Kansas Street. There were several young and newly married couples in Norton and they enjoyed going to dances and parties and playing bridge together, as well as being leaders in the town. Mother and Dad were young and in love and happy. Mother told me their 'song' then was "Who?" (Kern, Harbach, Hammerstein): "Who stole my heart away? Who makes me dream all day? Who means my happiness? Who? Who? No one, but you!" When Jerry was born, Mother said their theme song became "My Blue Heaven" (Donaldson, Whiting): "Just Molly and me, and baby makes three, We're so happy in My Blue Heaven." Dad's practice did very well in Norton, but when a woman doctor offered him quite a lot of money to buy his practice in Norton, it seemed like a good time to go home to Nebraska, where he had grown up. So, in the early 1930s, after Jerry and Beverly were born but before I was born, Dad sold his practice in Norton and bought a practice in Stromsborg, Nebraska. They felt like they were rolling in money and even went on a vacation to Minnesota, the Land of Lakes, before moving to Stromsborg. Unfortunately, the woman osteopath had lied about how well her practice was doing there and had not told him that the people from Stromsborg went to York or Lincoln when they needed a doctor. So, when Dad opened his office in Nebraska, patients did not come. Standing in his office waiting for patients that never appeared was disheartening. In addition, the house that they rented looked okay from the outside, but at night, they heard scratching noises and the pitter-patter of little feet in the attic and in the walls. When they cautiously peeked downstairs, they discovered big rats gnawing on some of their belongings. They packed up their belongings and set off again to find someplace where Dad could set up his practice. After looking in Junction City and other possible towns, Mother just wanted to go home to Norton. Since Dad had signed an agreement with the woman doctor that he would not practice in Norton for a certain number of years, he could not re-open his practice in Norton and had to take a job at a gas station to make ends meet. They moved into the house that Mother's Grandpa Corfman had built at 209 North Wabash. After a few years, the woman Osteopath was not successful in Norton and decided to leave; Dad was able to set up his practice again.

Norton was growing by the late 1920s. After the old courthouse burned down, a new one, still standing today, was built in 1929. A sewer system and a water system were built with a water tower (we always referred to it as the 'standpipe') to store the water for the town. Before then people had private wells in their yards with hand pumps to provide water. The sewer system made it possible for people to have indoor bathrooms, a nice change from outhouses.

The 1930s brought many challenges for Mother and Dad. Jerry was born in 1929, just before the stock market crashed and the Great Depression began, Beverly in 1931, and I in 1934, just as severe drought caused the soil to turn to dust. The 'dust bowl' of the 'dirty thirties' combined with financial depression are well-documented events. Mother described how great clouds of dust would suddenly sweep through the air, burying everything in a layer of dust. At that time, there was no NOAA weather to warn people that a dust storm was coming. She said that one evening, she and Dad and another couple had gone to the movies, but the movie was halted and everyone was told to go home, because the wind had started to blow clouds of dust through the streets. When they came out of the theater, the wind was blowing so strongly that they could barely stand up, and by the time they got home, their hair and clothing were covered with dust and it was in their eyes and mouth. When the storms hit, you could see the sky filled with roiling, black clouds of dust. She would cover my crib with wet sheets to keep the dust off of me, lay wet towels and sheets along the window and door sills, and hang wet sheets over the windows in an effort to keep the dust out. After the storms passed, dust was thick on everything. Cleaning up must have been backbreaking. The blowing dust, and then the clean up afterward, caused many people to get dust-pneumonia. Perhaps that is why Beverly and I have scars on the bottom of our lungs!

At this time, we were living in the house at 209 North Wabash (the second house south of the Burlington railroad tracks), and Grandma and Grandpa Drummond were living at 211 North Wabash in the house closest to the railroad tracks and by the viaduct that went over the Burlington tracks. Beverly remembers that hobos, who 'rode the rails' looking for work, would climb up from the railroad tracks that went under the bridge and come to our door, asking for food. Mother always tried to find something to give them, even if it was just some bread or crackers. I suspect that the hobos marked our house with their special codes to let other hobos know that Mother would have something to give them.

Grandpa Abraham Lincoln Drummond had pernicious anemia and, at that time, there were no vitamin B-12 shots to give him; the treatment was to eat raw liver! Mother remembered him trying to mash the raw liver so that he could swallow it whole, without chewing and without tasting it. He died in November of 1936, when I was almost two and one-half years old. Yet, I remember him. I have this mental image of him, from the point of view of being close to the floor and looking up, sitting in a rocking chair in the great room of the house on North Wabash. He seemed very gentle and kind to me, and I have warm feelings for him just from that brief memory.

After Grandpa Drummond died, we moved in with Grandma Minnie Drummond in the house next to the railroad tracks. Grandma Drummond was probably not thrilled to have all of us in one house. Since she had not approved of Mother marrying Dad, to live in the same house eight years later must have been stressful. She had several physical ailments as well as some mental decline, and her health problems were becoming worse. She began to wander away from the house and not know how to get home. Someone would call and say that Minnie Drummond was somewhere and did not know how she got there or how to get home. So, Dad would go and bring her home. Beverly and Jerry remember peeking at her as she would stand in front of the floor mirror in the bedroom and talk to her friend in the mirror (I don't remember seeing her do that). Since she had been a milliner for many years, she might have had some mercury poisoning from working with felt and furs that had been treated with mercury. Mother and Dad (but mostly Dad, according to Mother) felt that Grandma Drummond needed to go to a home where she could be watched over better. The 'home' was a state institution in Larned, Kansas. It broke my mother's heart to take her there, and she felt guilty about doing so the rest of her life. This was about 1939 or 1940. Mother told me later that when her mother had a physical exam at Larned, they found that her uterus was "almost falling out of her", prolapsed, as it is called now. Medical science was not what it is now. Antibiotics were not yet available, and there were few doctors in small towns. People did not go to a doctor for a 'check-up', and most problems such as flu, pneumonia, digestive problems, or 'female' problems were treated with bedrest, soup, tea, and hope. Mother wondered if having to deal with that in silence caused some of her mental decline.

In addition to Mother's parents, Dad's parents also required care during those years. Dad's father died of stomach cancer before I was born, and Dad did what he could to help him cope with the pain. I remember Mother saying that he craved pork, and she wondered if pork contained something that his body needed and if the craving had something to do with the cancer.

Therefore, throughout the 1930s, Mother and Dad were raising three children, taking care of her parents and sometimes his parents, in a small house with a coal stove and no indoor bathroom for most of the time, during the depression and during the dust bowl years. Mother was only five foot two and never weighed more than a hundred pounds. When she was in sixth grade, she had mastoiditis and missed a whole year of school. Doctors through the years told her that she was not strong, so she thought of herself as being fragile and not being able to do things, but she proved herself, again and again, to be tough and resilient.

After Grandpa Drummond died and Grandma Drummond was at Larned, Mother noticed that some items of their furniture and other things had disappeared. Mother felt that Dad wanted to get money out of them and had either sold them to Aunt Ruby or someone else, but neither he nor Aunt Ruby would admit to anything. The furnishings that Mother had grown up with were very dear to her heart, and some bitter feelings arose over where things had gone and whether Aunt Ruby had sold things.

Mother had little help taking care of her parents from Aunt Ruby or Uncle John. I never met my Uncle John, who was thirteen years older than Mother. He married Anna Van Cleve in Detroit, and they had three daughters, Lois, Doris, and Helen. John Drummond was a musician and had an orchestra when Mother was growing up, as well as a photography studio in Norton. Mother thought her brother was wonderful; apparently, he was quite charming. There is a photo of him in military uniform during World War I at Fort Riley, but Mother never talked about his being in the Army. He worked as a telegraph operator on the old CB&Q railroad and was the station agent at Republican City, Nebraska when he left his family and "ran off" to California. The family was living in the second floor apartment at the Depot, which was customary at the time, when he disappeared. He never made contact with any of his family, although there were rumors every now and then of where he might be and a supposition that he was living in California with a woman from Norton. It was believed that he died in California of diabetes in the late 1940s, but I have no facts as to when or where.

Aunt Ruby was something of a gypsy, too. She was eleven years older than Mother. She "ran off" and married someone at age seventeen or eighteen, but she came home again quickly. Years later, she told me what happened. She said that when they got ready to go to bed on their wedding night, he took off his pants and his penis hung down to his knees! "It was huge!" She "took one look at it and ran screaming from the room"; that marriage was annulled. Later, she married Roy Dean and had five children: Donald, Dixie, Phyllis, Shirley, and Judy. Roy was a barber in Norton and died of emphysema or lung problems aggravated by all the hair debris that he had inhaled over the years. He died when Judy was around ten years old, and Aunt Ruby left her with us at the house on North Wabash for a short time while Aunt Ruby looked for a way to provide for five children. Judy lived with us when I was in kindergarten. When I visited her in the 1990s and told her how much I enjoyed Aunt Ruby, she said, "Yes, mother was a lot of fun, but she wasn't a very good mother." I suspect that Judy deeply felt the disruption in her life that came from losing her father and the difficulty her mother faced carrying on alone.

The left photo shows Judy Dean, Beverly, and me on south side porch at 211 North Wabash. Notice the camera I am holding. It is a Kodak box camera, which probably did not work, if I was allowed to touch it. On the right is Aunt Ruby in her nursing uniform.

Aunt Ruby led a somewhat nomadic life as she tried to make a living to support her five children. She worked as a nurse most of the time. When I was in junior high and high school, she was working at the tuberculosis Sanatorium in Norton...'the San' or 'The Farm', as we referred to it. I loved having her come stay with us on weekends, because she was so much fun. She always had a funny story to tell, and she encouraged me and influenced me, too. Dad thought she threw her money away on unnecessary things. One time we were talking about this, and Aunt Ruby said, "But, that's what money is for...to buy the things you want. That's why you work." I had never thought about money this way, and I still have trouble with that concept. The fear of not having enough and the idea that your value is based on how much money you have are in opposition to the rational thought that money is to buy what will make you happy. Need versus want. Value versus self-respect.

CHAPTER 2

My Mother, Dorothy Ruth Drummond Butler

MOTHER HAD A WONDERFUL ATTITUDE toward life. She never was one to blame or criticize anyone. For example, I dropped a small glass of milk one time, and the glass broke and milk went everywhere. I was extremely upset at my clumsiness, but Mother put her arms around me and said it was okay... it was just some milk and an unimportant glass. I felt such relief, and surprise, and release from the fear of making a mistake. The feeling that Mother would not criticize me for small goofs always made it easy to be with her and created a close bond, a comfort zone, and an openness to be myself and comfortable in my own skin.

Of course, Mother could also let me know when I did something inappropriate. One day when I was about five or six, we were in Virtues, a small department store downtown, and I had my doll, Gretchen, with me. I do not know what I did that upset her, but I do remember her giving me a little swat on my bottom to set me straight. I was mortified! As a result, the rest of my life, I always did whatever she told me to do! (Really! I did!)

When I was five, Mother made Raggedy Ann and Andy dolls for me...I still have them. She made most of our clothes, too. One that I remember was a Sailor Middy top that was navy blue with the big collar hanging down the back. Alice Isaac made one for Sandra, and we wore them to the county fair. She continued being creative throughout her life. For a luncheon, she made mini-hats for place markers, and she made decorative, fabric covers to put over 'ugly' lampshades. In the 1960s, she made a beautiful velvet patchwork long skirt for me to wear to a party at Lake Quivira, and she made patchwork skirts for all of her granddaughters; later, when they outgrew them, she made the skirts into quilts for them. In addition, she painted and made crewel-work pieces. I have several of her paintings and several crewel works: two works with red poppies, the RCA dog, Nipper, sitting in front of the antique Victrola, and two flowered decorative pillows that she created. She never stopped 'creating' and made an embroidery Bible cover when she was living in the Andbe Home.

Mother was also sneaky. Every day when I got home from kindergarten, she would have a little table set up in the great room with graham crackers or cookies and a little glass of grape juice, and we would have a 'tea party'. I thought it was such fun and it tasted so good. Only much later did I find out that in that glass of grape juice was cod liver oil! Well, I am glad she did! That cod liver oil probably kept me healthy! Mother was devious; I was naïve, trusting, and completely accepting of everything.

It seems everyone has some kind of innate fear. A flying wasp petrified me, and I would hit the floor if one flew into the house. Although Mother had a fear of birds and cringed if a bird flew too close to her head, she had no fear of wasps. As I cowered and screamed in fear, she would get her long scissors from the drawer, wait for the wasp to land, reach over and snip the wasp in two. My hero!

Mother was a wonderful pianist, playing by ear and with such joy. Mother had played the piano for the silent movies for many years in the 1920s. When playing for silent movies, the pianist watches the movie and plays something that enhances the movie action. However, one night, Mother was not paying attention to the movie and was just playing whatever came into her mind. She was playing "Ain't We Got Fun" when she looked up and realized that they were hanging a man in the movie. She quickly switched to something more appropriate.

Someone was always playing music in our house. Gathering around the piano and singing together was a frequent event. We had many jam sessions, not just with our immediate family but also with other musicians around town. Bill Krehbiel played a great soprano sax, Irene Hollinger would come over and play drums on a suitcase, Beverly and Dad would sing. Jerry, Mother and I would take turns at the piano, and Jerry would play guitar when he was not at the piano. I was delighted when Bill Krehbiel wrote "To a Hepcat", when he signed my 1950 annual.

Mother cooked, she sewed, she took care of three children, and she worked downtown most of the time when I was growing up. She worked first at Muir's Music store, and then at the Cottage Style Shop for Mrs. Neva Funk when I was in junior high and high school. When I was at the University of Kansas, she was working at Worden's Jewelry shop. She paid for my clothes, her clothes, and probably Beverly's and Jerry's from the money she earned at the Cottage Shop and Worden's. And, she dressed us well! It was always exciting when the new spring or fall clothing lines came in. When Mother worked at the Cottage Shop, we had first pick of the new styles each season. She never wanted to buy anything off a 'sale rack' because those were leftovers and last year's styles. She wanted the styles of the new season! At that time, there were sales only at the end of a season, such as after Christmas or at the end of summer. The magazine, "Seventeen", started publishing in 1944, when I was ten. It, "Glamour", and "Vogue" were the fashion bibles that we bought as soon as they came into the drug store. We would pore over them together, and Mother would "ooh and aah" over the wonderful fashions and say, "Marlyn, you must have this!" She bought a plaid skirt for me when I was in junior high that I felt very fashionable wearing. Another outfit was an off-white Orlon suit, a new fabric in 1950...it looked like wool, but was washable! I still have it (but I've never tried washing it!), as well as the tweed wool skirt she got for me when I was leaving for Kansas University, a black cocktail/formal dress, and the remains of a teal, silky moiré dress. The summer of 1948, before I was a freshman in high school, she bought for me a turquoise corduroy gathered skirt with an off-white wool, long-sleeved sweater and a brown leather wide belt. The Norton County Fair was in August, and it was warm, but fashion came first. Mother told me that when the sun went down it would be cool in Elmwood Park, so I wore that outfit to the fair on a very hot night when I had a date with Jimmy for the dance on the tennis court. When I was in college, Mother bought my clothes and Dad paid the housing bill and tuition.

Mother always had 'style'. She loved the Early American style of house decor, probably because the antiques she inherited were close to her heart, and throughout her life, she enjoyed going to antique shops and finding treasures. Some treasures she bought included a wine press, a child's cradle, a brass bed warmer, a walking spinning wheel, an iron water pump that she painted red, iron skillets and flat irons. She liked oval braided rugs over the pine floors. In fabric designs, her favorites were polka dots, ginghams, flowered chintz, and black and white checks. She had a wonderful fashion sense and looked forward to each season and the new styles. Often today, I will see something in a store and think, "Mother would have liked that!"

Mother's idea of a Sunday drive was to drive around town and look at the windows in the stores downtown or see the decorations and flowers in people's yards. Dad's idea of a Sunday drive was to go over back roads out in the country. Mother would say, "Why do you want to drive over bumpy roads out in the country where there's nothing to see?!" On one Sunday drive, I remember Dad spotted plums growing beside the road, and we stopped and picked some. Gooseberries and blackberries were always a treat to find; gooseberry pie was a favorite at our house. There was no air-conditioning in cars (or in houses!) at that time, so the windows had to be rolled down manually to get any air, and the dust and wind would rush and gush through the car if you drove very fast.

Mother was always fun and very sociable, and she loved to laugh. In the 1940s, it was the 'thing to do' to dress up in high heels, a hat, and gloves, and go downtown in the afternoon, meet friends at the drugstore, and have a fountain Coke. She usually wore her hair pulled back from her face into a chignon. She would brush her dark hair back into a pony tail, and then pull the tail through a "bun" (a purchased donut-shaped roll about three inches in diameter with a hole in the middle) and then place her hair evenly around the bun, cover it with a hair net and keep it in place with hairpins. It was a sophisticated-looking style and she always looked elegant.

Until the 1950s, Mother always wore dresses, called 'house dresses' or 'dusters'. She liked yellow for summer; once she had a yellow canvas cloth wraparound dress and another summer a yellow 'peasant' skirt and top in crinkled cotton crepe. Incidentally, Mother knew her fabrics! I absorbed the names of about every fabric there is as I was growing up. The type and quality of clothing was important to Mother's fashion sense. She never wore slacks until stretch knit came into style in the 1960s; even then, she never wore blue jeans. Nor would she ever wear sneakers. She did condescend to wear Grasshoppers or Keds by the 1970s, but preferred Espadrilles (a canvas Wedgie) in the summer. However, running shoes or sneakers were out of the question...they were much too ugly! Even when she was in a wheelchair and could barely walk, she wanted at least a one and a half inch heel, preferably higher. She wore a size four and a half or five, so finding shoes both stylish and that would fit her was always a problem. Knee-high hose were not on the market yet, so she rolled her stockings. Thick stretchy round bands were available for this purpose. She would pull the band up over her leg to the top of the stocking, fold the stocking over the band, and then roll down over and over to wherever she wanted the stocking to be held, usually just above the knee.

She could always find something to laugh at in whatever situation occurred and could make lemonade out of any lemons that came her way. For example, Mother was wonderful at decorating, and she recycled many things when redoing the house. After World War II, she decided that the new style of bedroom furniture was a smooth look for the end of the bed. However, her bed had tall posts on the footboard. No problem. She got the bread knife out of the kitchen drawer and she and Beverly proceeded to saw off the out-of-date posts! Then she covered the stumps with a chenille bedspread.

When I was visiting Norton with Pamela and John in the mid-1960s, we were in bed and trying to go to sleep. Instead, we kept talking and laughing over silly things. It was getting very late and Mother finally said, "This time we really are going to sleep. Good night." About thirty seconds later, the Seth Thomas clock in the hall started striking and we all started counting in our heads. One, two, three... When the clock struck thirteen, we all burst into laughter.

Mother and Dad went to Kansas City for a medical convention in the late 1940s, and Mother had put a container of Metamucil into the suitcase. She was following Dad into the hotel when she noticed something leaking out of the suitcase. The Metamucil container had broken and with every step that Dad took, Metamucil was squirting out of the seam of the suitcase, leaving a white, powdery trail through the lobby. She did not tell Dad that he was leaving a trail; some things are better not known.

On another trip to Kansas City with Bill and Alice Isaac, they went to dinner at a lovely restaurant. Mother was wearing a black hat with a lace veil that came down over her nose (yes, at that time, women dressed elegantly and wore long gloves and hats for such occasions). Mother ordered a Pink Lady cocktail and asked Dad for a cigarette. (It was very sophisticated to smoke.) When she went to light it, the veil of her hat caught on fire and sent a flame up in front of her face! She screamed and quickly took off the hat, and, of course, she laughed about that for a long time. I think Lucille Ball could have gotten some of her skits from Mother!

Mother had a way of enjoying and creating fun out of simple things, and she loved talking with people she might meet somewhere. In the 1960s when we lived at Lake Quivira, near Kansas City, we often picked her up in the summer and took her with us to visit Beverly in Kimball, Nebraska. On the way home on a Sunday afternoon, we stopped in McCook at a restaurant for lunch and Mother struck up a conversation with a local patron. She told us that a local church was having an ice cream social and said we should stop by and join them. Mother thought that sounded enjoyable, so we all went to the ice cream social and talked to the local people and ate ice cream and had a delightful time. We remembered and reminisced about that afternoon in McCook for years.

By the early 1980s, Dad's health was becoming worse. I remember him lying on his treating table and hurting, with no osteopath to help him. He even went to the chiropractor in town trying to find relief. He had never taken care of himself, but I do not know exactly what his health condition was other than being in a lot of pain. Beverly finally talked him into going to the nursing home in Kimball, even though he felt responsible for Mother and was concerned about her being alone. With assurance from Beverly and Jerry that Mother would be okay, he finally agreed to go, and Jerry drove him to Kimball. He said that Dad lay down in the back seat the whole way because he hurt so much.

I thought maybe Mother would like to come to Corpus Christi and live with us, but she felt uncomfortable there. With the high population of Hispanics and a 'Texan' culture, Corpus Christi seemed like a foreign country to her. While she was there, she asked me several times if I had the radio on, because she kept hearing a radio. There was no radio playing. This was the first incident of 'hearing voices', which got worse over the next ten years. After three weeks in Corpus Christi, she told me, "I just want to go home to Norton". I drove her back home to Norton and she tried to live by herself for a while. She had Meals on Wheels delivered and, like many people, she would forget to put what she had not eaten in the refrigerator. Then she ate more of it for dinner. As a result, she had quite a few attacks of food poisoning. Finally, Jerry suggested that she should move to Goodland and live at the Manor, where he was the director. She was very excited about this, first because the Manor was very nice, but also because she would be near Jerry. However, within a year, the voices got worse and she was homesick for Norton. Therefore, she moved in to the Andbe Home in 1985. Since she could not take much furniture to the Andbe Home, Hank (my husband) and I pulled a big trailer to Goodland. Beverly, Jerry, and I divided the furniture and all of Mother's things by drawing straws and then taking turns picking items that each of us wanted. Beverly drew first and wanted the walnut Secretary desk, I chose the corner cupboard that Great-Grandpa Corfman had built; I believe that Jerry's first choice was the Duncan Phyfe dining room table and chairs. I also picked the walnut chest of drawers that Great-Grandpa Corfman made. One of the things that neither Beverly nor Jerry wanted was Dad's desk, because it was literally falling apart. I brought the pieces back to Corpus Christi thinking I could refinish it myself. However, when I started cleaning the top of the desk, I was shocked at the layers of yellow and brown nicotine and tar residue that clung to the top of it, as well as the extent of the rebuilding that would be necessary to restore it. I hired a furniture restorer to put it back together and refinish it.

Jerry was able to visit Mother at the Andbe Home usually weekly since he was just a couple hours away. Beverly was about six hours away and was swamped, trying to run two dress shops as well as deal with the farm crisis going on at that time (falling crop prices, a grain embargo against the Soviet Union, high interest rates on loans, high fuel costs, and falling land prices caused many farm foreclosures). I lived two days away, and we were having major problems with our business situation. As a result, I got up to Norton only two or three times a year. This was frustrating and guilt producing because there was little I could do to be of help.

Mother had a saying, "If you can't say anything nice, don't say anything at all". Although she generally did live by this, she could let little snide remarks slip out now and then. She used 'teasing' as a form of commenting on how she felt about things. For example, when Beverly came to visit her at the Andbe Home one time, she was dressed in culottes, which stopped above the knees. Beverly always dressed very well...a fashion plate of style. But, Mother looked at her and said, "Well, I know it's the fashion, but I sure don't like it!" One of her worst teasing remarks was to me. I had put on some weight in Corpus Christi, and on one visit at the Andbe Home, she looked at me and said, "Marlyn! Are you pregnant?!" She thought she was being funny; I was appalled!

She was having trouble with her teeth and had to have some pulled. When she complained about it, I reminded her that she had never liked to brush her teeth and had never flossed them, and I said that perhaps if she had taken care of them maybe she would not be having so many problems. Her answer: "Well, now you tell me!"

One day she was bemoaning how many people had died at the Andbe home and worrying about it. When we reminded her that the people who had died were all over ninety years old, she said, "Oh. I never thought of that."

Mother gave me several things: a sense of humor and the gift of laughter, the gift of music, the gift of forgetfulness, the gift of style, the gift of creativity, the gift of small moments, the gift of sharing herself and her memories, the sense of family with tales of her childhood and family stories, the love of home.

CHAPTER 3

My Dad, Dr. Howard
Gustav Butler

WHEN DAD WAS ABLE TO set up his practice in Norton again, after the move to Nebraska was not successful, he did well. During World War II he was usually paid in cash, and when Mother and Dad moved the house from Oronoque to Norton and rebuilt it, he usually paid the workers in cash. He did get loans from the First State Bank (Bill Rouse was bank President there from at least the early 1940s until he died) for the lot. Sometimes, however, Dad was paid in chickens or other services, and, quite often, he never did receive payments from his patients. When Jerry, Beverly, and I looked at the ledgers that he had kept throughout the years, we realized that he never collected many thousands of dollars that his patients owed him.

Dad was an excellent doctor and diagnostician. He said he could diagnose diabetes by the smell of the urine, for example. At noon, he often brought home brown sacks with a patients urine in a bottle inside, which he then took up to the hospital for analysis. Dad was extremely intelligent. He had earned top grades at the Kirksville College of Osteopathic Medicine and, when he was fifty years old, he was able to pass the newly required medical accreditation test in the state of Kansas.

His patients often told Mother how wonderful he was, and how he had helped them; and a high school coach told my sister, Beverly, that Dad had helped so many people as well as the many athletes who the coach had brought to him.

Beverly, Jerry, and I all grew up getting osteopathic treatments when we had any aches or pains and, of course, various treatments for sore throats and infections. When I was in college, I came home one time with a very sore throat. Dad took me down to his office to look at it and, before I realized what he was doing, he painted my throat with some red medicine! Merthiolate? Mercurochrome? I wonder! Mercurochrome was the go-to antiseptic when I was growing up. It came in a small bottle with a narrow glass stem that was used to daub the red liquid all over any cut or scrape. When we got an upset stomach, he would bring a glass of warm water with a teaspoon of baking soda stirred up in it for us to drink. It would come back up quickly and then he would bring another glass of baking soda to drink. After a couple of glasses, our stomachs would be pretty well cleaned out, and we would recover. Some of our stomach upsets were likely from food poisoning due to keeping refrigerated food too long in a refrigerator that was not as cold as it should be. The feeling that wasting food was throwing away money could be blamed on the depression, but Dad told the story of his mother making him, as a child, eat a rotten egg (which he promptly threw up) rather than waste it. So 'waste not, want not' is a very old attitude. Maybe that is why we all got the lecture about the starving children in India or China. The feeling that I could save all those children by eating the food on which my parents had spent their hard-earned money resulted in instant guilt if I didn't eat it...at least until rational thought developed in my thinking.

Dad would also always rub our abdomens, right under our right ribs, to get the bile from the gallbladder flowing. He had a little magic green pill that he would give us to help the gallbladder work. Later he introduced us to a little white pill that was a wonderful digestive aid and always helped the stomach feel better.

Dad loved to conduct the big band music played on the radio...and was quite good at it. He had played the baritone horn growing up and loved to sing. He was a good dancer, and I loved to watch Mother and Dad dance together. But, I found it difficult to follow him because his dance steps seemed free-form and varied to me, and, also, I felt inadequate and was intimidated by the fear that he would think I was a bad dancer!

Dad, as was the custom for men, always wore a hat when he left the house. He did not buy many clothes, since they just were not high on his list of priorities, but dress pants, a white shirt, tie, and jacket is what I remember him wearing daily.

When I was fourteen in 1948, he saw an advertisement for a doctor needed in North Carolina and was very excited about the prospects. However, Mother refused to go. She remembered Dad selling his practice in Norton to move to Nebraska and the promise of a wonderful practice in the early 1930s. The 'wonderful practice' was sold without full disclosure of the problems there, and it turned out badly. Therefore, Mother was not willing to leave Norton again. I thought moving was a good idea and imagined an exciting new adventure. I was sure that I would meet my 'soulmate' and my 'real life' would begin when I left Norton, since it seemed at the time that 'my true love' was not going to be found in Norton. However, Mother ruled, and we stayed in Norton. Looking back, moving to North Carolina would have been a disastrous move. The cultural shift between Norton, Kansas and the Deep South would have been an impossible chasm for Mother to cross. She loved Norton; it was home.

Dad was on the school board for many years, before and throughout my high school and college years. Dad was on the school board with Bonnie's dad (Burchie Underwood), Judy's dad (Bill Rouse), and Ronnie Allen's grandfather (E.H. Allen), when the gymnasium and other additions were built around 1952. He was also a very active member of the Lions Club, the Norton County Fair Board, and the Masonic Lodge.

Dad drove carloads of kids to out-of-town football and basketball games while I was in junior high and high school. Norton was in the Northwest Kansas league, which included Oberlin, Goodland, Colby, Saint Francis, Atwood, Hoxie, and Phillipsburg; we also played Smith Center and Wakeeny but I am not sure they were in the league. Games were played on Friday nights and, after the game, there would be a dance in the gym of the host high school. The community supported the games, and there was always a large contingent of Nortonites traveling to the out-of-town games. The roads were two-lane, cars had no seat belts, the cars were always full of teenagers, and most men would always have a beer or two. Bill Isaac was the driver to a Friday night football game in Phillipsburg when I was a sophomore. On the way home on Highway 36, he came over a hill and saw a mother skunk followed by three baby skunks. He slammed on the brakes, but it was too late and the car ran over them. Pee-ewy! When I walked in the front door, Mother was upstairs and I heard her scream, "Marlyn! What in the world?!" She told me to get my clothes off and get in the tub immediately. My clothes spent the night outside and, even though she sent my beautiful new red wool, double-breasted coat to the cleaners several times, the smell never came out and the coat had to be discarded. Bill never got the smell out of his car either.

Dad did not participate in child rearing in any direct way. I do not remember Dad telling me to do anything nor counseling me about life in any way; that was Mother's job. Nor did he yell at me. I do not know if he was disappointed in me or pleased with me. As gentle and empathetic as he was when we were not feeling well, he just was not one to give hugs or express outward affection. It was not easy for me to talk with him as a child or even later as an adult. He would come home at noon for 'dinner', but usually talked very little during the meal. With three children and Mother talking, maybe he just could not get into the conversation. If he wanted something, he would point to it until someone passed it to him. I do remember a compliment that Dad gave me once. In the summer, the high school band played in front of the Courthouse once a week. As we were getting ready to go one evening, Mother had braided my hair and wound the braids across the top of my head. Dad looked at me and said, "You look a lot like your mother." I took that as a compliment because Mother was beautiful.

Dad always seemed to have a chip on his shoulder. When "All in the Family" came on TV, I saw my Dad in Archie Bunker's character. Although he cared deeply about his family and on occasion showed his sentimental and tender side, he could also be a bit (or a lot!) crotchety and gruff. One time when we were driving to Geneva we got behind a very slow-moving, and long, funeral procession. You were not supposed to pass a funeral procession, and Dad became more and more impatient, grumbling and cursing under his breath. Mother said, "Howard! Be nice! Someone died!" In true Archie Bunker mode Dad growled back, "Well, why did he have to die here?!"

Dad started drinking at parties when he was in college, as many students do. He usually drank beer, but one time he drank too much vodka, which seemed to affect him differently, and went on a crying jag. It was shortly after World War II began, and I remember him sitting at the dining room table in the Hale house, crying. Mother tried to assure us that he was okay, and said the reason he was upset was that he had tried to enlist in the Army and was turned down. Dad had been too young to fight in World War I, and he was terribly disappointed and frustrated to be told now that he was too old.

That was the first time I was aware of anyone drinking alcohol. Mother said that when they would go to parties or dances, everyone would be drinking and having a good time, but when Dad drank his temper could flare and he would often end up in a fight with someone. Even with Dad's drinking and short temper, they were happy and had fun with the group of people their age: Tommy and Lucile Thomason, Bill and Alice Isaac, Mae and Les Mason, Sandy and Ione Jordan, and others. They belonged to the Country Club. Dad played a lot of golf on that course, which had buffalo grass and sand greens, and Mother talked about the many wonderful parties they went to at the Country Club in the 1930s and early 1940s. She laughed about a Halloween costume party when Bill Isaacs was dressed in red long johns, and being a bit tipsy, he would dash across the floor and jump onto the top of the big cornstalk decoration and then slide down. Then he would get up and do it again. Parties often ended with Mother at the piano and everyone gathered around singing the popular songs of the day.

I remember three of Dad's offices in Norton. The first one I remember was in the duplex on State Street and one, when I was in third grade, was up a long enclosed flight of narrow stairs to the second floor, where a door opened to a landing, which led to several offices. By the time I was nine, Dad had moved to an office facing west on State Street in the heart of downtown Norton. This had been Bill Lathrop's Dad's dental office before Dr. Lathrop was called into the Air Force as a Major in 1943. In the other half of the space was Dr. Les Mason, optometrist. I always liked Dr. Mason. He would slip a nickel into my hand and whisper, "Go get an ice cream cone". I would look up at his smiling face in disbelief and run to Stapleton's drug store for that chocolate ice cream cone.

These two offices had a recessed area below the second floor with Dad's office on the left (north) and Dr. Mason's office on the right. Large picture windows, about a foot from the floor, surrounded a sitting area that came out to the sidewalk on each side of the inset entrance. Dad hung heavy, tan-colored woven curtains on curtain rods about three feet above the window base. I can still picture him standing with his foot on the low sill, looking out the window as he waited for patients to come until five o'clock, when he would leave the office. His patients came from Norton, Edmond, Almena, Norcatur, Lenora, and surrounding areas. Many of them were farmers or other manual laborers and often smelled of sweat and soil.

The office on State Street is where he took my daughter, Pamela, one Saturday night when she was about six and had gotten a big splinter in her leg while sliding on the upstairs wooden floor at 411 North Grant. Mother and I stayed home with my son, John, while Hank and Dad took Pamela to his office for treatment. They said that Pamela yelled and screamed and put up quite a fight with it taking both of them to hold her down while Dad got the splinter out and gave her a tetanus shot. When she got home, Pamela was very calm, however, and told her Grandma Butler and me that she had been very brave and did not even cry. Since the stores were open in Norton on Saturday nights, many people heard her screaming and later asked Mother and Dad what had happened in the office that night.

We always had only one car, so when Mother needed to take me to some school-related event, Mother had to keep the car to get me there. However, Dad insisted on having the car when he shut his office at five o'clock, because his routine for unwinding at the end of the day was to take a drive in the country, with a can of beer in his hand, before coming home. If Mother was not ready to leave the Cottage Shop when he got back from his drive, he would go to Delphia's pool hall and play Snooker until The Cottage Shop closed. I would often go downtown and wait at the Cottage Shop till Mother got off work at six o'clock, and then we would wait in the car for Dad to come out of the pool hall. If he did not come out by 6:15, Mother would send me into the pool hall to get him. I cannot blame her for having me go in, but I hated doing that. The smell of smoke and beer, the dim lights and slowly-turning fans above the pool tables, and all the men looking at me (I know that young girls were NOT welcome in the pool hall, and maybe older women weren't either, since I don't remember any women in there!)...well, it was an unpleasant experience! That distinct smell of beer and cigarettes is still imprinted on my mind. Dad was generally not pleased when I came in, interrupting his game of Snooker or Pool, and his scrunched brow caused me to wince. For self-protection, I retreated into my shell and a quiet ride home.

Cursing was a part of Dad's language. Today that seems to be the norm, and one cannot watch primetime or family time TV without hearing this type of language. Maybe Dad was just ahead of his time, language-wise! I don't know when it became a habit with him, but it seems to start as early as junior high today when one-upmanship often sets the 'wimps' apart from the 'macho men'. Not being a man, I have not been a member of a 'men's club', but if movie scripts and books about War, the Government, and major sports are true, cursing is a mark of membership, the 'lingo' of belonging. Even though Dad cursed often, it was aimed at some imaginary person who was not there and consisted of basic curse words; I never heard him say sh*! or the 'f' word. I wrote very little about Dad's yelling, anger, and cursing in my diary, maybe because I was in denial about the angst it caused. A few comments I wrote were: "Dad's on the rampage" and "Mother slept with me tonight" and "Dad wasn't happy". Beverly and I talked about Dad's behavior once and realized that we thought it was common for men to be angry, to curse, and to act whatever way they wanted, and we were never to complain or suggest that they were acting badly. What we came to believe was that this was normal 'blowing-off-steam' behavior, the anger would pass, and then you would go back to pretending that everything was okay. Interestingly, Jerry, Beverly, and I did not pick up the constant cursing, being angry, and lashing out habit. (I guess I must qualify that a bit, since a "da.." and an "oh, sh.." have been known to cross my lips on occasion.) Maybe we found it painful and unpleasant to hear; I still find cursing and people yelling at others in movies and TV shows nerve jarring and a turn off, which is what I do: turn them off. It may be realistic and the way some people talk, but I do not personally know anyone today who curses much...at least in my presence.

On Saturday afternoons, when I was in grade school, The Cozy Theatre showed a western movie and a serial of some kind. It cost twelve cents to go. Mother would be working at the Cottage Shop and would send me into Dad's office to ask for the twelve cents. Dad was always on the frugal side, just like his mother, and did not like to waste money. He acted as if he did not want to give me money for something as frivolous as a Saturday afternoon movie, and I could sense his reluctance to place the dime and two pennies in my hand. We can get all sorts of feelings mixed up with our reactions to money. Money can represent security, power, freedom, love, control, God's bounty, God's punishment, loneliness, alienation, etc. Even though I rationally knew that money was always a worry for Dad, the feeling that I was not worth twelve cents stayed with me for years. My friends (Sandra Isaac, Judy Rouse, and Pat Melroy) all received allowances and could buy popcorn at the movies; I pleaded with Dad to give me an allowance of twenty-five cents a week, so I would not have to ask him for twelve cents, but he refused. Even when I went to college, Dad still did not want me to handle money. He instructed me to write checks for what was needed (Sellards Hall, tuition, books, miscellaneous) and he would cover the checks as they came in to the First State Bank. I was conscientious about spending and did not buy anything other than necessities. When Hank and I were first married, Hank worried about my ability to handle money, because I had never been asked to keep track of what I spent, nor had I ever balanced a checkbook. He was afraid that I would write checks and forget to record them; as a result, a check would bounce and his military record would be tarnished. Maybe because of all this, I still feel that popcorn at a movie is an unnecessary luxury, and my family teases me about being frugal.

As Dad got older, he did not seem to smile much. I remember him with knitted brows and frowning a lot. I know he was starting to have pain in his back from standing and bending over the treating table day every day. He had gone to a doctor in Kansas City who told him he had an enlarged heart; being young and not knowing what that meant, I expected him to keel over at any moment. He was a heavy smoker, probably three packs a day, and he always seemed to have a cigarette in his hand. I often smelled cigarette smoke in the night, because he would light a cigarette when he got up to go to the bathroom.

By the 1970s, the cost of malpractice insurance for doctors was skyrocketing. To cut down on expenses, and because the pain in Dad's back was getting so bad that he was thinking of semi-retirement anyway, he moved his office to the house on North Grant. The downstairs bedroom, which had been Mother and Dad's bedroom when we moved in, became his office. A door was installed where the window to the back porch had been and the porch was completely enclosed, so that patients could come in through the porch area rather than through the living area of the house. Dad set up his treating table in the bedroom and had his diathermy machine and other equipment in there, too. Some chairs were set up on the enclosed porch for any waiting patients. In not too many years, however, malpractice insurance cost more than Dad could earn in a year. It was truly exorbitant, and there was no provision for someone practicing part time. This forced him to retire fully. However, he still agreed to give an occasional treatment to the many patients who came and begged him to help them.

One of the lessons I learned from Dad was about the different roles that men and women played: men were served first, men could do and say whatever they wanted without reprisal, and men did not need to justify spending money. These 'lessons' may sound cynical, disparaging, even mocking, but these attitudes about the role of women were prevalent at the time and were reinforced by the movies that I saw growing up. These were the subtle and unspoken rules that were deeply ingrained in little girls, difficult to recognize, and which were revolted against by the women's lib movement (still in progress).

Reflecting on my Dad, I have wondered why he frowned so much and seemed angry. He apparently had a quick temper and a tendency to anger as a child; Grandma Ida told Mother that when she was pregnant with Dad that their hired man on the farm had a terrible temper and would drink and then rant and rave. She wondered if he had somehow 'marked' Dad when he was in the womb or had put a curse on him. I thought perhaps he was allergic to alcohol or an ingredient in it...yeast or hops, for example. I had read that allergic reactions could cause violent or erratic behavior as well as be the reason some people become alcoholics when they drink and some do not. Or, maybe he was an undiagnosed diabetic, since we were told he went into diabetic shock and a coma while in the retirement home in Kimball, shortly before he died. Bill Rouse, who was always mild-mannered and seemed the epitome of decorum, was diagnosed with diabetes after he suddenly went into a rage, throwing things and threatening Winifred to the point that she called the police. Evidently, sudden drops in blood sugar can bring on this kind of behavior. Whatever the real cause of this 'quirk' in his personality, I suspect that Dad was very frustrated by the lack of respect that Doctors of Osteopathy received in the medical world at that time. The AMA was waging a 'war' against Osteopaths at that time and protected their turf fiercely by denying Osteopaths hospital rights, for example.

Dr. Butler celebrates 50 years as Osteopath

Dr. H.G. Butler has recently celebrated his 50th year of practice of osteopathy. He has spent more than 48 of those years in Norton. "For the foreseeable future, I'm going to continue practicing," said Butler.

Butler, 73, a native of Hebron, Neb., received his medical training at the American School of Osteopathy in Kirksville, Mo. When he graduated in the spring of 1924, Butler went to Nelson, Neb., where he practiced his trade for one and a half years.

In December of 1925, Butler came to Norton to meet Dr. Brown, also an Osteopath who was trying to sell his office. "I met Dr. Brown and I liked the town," said Butler, "I jumped at the opportunity to buy his office."

Dr. Brown later moved his office to Beaver City and died sometime in the early 1940's.

In 1926 Dr. Butler met Dorthy Drummond, daughter of Mr. and Mrs. A.L. "Link" Drummond and they were married July 23, 1927.

Since 1925, Butler has had a steady practice in Norton. He now practices out of his home at 411 N. Grant.

Butler likes to fish and he used to play golf. "I used to be a golfer, until I got too close to the ball after I hit it."

Butler has been a Mason for over 30 years. He is a Past Master of Norton Lodge 199 and Past High Priest of RAM Norton chapter No. 93.

Butler and his wife are members of the Norton United Methodist Church. Butler has served on the Chamber of Commerce and was a member of the High School Board when there was remodeling done in 1946.

Butler was a member of the Norton County Fair Board and was the horse racing secretary. "When they brought in the motorcycles and cars, I went," said Butler.

The Butlers have two daughters and a son, Beverly Hisey, Kimball, Neb.; Marlyn Evers, Lake Quivera in Kansas City, Kan. and Jerry Butler of Goodland. They have 10 grandchildren and one great grandchild.

The centennial for Osteopathic medicine is this year, and Butler plans to go visit to his alma mater, now called Kirksville College of Osteopathic Medicine, to receive a certificate for practicing 50 years. Founders Day at the college will be October 10 and Dr. and Mrs. Butler plan to make the trip.

DR. H.G. BUTLER stands by the diploma that he earned fifty years ago this month at the American School of Osteopathy in Kirksville, Mo.
Butler has been practicing osteopathy in Norton for 48 of those 50 years and continues to practice from his home.

CHAPTER 4

Granddaughters Remember

My daughter, Pamela, and her cousin, Laura Lei Butler (Jerry's daughter) emailed back and forth several years ago, talking about their memories of visiting their Grandma Butler and Grandpa Doc in Norton. Here are excerpts from their emails:

Pam: I remember walking to the Hillside Grocery almost every day since G&G didn't keep much in their fridge...and rightly so since it didn't work so well. The Hillside didn't have much, but they did have a cooler of soda and I loved getting a grape Nehi or orange soda. I'd always try to pick up a pack of Juicy Fruit gum for Grandma and pretzels for Grandpa.

Laura: A grape Nehi is still the best. Juicy Fruit reminds me of Grandma every time I see it. I remember that refrigerator sounding as though it was working terribly hard! When you'd open it, it was almost warm air rushing out instead of very cold. Remember Grandpa's beer in there? And Grandma's cottage cheese? And how Grandpa knew when there was a beer missing?

Pam: I do remember that about the missing beer. Hey, I wasn't taking it...hmmm.

Laura: I remember the cracks in the sidewalk on the way to the Hillside Grocery! Remember how you had to watch your step or you'd stumble on the heaved portions of the sidewalk?

Pam: I thought we were missing the cracks to avoid breaking our mothers' backs.

Laura: And I remember something about blackjack gum and some clove-flavored gum that I only saw at Grandma's - seems like it was a white wrapper with red printing.

Pam: I don't remember the Blackjack gum, though I know I've seen it.

Laura: Yep...I really liked the Clove gum, though hated licorice so hated Blackjack.

Pam: Going fishing with Grandpa at those cow ponds was such fun. I loved walking the cow paths and pretending I was on a horse rounding up cattle. I really liked watching the cattle more than fishing. What a goof. I didn't like to hook a worm on a line, but was fine with stinky cheese! HA. Poor Grandpa...he never really got to fish when he was with us kids; one of us was always having trouble with our line.

Laura: Yes, I always felt like we were going fishing to entertain Grandpa, but in reality of course, he was trying to entertain us because you are right...he never got much fishing done when we were along! Try as we might, we just couldn't keep our lines straight! I remember riding in his car to fetch the worms and then on out to fish. It always seemed such a sturdy car clanking along over those rough, washboard, dirt roads (and his car always smelled so smoky!) I also remember catching croppy off a boat dock and fishing at the Norton Dam.

Pam: Was the bait shop in that weird little green building at the corner of State and Hwy 36 that also had a little café? I can still remember the smell of the cigarette smoke.

Laura: The car really did smell, didn't it! Fish and beer and smoke and Old Spice cologne and dust. HA.

Pam: Probably my fondest memory is going to Station 15 with Grandma and Grandpa. I knew Billy the Kid, you know (okay, a former life...I'm not that old), and he lived in Norton as a kid when his Mom was the station manager there. I always felt a strong connection to Station 15. Okay, a bit weird, but real for me. Just remembering this brings back all the smells and sounds. I'm having flashbacks!

Laura: Oh, how could I forget Station 15? I LOVED it...I don't know why now when I think about it. It wasn't really much of anything, but at the time seemed so special! Looking in those windows you could be transported back into a time that I always loved to pretend I was in! Sometimes I would sit by the open window in Grandpa's bedroom upstairs and pretend it was Victorian times and there were fancy ladies in big hats sipping drinks out in the yard and you could hear a party going on...until the festivities were shattered by a gun shot from a rebel cowboy who rode in on his horse! Ha! I would pretend I was a girl dressed up like a boy so I could escape and ride away with that rebel cowboy!

Pam: I think that's why I have three Victorian costumes in my wardrobe!

Laura: Maybe we both knew Billy the Kid...or maybe we were Pony Express riders and stopped at Station 15?

Pam: Remember 'helping' Grandpa clean the fish? He'd sit out on the driveway in those metal chairs with a bucket of water, gut the fish, and then take the pliers and skin the fish. Oddly, I particularly remember one time when I pulled out the spinal cords of the fish he'd cleaned and thinking that was cool, then noticing that the fish didn't move anymore from reflex when Grandma salted them in the pan. I remember asking Grandpa about that and he explained about the nervous system and spinal cords, etc. My first important anatomy lesson. I really started reading all of Grandpa's medical journals after that. I liked helping Grandma fry the fish, too. Oh, yeah, and EATING them. Haven't had fish as good as those bullheads since.

Laura: I remember the first time he pulled the clusters of pink eggs out. He fried them up and I really didn't want to taste them, but they turned out to be really delicious! I don't think I've had fish eggs since then...but only because of lack of opportunity, not because they weren't good! Yes, the fish were delicious. I remember that too...so white and flaky.

Pam: Eeesh. Still won't eat fish eggs. Remember the Jam sessions in the living room! Grandma, Mom, Jerry...great fun. Okay, maybe it was more like they played the piano and we all sang, but still GREAT fun. We need to do that again.

Laura: Oh, yes!

Pam: I got my tonsils out while at G&G's. Don't know why I got them out there, but I did. Age 4. Evidently I threw up on Grandma's couch. Oops! I also remember being sick while at Uncle Jerry's and Aunt Lena's...don't know when, why, or anything, but do remember the lamp with the Black "Moroccan" guy with red pants and thinking "weird...where'd that guy come from? Where am I?" I was also sick at Aunt Beverly's once...equality, I guess

Laura: I didn't know you had your tonsils out in Norton! And, I don't remember you being sick at our house. I do remember

the lamp you are talking about...I think Mom and Dad may still have that! That would be something that someone delirious would puzzle on for sure!

Pam: When I came down the stairs at Christmas in Norton...about age 4 or 5...I saw the gray stuffed dachshund (still have it!), the metal dollhouse (probably still have it in the garage), and the lights on the tree, and I was thinking "this is just like the storybook!" I still have the storybook!)

Laura: Oh, what a lovely memory!

Pam: I loved to sit on Grandpa's office floor and read those magazines. I learned a lot. I also remember Grandpa's old office downtown, the one with the really cool cane furniture. Whatever happened to that furniture? I hope it is being loved and wasn't just taken to the dump like G&G's old fridge.

Laura: I don't think I ever saw Grandpa's office downtown! I don't have any memory of the furniture you are talking about! I do remember walking downtown to see a movie once. I always wondered what happened to the old fridge. We should have salvaged it and turned it into a unique storage cabinet.

Pam: When I was in college, our folks pitched in to get G&G a new fridge. I wanted that old fridge, but didn't have a place yet, so off it went to the dump; probably still there buried by a couple decades of trash. I remember also sitting on the upstairs hallway floor and reading G&G's Books of Knowledge. I learned SO MUCH. Still have those books...they are one of my most treasured possessions. They are in my living room in the same bookshelf they came in. I learned animal breeds, science, farming (well, not nearly as much as I did from Uncle Al), geography, history...perhaps my best education ever.

Laura: Were those the books up in the attic behind Grandpa's bedroom (this is a very fuzzy memory...was there an attic or just a closet?) I remember those books as well. I am glad you have kept them safe and treasured!

Pam: The books were in the hallway upstairs; now they are next to my piano! And, NOBODY gave a better osteopathic treatment than Grandpa and NOBODY ever will. Grandpa not only was a brilliant osteopath, he was a brilliant and highly intuitive diagnostician. He never got the recognition he deserved from the MDs in town, but they sure relied on him for assistance when they couldn't figure out a medical problem.

Laura: I SO remember the treatments! And when he would "crack" your neck. You knew it was coming and you knew it was going to feel so good, but somehow the anticipation would make you tense up and Grandpa would have to work so hard to relax you first. And then suddenly...unexpectedly, but not really..."craaaaaaaack"! Yes, Grandpa was in the wrong time period. He'd be well-respected now (well, more so anyway, in this more accepting age). I remember Dad saying that when they were looking at his old records, how many times he had taken chickens or other such things in lieu of payment and how much money he had just never collected. Somehow, I always got the impression he wasn't in it just for the money...that he got other satisfaction from his work. I formulated that image as a child before I would have been able to put that image into quantitative terms or understand exactly what that thought really meant, but now I know it was about the kind of person Grandpa was and had little to do with it being just about a job for him.

Pam: Yes, he would be well-respected now. I've no doubt that his profession was far more to him than money. Mom has Grandpa's ledgers...yes, he often took chickens, corn, potatoes, beans...and most of his ledger shows unpaid debts from his patients. I had him write in a journal once and he said that he became an osteopath because of an osteopath who was a friend of his parents and whom he knew as a teen. He believed being a D.O. was a way to really help people. Being a doctor was a calling to him, not just a job and certainly not for the money. However, I know that not receiving the respect from MDs really ate at him. To this day, MDs look down on DOs despite the fact that DOs have just as much (actually, more) training than most MDs. Kirksville, where Grandpa studied, is still the premier school of Osteopathy. Do you remember our matching skirts for the Norton Centennial Celebration? I had my arm in a cast because I'd gotten injured from a fall from a horse. Do you remember the barbecued brisket that they roasted in a pit for days before the Fair? Wow! Almost (but NOT quite) as good as Uncle Al's chicken fried steak. Got me hooked on barbecued brisket for life.

Laura: Oh, my gosh! I forgot about the matching skirts! And I do vaguely remember the roasting pit. We never spent any time up at Aunt Beverly's and Uncle Al's in Kimball...but I wish we had.

Pam: You would have loved spending time up there. I rounded up cattle, watched buffalo on the range, rode a calf, gathered chicken eggs, slopped hogs, and drove a tractor, a wheat truck, a power wagon, and a combine. We stayed in the house that had the milk separator in it. Which reminds me...one time we were milking the cows and aimed the milk coming out of the udder at the flies and shot them into the milk. That probably wasn't smart...but it was fun. Always so much fun there! Except when Richard convinced me that the "cement pile" was solid and I jumped on it, but it turned out to be one very large pile of cow dung and only "hard" on the outside. Yuck...Bad Richard!

Laura: That's funny!

Pam: How about the goat swing? Okay, it was next door at the Moody's, but all the same it was part of being at Grandma's and Grandpa's.

Laura: Did you every smash into the tree trunk? I always felt like that tree was watching over us in a way.

Pam: I never hit the tree, and yes, I believe the tree watched over us.

Laura: Remember when Mr. Moody died? I remember that Mrs. Moody died very soon after and how Grandma said she wasn't sick, that she died of a broken heart...she just wanted to be with Mr. Moody.

Pam: I do remember that. I was very sad and missed them. Dying of a broken heart often happens, I think. Sad and beautiful all at the same time. Remember talking late at night during summer with the windows open and the crickets and cicadas humming away? I can still make the sound of the Norton cicadas...sssooosssssoooooossssssoooo.

Laura: Bugs! How can bugs be so darned special? I used to keep cicada shells.

Pam: I remember bending over the bathtub to wash my hair under the faucet and thinking there must be a better way. I liked the vanity Grandma had in the bathroom...it always smelled good!

Laura: Oh, yes! I always thought only the fanciest of ladies actually had a special spot for putting on makeup and to me Grandma seemed like a very fancy lady! I don't think I ever saw her without her lipstick on! I also use to marvel at how very tiny her feet were. And her purses (to even have more than one seemed interesting to me) always matched her shoes; and she had so many hats!

Pam: Grandma NEVER went out without earrings and lipstick on... bright red. Candy apple red, Revlon, I think. She wore size 4½ shoes. To this day, I see a pair of size 4½ shoes and think of Grandma. She had this pair of shoes that looked like almond shells to me, and she always had a pair of red heels on hand! She loved to come to KC and shop at Harzfeld's for shoes. And yes, matching purse and shoes were absolutely essential.

Laura: I LOVED the closets behind the bathroom and in Grandma's room. So full of interesting things. We'd get out stuff and play dress-up, and Grandma would tell us stories about the things.

Pam: When I read the Chronicles of Narnia...The Lion, The Witch, and the Wardrobe...somehow Grandma's closets came to mind. I'm sure they were magic...I know I found doorways to other worlds in there!

Laura: I didn't read the Chronicles of Narnia until I read them to MiKi when she was little...and I thought of Grandma's closet then! I thought it was magical as well. I remember one night when we were there and there were tornado warnings but I would just hide in that closet and feel perfectly safe in there if a tornado came.

Pam: How about our doing 'shows' in the basement? I don't remember if anyone actually saw our 'shows', but we had fun creating them. The basement also was a 'magical' place and I'm sure there were treasures in that crawlspace. Either treasures or really creepy things. Either way, fascinating! I recently saw "War of the Worlds" (the Tom Cruise version) and the basement in the movie reminded me of G&G's basement.

Laura: Yeah. We were such BIG talents! Ha! Don't you remember the time when they all watched us do our show in front of the live stink bug?

Pam: Oh, my gosh! The Stink Bug Show! Didn't we come up with some song about the stink bug? What fun we had. And I loved to play Flinch around G&G's dining table. Greg always cheated, yet he always looked so innocent. How did he do that?

Laura: Yes, and so much giggling!

Pam: And, all the celebrations at G&G's. Birthday cakes, Thanksgiving dinners, Easter...Grandma sure got a kick out of my Easter bunny makeup and ears when I visited for Easter while at K-State. Of course the drunks in PBurg were a bit shocked when they came out of the corner bar and saw a rabbit sitting in a Capri at the stop light...they went right back into the bar! I laughed all the way from PBurg to Norton...a miracle my makeup didn't wash off with the tears of laughter.

Laura: I remember your Easter Bunny! I could not believe how much like a bunny you really did look! I thought that was amazing!

Pam: Speaking of dinners...which I am now...Grandma's green jell-o salad with marshmallows...her potato salad...the roast turkey and gravy...mashed potatoes...Grandma's fried chicken and fried fish... now THAT's comfort food!

Laura: It sure is!

Pam: I also remember cleaning the chandelier, which Grandma convinced us to do every summer. I remember thinking it was fun. Now I know better.

Laura: I don't remember ever doing that! I think you got snookered! Ha!

Pam: Hey! Actually, Grandma was sooooooo good at making everything FUN. I've never known anybody as good at FUN as Grandma. She could always laugh and sometimes when I'm down I feel as if Grandma is poking me on the arm (like she did) and giving me one of her pursed lips looks...and then laughing.

Laura: I remember her doing her 'pursed lips and laughing'. It's on the tip of my brain...I so wish we had video back then! I'd go revisit it right now! Okay. Here's a weird memory that I just thought of...I remember Grandma saying that "Pam has the most beautiful hands". I remember her remarking at how perfectly long and slender your fingers are and how nice you kept your fingernails. I do remember that I felt so jealous! Grandma would find the oddest things to comment on, but her comments always made me really think about things in a different way!

Pam: I remember Grandma saying how wonderful your hair was and being jealous of that. You had hair like Mom's, which was always thick and curly. Mine was just straight and drippy. Dippy? Yeah, I sure wish we'd had video then. I could have made feature films of things Grandma said and did. I remember that she could be pretty... uh ...biting sometimes. Once when we visited Grandma at the nursing home, Mom wore a wonderful ethnic type skirt; black with colorful accents and very stylish. Mom walked in and Grandma said, "Marlyn! Why are you dressed like a gypsy?" Grandma could be such a snot! And yet, at the same time, so darned funny!

Laura: Yes, she always made me laugh.

Pam: I think of Grandpa whenever I play solitaire on the computer, see a roll-top desk or a chair like he had (the kind I'm scared to sit in for fear of falling backwards), have to use my knowledge of medicine for my law clients (he's always there to assist, I do believe), smell the smoke of whatever cigarette he used to smoke, drink beer, see sausage (salami? Pepperoni?), or hear polka music. Do you remember how he would 'direct' the music on the TV or radio?

Laura: Oh, I DO remember him directing in the air! And playing solitaire at his desk. I remember his desk and chair as well. I assume somebody in the family ended up with those? It would be fun to see those again someday.

Pam: Mom has the roll-top desk and chair. She treasures those 2 pieces of furniture. Don't know if you know, but there was always a dispute about whether the desk came from Great-Grandpa Drummond (Grandma claimed it was her Dad's law office desk) or whether Grandpa bought it himself. I think of Grandma whenever I see polka dots, hats (especially red ones!), antique furniture, milk glass chicken-shaped candy dishes, spinning wheels, a plaid sofa, lace curtains, red geraniums, sunflowers, great decorating or design, white gloves, and black patent shoes, or hear stride piano, especially Alley Cat.

Laura: Oh, yes! Alley Cat! Travis and I played that as a duet in a piano recital a few years back and I thought about Grandma and how she always seemed to have such joy playing it!

Pam: She LOVED that song. I bet she was up in heaven smiling wide when you two were playing it! She probably poked God in the arm and said, "That's my granddaughter and great-grandson!" I could go on and on...I have to say that my memories of Grandma and Grandpa, as well as of my Aunts and Uncles and Cousins, are so dear to me. I believe I am who I am because of my family. I had a wonderful childhood because of my large and very loving extended family. Norton and Kansas will always be home to me more than anyplace on this planet.

Laura: I hope Miki's childhood memories are as sweet as mine! I hope she has treasured memories of Kansas, too. But, I keep thinking we should have baked more cookies!

Pam: You did bake enough cookies. Even a moment is enough when you remember it. And, if we hand down stories of family, Grandma and Grandpa will live forever.

Laura: It's has been fun remembering things today! Love ya!

CHAPTER 5

The Only Grandparent I Knew, Ida Duerfeldt Butler

MY GRANDMA IDY (IDA BUTLER) was the only grandparent I remember well. She and Elmer Butler lived on a farm near Barada, in Richardson County in southeast Nebraska until 1911 when they moved west to a farm one-a-half miles north of Hebron in Thayer Country. In 1920 after the two older boys, Henry and Ralph, had left home and my dad, Howard, was graduating from high school and had no interest in farming (he already wanted to become a doctor), they moved into the town of Hebron where they lived until Elmer died of stomach cancer in 1931.

I remember Grandma Idy as being very kind, rather quiet, with gentle eyes, patient, and always trying to be helpful. I do not remember her smiling or laughing out loud, but she had a pleasant, comforting expression on her face. She lived in Falls City and Geneva most of the time that I was growing up, and sometimes in Norton, too. In my memory, I see Grandma Idy in a print dress and always wearing an apron. She wore metal rimmed glasses...yes, the kind that became known as 'granny glasses' in the 1970s.

When I was about nine, Beverly, Jerry, and I visited our Grandma Ida Butler in Geneva, where Aunt Blanche and Dr. Harold Rosenau also lived. Something I ate made me ill, and my stomach was hurting badly. Grandma Idy fixed me a hot toddy with some kind of alcohol in it to cure me. Maybe it did...I vomited immediately and did recover.

When Mother and Dad went to Albuquerque while we were in the Hale house in the early 1940s (either they took Aunt Ruby there or went to get her), Grandma Idy came and stayed with Beverly, Jerry, and me while they were gone. She was conscientious and tried to take good care of us. Being penny-wise, as it was necessary to be during the War, she did not like to waste anything. She served cottage cheese at one meal, but none of us liked it, and we did not eat it. So, the next day, she added cocoa to it, thinking we would like anything chocolate. But, we weren't fooled; it was still cottage cheese! When the folks got back from Albuquerque, they brought Jerry a huge Indian chief's headdress and a bullwhip. They brought Beverly a doll...an Indian mother holding her papoose with an Indian blanket wrapped around the mother's shoulders. Oddly, I do not remember what they brought me! Was I coveting?!

When we lived in the house on North Second Street, from mid-1944 until September of 1945, Beverly and I slept in the center bedroom. While we were there, Grandma Idy came to live with us and a bed for her was set up in the bedroom that Beverly and I shared. She had gallbladder problems and, before she went to bed each night, she would sit on her bed and rub her belly, bringing up long and loud burps. This grossed me out, because it sounded like she was vomiting, which caused me to gag. I hated to vomit, so I would wrap my pillow tight around my head trying to drown out the sound.

When we moved to 411 North Grant in September of 1945, she moved into the duplex on State Street, north of the Methodist Church. On the morning of January 26, 1947, Dad found her dead on the floor when he went to check on her. It was presumed that she had a heart attack, but it was rare to have an autopsy done at that time and the sophisticated heart tests, such as CT Scans and echocardiograms, were not available then. Since I had a Penetrating Aortic Ulcer, Jerry has an aneurysm that is being watched, and it was discovered that Dad had an aortic aneurysm shortly before he died, I have wondered if Grandma Idy actually died of a burst aneurysm.

The funeral was held in Nebraska where she had grown up and spent most of her life. As we set out for Nebraska in our car it was starting to snow, and the storm got worse as the hours went by. By the time we got to Nebraska, the snowstorm had become a raging blizzard with blinding, wind-driven snow, and visibility next to zero. Dad was driving slowly and as the road began rising slightly, he suddenly sensed that we were approaching a train track. He hesitated and suddenly, in that moment, a ground tremor slightly shook the car, a rumbling sound swelled louder, and the freight train roared down the track just a few feet in front of our car. With the howling wind and the snow, none of us heard it or saw it until just before it was upon us. We all sat in stunned silence as we realized how close we had come to being hit. A very scary moment!

Grandma Idy's funeral service took place in a small, country church in Hebron, and she was buried in the cemetery there beside Elmer. A big, coal-burning stove glowed in the corner of the church, but it was still very cold inside the church. A women's trio sang "In the Garden", one of Grandma's favorite hymns. I still think of Grandma Idy when I hear that hymn today.

Years later, I had a psychic reading in Sedona, Arizona, and Robert Petro said that he saw a kind-looking woman with metal-rimmed glasses and wearing an apron standing behind me; she told the psychic that she had loved to brush my hair when I was a child. I like to believe it was Grandma Idy.

CHAPTER 6

Siblings: A Simple Word
For Timeless Bonds

I SPEAK OF MEMORIES OF Beverly and Jerry in other places of my memoirs, but I want to give a brief 'essence' of who they were and are. As I was growing up, I was always an 'observer'. Being the youngest in my family (and among all my cousins), I did not feel that I fit in with my older relatives. I stood back and watched what my older sister, brother, cousins, as well as others, did. To me, they seemed very sure of themselves. Beverly was social and outgoing, and Jerry was daring and musically talented: two great talents to absorb by watching them. I always felt happy and honored when they included me in their activities.

A. JERRY MILTON BUTLER

Jerry was five years older than I was, so I viewed him 'from afar' when I was little. He was adventurous and creative from the time he was young, which got him into trouble often... for example, the accidents talked about below. He was, and still is, very intelligent, and school was not a challenge to him. Even though he got the highest score ever received (up to that time) by anyone in Norton on a test given to graduating seniors, he was not interested in studying or competing for top grades in school. I assume he completed the assignments when he was in high school, but I do not think he ever opened a book to study. (The photo must have been posed for the NCHS Annual.) School started at eight o'clock and Jerry would sleep until 7:30 or later, dress, grab a sweet roll or some toast, and leave the house about five minutes before eight!

He did like to do 'experiments' that he'd read about and create things. One time he made something that smelled like rotten eggs, which Mother was not happy about. While living in the house on North Wabash, he spent hours building an oil derrick out of balsa wood and toothpicks only to have it destroyed when our dog, Tag, jumped onto the table and knocked it off.

Jerry, like all boys I suppose, had a few accidents growing up. He got a concussion while living on North Wabash, and when we lived at the Hale house on

West Waverly, he and Billy Cutting had gone to a Tarzan movie and then tried to emulate Tarzan by jumping from limb to limb. Jerry fell head first onto the curb, fracturing the bones in his forehead and breaking his right arm just above the wrist. When he was in high school, he was playing third base on the local Norton baseball team when an opponent charged him; the blow broke his collarbone. Jerry said he watched the fluoroscope as Dad and Dr. Kennedy each took one of his arms, felt with their hands to find the broken collarbone, and then "pulled me apart" in order to set it. To quote Jerry, "That hurt!!!"

While in high school and after graduating in May of 1947, Jerry worked at the First State Bank. One day as he walked past the CB&Q railroad station on his way to the bank, the Station Agent stopped him and offered him a job at twice the salary he was getting at the bank: six days a week at $7 a day! That was an easy decision to make. One of his jobs at the Burlington railroad was loading and unloading heavy cream cans on and off the freight cars; he built up some muscles doing that. He also started learning telegraphy.

Telegraphy was the way communications were transmitted between railroad stations regarding train locations, cargo, mail, etc. Morse code was used to input the information by tapping a 'key' on the transmitter to 'type in' the words, letter by letter, using dits and dahs (or dots and dashes). The sound of a telegrapher at work was endemic to war movies or to news reports and always conveyed a sense of urgency to what was being relayed. Knowing that telegraphy would help him get assignments to more desirable job locations, Jerry worked to become adept at telegraphy.

Chillicothe Business School in Missouri offered a course in telegraphy, so he went there from January to May 1948. He did extremely well in everything except penmanship. It is curious to me now to think that penmanship was a required class, but that was one subject at which Jerry did not excel. Maybe bad handwriting is genetic. Dad's handwriting was illegible, which we all attributed to his being a doctor, and both Jerry and I have poor handwriting; barely legible more accurately describes our style. I remember taking penmanship in grade school and hating it. I practiced those 'Os' over and over and could not get them to flow; I was given III's in penmanship, a very bad grade.

Jerry was, and still is a fantastic musician and played the piano by ear from the time he was young. Jerry continued working at the Burlington railroad until a blizzard in December 1948 stranded the Jack Everett Orchestra in Norton, and they recruited Jerry to play the trumpet in the band. Norton was proud of his accomplishments in this area because, after all, this was the era of the Big Bands. Jerry travelled with the band by bus all over the Mid-West for about seven months, and he found that being a touring musician was not as glamourous and exciting as it sounds. He decided that playing one-night gigs, packing up the bus, riding in the bus all night to the next gig was not a comfortable way to live. He said, "I left the Band in Keokuk, Iowa the middle of July, 1949, and rode the CB&Q local all the way to McCook, then took a taxi to Norton and got home with $5 left." He then started working as a telegrapher for the Rock Island railroad on August 5, 1949.

When the Korean War began in June of 1950, Jerry was drafted into the Army. Fortunately, he went to Germany instead of Korea! Even more fortunately, he went into the Special Services and played music: in the band, in a small combo, and as the bugler.

After getting out of the Army in 1952, the GI Bill gave veterans the opportunity to go to college. I was at the University of Kansas at the time, and he came there for the spring 1953 semester. College was slow for someone like Jerry who learns fast and does not like to waste time, so he got a job again with the Rock Island railroad, this time in Kansas City. He took a CPA correspondence course and finished the two-year course in one year since the 'third trick' (overnight) on a railroad has a lot of 'waiting time'. In June of 1954, he took the CPA exam at an accounting firm in Topeka, passed it the first time he took it, and the firm offered him a job at $250 month. Since he was making $450 a month on the Railroad, it was again an easy decision.

Jerry had a great laugh, sort of a cross between a mad scientist and a triumphant 'gotcha' chortle. He did like to tease and pull fast ones on his little sisters. In spite of this, Jerry was a thoughtful brother always. When I was nine, Jerry got a paper doll book, cut the doll form out of wood, and glued the paper doll to the form to give me for Christmas, along with the paper clothes from the book. That doll was dear to my heart! There was a small, dugout root or storm cellar under the kitchen part of the 'Hale' house, and the sides of the room were built with large, uneven rocks or stones, piled and layered on top of each other to create the walls. The only light was from candles or any daylight coming in when the storm doors were open. And, there were huge, ugly centipedes down there! They must have been three or four inches long! Jerry and a friend decided to have a 'saloon' there, so they cleaned it out, set up a bar, and put empty liquor bottles that they had found in the alley on the ledges of the rocks. I was surprised and so happy when Jerry invited me down to see it! He had a way of making me feel special and accepted.

In 1951, I was a junior in high school and he was in the Army, stationed at Ft. Sill, Oklahoma. When Mother and I had not been able to find a formal for me to wear to the Junior-Senior Prom, he went to the PX and bought a beautiful white formal gown for me to wear. Mother made a matching net duster to wear over it.

Later, he sent me a gorgeous pink, two-piece suit! In addition, when he was in the Army and stationed in Europe, he sent me a bottle of Channel No. 5. I thought I was the most elegant and sophisticated young lady ever when I dabbed it behind my ears and on my wrists with the glass stopper! Jerry also taught me about chords and techniques for playing 'Jazz' and popular music. One other thing about Jerry...it was impossible to get a good photo of him! If I raised my Brownie camera and aimed it at him, he would make an awful face, cross his eyes, stick out his tongue...anything to thwart me! Dad took this photo when Jerry was home overnight because the Jack Everett Orchestra played for a dance in Jennings, Kansas, not far from Norton. He grew a mustache and combed his hair back to have that 'musician' look, but he said he was glad to shave off the mustache after he left the band.

B. BEVERLY JEAN BUTLER HISEY

Beverly was a great role model for me of what a 'girl' is supposed to be. She has always been outgoing, able to make friends quickly, cheerful and friendly. I have always wanted to be able to 'bubble' like Beverly! She is a warm and caring person and has an ability to make people feel comfortable. She was active in all kinds of social groups and was elected President of Y-Teens. She also always had many boyfriends.

When Beverly was about five years old, in the mid-1930s, Mother and Mrs. Abe Schneider would drive to Hays, about 100 miles, so that Don Schneider and Beverly could take acrobatic lessons. I do not know why it was important enough to drive several hours in a hot car (no air-conditioning yet!) and pay for lessons, but Beverly and Don were apparently quite the 'adagio team', and Beverly could do cartwheels, the splits, and back-bends with ease. I was not envious at the time (because I was too young), but later I did not really understand why I could not get the tap dance lessons I 'really, really' wanted when I was in grade school. Perhaps, it was because a World War had taken place and times had changed by then.

Beverly and I shared a room, and a double bed, while growing up. Beverly, even as a young girl, seemed to like cleaning and keeping her space orderly and neat. Since I did not share her zeal and was not a particularly neat roommate, this was a point of friction. One time she told me to clean up my half of the room while she was gone or she would do it for me when she got back. When she returned, she was surprised and pleased to see a clean and neat room; that is, until she discovered that I had solved the problem by putting everything under the bed. I still have things under my bed, but she admits that now she does, too!

Beverly was always conscientious and dependable. When Mother and I went to Albuquerque in 1948, Beverly had just started a job at Stapleton's drug store and assured us that it was okay for us to go without her. She said, "I'll stay home and take care of Dad." She did her best to plan meals and cook dinner for him every day. (Of course, she may have enjoyed the freedom that summer when was seventeen.) Beverly commented many years later that Dad had stayed home every evening while Mother and I were gone rather than go to the pool hall and play snooker. He was a conscientious father!

I do not remember ever fighting with Beverly in any big way, although I am sure we had minor skirmishes now and then. The bedroom that Beverly and I shared in the 'Hale' house had a narrow, but deep, walk-in closet with a curtain hung across the opening (no door). One day we were arguing about something and Mother disciplined us by making us sit in the closet until we could be nice to each other. Wily Beverly said, "Let's pretend that we don't care" that

Mother scolded us and "let's just play in here". Before long Mother came to see what all the laughing was about and she let us come out of the closet, since it was not being much of a punishment! Beverly was clever...and cunning! Beverly was also a wonderful mentor to guide me through junior high and high school. For example, one morning when I was a freshman, I woke up with a huge, red zit right on the bridge of my nose. I was about to head out the door to walk to school, when Beverly pulled me back and said, "For heaven's sake! Put a Band-Aid over that thing!"

I got hand-me-down clothes from Beverly, of course. I remember a few of them fondly. One was a deep rose two-piece outfit with a straight skirt and a mock turtleneck top that came down over the skirt; I thought it was very pretty and sophisticated. Another was a two-piece skirt and top, similar in design to the rose-colored dress, but in black velvet. I wore it to Jerry's high school graduation in 1947. As I was getting dressed, Mother looked at me and said, "Marlyn, I think you need a bra!" I felt so grown up, even though the hand-me-down bra that Mother got out of the dresser drawer was quite uncomfortable to wear throughout the graduation ceremony! Mother always said, "You have to suffer to be beautiful!" When Beverly was a senior in high school, she had a dress that was covered in roses, and one of the roses sat directly on her breast. Alvin Hisey, her boyfriend (and later husband), gave her the nickname of Rosie when she wore it. I thought that was so funny!

When Alvin was in the Air Force, he was stationed in Alaska and would complain about not getting letters from Beverly. A popular song at the time was "No Letter Today" (recorded by Hank Snow), which seemed to be a theme song for them. Also popular was "Far Away Places" (Kramer and Whitney), which was appropriate since he was so far away.

After graduating from high school, Beverly went to Chillicothe Business School in Missouri. Dorothy Harris, a Norton classmate, also went, so they were roommates. Beverly made many friends there and met a young man who asked her to marry him. However, after graduating from Chillicothe, Beverly came back to Norton, became secretary to Gerald Travis, the Principal of the high school, and reunited with Alvin; they were married in November of 1951.

PART II

Life From The 1930s to 1960s

*From the Great Depression, through the Dust Bowl years
and World War II, through a Boom time and another war,
life molded us with the push/pull of changes, the fear and
excitement of new experiences, and our reactions to problems
and opportunities. Hang on! There is life to live!*

CHAPTER 7

Norton: The Way We Were

NORTON WAS FOUNDED IN 1872. It lies in a valley between Highway 36 on the north and a hill on Highway 283 a few miles south of town. That may not be the official description of what makes up Norton, but that is the way I remember Norton and the way it was when I grew up. Whenever we return to Norton for a visit, I feel a sense of belonging, of roots, when driving into Norton from the south and seeing the town spread out in the valley below as we come over the top of that hill. I am 'home' again. The north half of Norton was built on a hill rising from the center of town (the intersection of State Street and Main Street) over a length of about five blocks up to Highway 36. That hill was wonderful for sledding in the winter and caused long walks uphill from downtown to our home. A nice thing about a small town is that you know most people and folks help others, so it wasn't unusual for a driver of a car to see someone trudging northward and offer to bring them 'up the hill'.

Life in Norton when I was growing up was typical for the many small towns across the Midwest during the 1930s, '40s, and '50s. Norton was a farm-economy based community and was in its prime then. The dust storms and the depression of the 1930s, followed by World War II, slowed the growth of Norton during those years. However, after WWII ended, a boom took place in Norton, as it did across the United States. Building supplies were in short supply because of the war, but there was new construction in Norton as well as restoration of the downtown area.

Since we lived in town and many of my friends did, too, I was only vaguely aware that the town's financial well-being was based on farming. I knew that many of Dad's patients were farmers, but Mother worked at "The Cottage Shop", a dress shop owned by Neva Funk, and I was more aware of her customers who lived in Norton rather than on farms. Most of the children of farmers went to country schools until they got into junior high or high school. Ronnie Allen, Dick McChesney, Carol Rhoades, Harlan Conkey, Gretel Kopp, Gladys Hazlett, Myrna Kendall, and others spent early school years in one-room/all-grades country schools. Some of my classmates talked about their experiences and said the schools generally had no running water or indoor plumbing, and the walk to the outhouse was long and cold when the snow was blowing. Shirley Meyers, along with Carroll and Sherrill Jenkins went to a country school named "Hardscrabble" until they came to Norton for high school. Lawrence Wetter said the name of his school was "Frogpond", and others went to "Hillman" and "Lone Hand" schools. I knew very few kids who lived on farms while I was in grade school. Even in high school, when the kids from the country would drive to school, or have older brothers and sisters who drove them to town, most of them had to go home right after school because they had chores to do. Gladys VanDerWege, Sonya Sleffel, and Carol Deiter came to Norton to go to school starting in grade school. Carol lived not far out of town and had an older brother and sister who could drive her to school, so she was able to participate in more activities than many farm kids. She became one of my best friends from grade school on, and she had several parties at her house. It was at her farm where I almost got milk out of a cow, which was an exciting thing to do for a townie.

Norton had three Drug stores: Stapleton's, (Owned by Mrs. Nettie Stapleton; Oren Hollinger and Tommy Thomason were pharmacists there), Moffet's (Melvin Moffet, owner and pharmacist), and Raney's (Clarence "Squeak" Bower was the pharmacist and his wife, Mae, worked there, too). Raney's was the after-school hangout for Junior and Senior high kids. It was always fun to wander into Raney's and see who was sitting in the big red leather booths and to join friends for a Coke and some flirting and talking. I worked at all three drug stores as a soda jerk and sales clerk.

There were two banks in Norton: The First State Bank (Bill Rouse) and the First National Bank (Harold Kohfeld and Bill Smiley).

Although most people ate their meals at home, Norton did have several restaurants. Melroy's Café was on West Main, next to the Cozy Movie Theater, and was always busy at noon. Hannah Melroy (Mickey, John, and Leo Melroy's mother) had opened the café around 1920. John and Leo, along with his wife Emily, were operating the café by the time I started eating there around 1940. They served such things as roast beef, meat loaf, fried chicken, liver and onions, pork roast, all served with mashed potatoes and brown gravy, canned vegetables (peas, corn, green beans, butter beans), and a slice of bread and butter. Desserts included chocolate, cherry, lemon, and apple pies and pearl tapioca pudding. The price was thirty cents when I was in grade school. There was also a Serv-U-Well diner on the northwest corner of State Street and Main. Dad liked to go there for their ham and navy bean soup. Stapleton's Drug Store served sandwiches, fountain drinks, and milkshakes. For a fancier dinner, there was the Kent Hotel. The Lions Club and the Rotary Club had their weekly lunch meetings there. On Highway 36, north of town, the Lucky Strike Grill opened when I was in high school and lasted until the late 1980s. They served an excellent chicken fried steak, fried chicken, and ham and bean soup with corn bread.

Moline's Bakery, across the street south of the Courthouse, had wonderful maple and chocolate Long John rolls, Krispies, and cinnamon knots. McMahon's meat market and grocery store was near it on the southeast corner of East Washington and South Kansas Streets. Meat wasn't prepackaged then, so Mother would tell the butcher, Willie Kauten, that she wanted a three-pound chuck roast, and he would cut off a piece of meat from the hanging beef, weigh it, and wrap it in white, waxed butcher paper. Another grocery store (Safeway, I think) was in the middle of the main block downtown, and a small grocery store, Witt's was on North First Street about a block north of West Lincoln. Witt's became 'Wilson's' by the time I was old enough to walk down the hill from the Hale house in 1942. Mother allowed me to pick out a treat, which they would add to her bill. I loved the salted, unshelled sunflower seeds that came in small packages; I would put a few in my mouth and enjoy the saltiness before biting the sides of each one to crack open the shell and savor the small sunflower seed. They also had candy cigarettes, the little wax bottles filled with 'juice', and NRG candy wafers (these were not very tasty, but I imagined getting lots of energy when I ate them).

The Hillside grocery was on North Second Street way up the hill, a block and a half north of our house at 411 North Grant. All of these groceries were small, one-room stores with a minimal selection of products. Even so, they served to provide the can of peas or corn, or the piece of meat, or a few potatoes that we needed for dinner. On trips home to Norton over the years, all of the grandchildren enjoyed walking to the Hillside to buy a can of corn or something else that Mother sent them there to get. She always called ahead and told the owners that her grandchildren could buy some candy and just add it to the bill. The Hillside grocery burned down in March of 2014 and all the grandchildren (and I) felt a bit of nostalgic sadness at that news. Later, in the mid-1950s, a large Safeway opened on West Main and another locally owned grocery, Kellings, opened on the corner of West Lincoln and North Second Street.

Since home freezers were not widely available until the late 1950s, a Norton business provided large lockers, which could be rented to keep frozen food in. These were used mostly for large catches of fish or for sides of beef or pork bought from local ranchers. Ice, cubed or in large blocks, could also be purchased there.

Other stores in Norton at that time included Virtues, which was a general department store including menswear, women's and children's wear, shoes, and linens. This was just north of Raney's and ran the full width of the building, with entry doors on the west and on the east. Bower's Hardware was on Washington Street across the street south from Raney's. Years later, I happened to be visiting Norton when the hardware store was going out of business. I went in to see what might be inside, and there were treasures on the second floor. Items had been stored there since the 1920s! There was a new, full-leather fly-net coat for a draft horse! It was beautiful, and I wish I had bought it. I did buy a leather horse collar and an antique oven designed to sit on top of a coal-burning stove so the heat could rise into the oven for baking. It is now a decorative piece that reminds me of Norton. Kids look at it and think it must be an early microwave.

Many businesses moved to various locations in the downtown area over the years. For example, a business space across from Dad's office on State Street was occupied by Duckwall's in the late 1930s and early 40s, then Muir's Music store, and later it was a Penney's store. Muir's Music store was located in several different locations through the years before closing in the late 1940s. There were two barbershops: Hobe (rhymes with globe) Bower's was on State Street a couple doors south from Moffet's drug store; Gary Rowley's dad was a barber at that shop, too. Another barbershop was on Kansas Street north of Main Street; Marlin Bozarth (Bozie) had his barbershop there from the 1950s until he retired. There were also two lumberyards, Foster's and Newberry's. I am familiar with only Newberry's Lumber, which was on State Street a block north of Main Street, because that is where Mother went to buy paint, roller blinds, and such necessities. Sharon McClure was a year younger than I was and her parents had a small photography studio and bookstore just north of Browne's Clothing store on State Street. Casey Hardware was a fairly large store, also north of Browne's.

The residential areas of town were laid out with alleys at the back of lots, between the rows of houses. Most houses did not have an attached garage, so a freestanding garage was entered from the alley. When we built the house at 411 North Grant, we added a driveway from the street to the back of the house, but never added a garage or carport. Every house had a fifty-gallon metal drum at the alley where you put your trash. The trash collection trucks would then go through the alleys; the men would pick up the big barrels manually and dump the contents into the truck, and haul everything to the dump, which was north of town. I believe they burned the mounds of trash there periodically because I remember seeing wisps of smoke and smelling an odd odor. The dump was also the place to go to practice marksmanship. Jerry had a .22 pistol that he once let me practice shooting at bottles set up on a mound of trash at the dump; pellet guns and BB guns were also taken there for practice. When Dad would go fishing or hunting, Mother would insist that he take the 'entrails' to the dump immediately before they became too odiferous.

In 1945, a devastating fire destroyed the north end of the central block downtown. About 3 o'clock in the morning, the sound of fire sirens woke up everyone in town and, looking outside, we all saw the red and yellow glow of fire. Dad felt he needed to get downtown in case anyone was hurt, and Mother wanted to go see what was happening, too. Therefore, we all got dressed and drove toward town. The sight of the huge flames coming out of the stores was startling and frightening. Dad walked closer to the burning buildings, and Mother, Jerry, Beverly, and I sat on the curb half way up the next block for a while and then went upstairs above Browne's Clothing to watch while the fire-fighters fought the fire and finally declared that it was out. Mother let us stay home from school and sleep late the next morning; we went back to school after lunch. The fire destroyed the Western Auto store, which had been at the northern end of the block, as well as the Masonic Lodge, which had occupied the second floor above. Every store all the way down to Stapleton's drug store in the middle of the block was gone by daybreak. Slowly that end of the block was rebuilt and remodeled and new stores filled the spaces.

One of the stores built or rebuilt after the fire was Horney's Appliances. Lee Horney stocked household appliances such as toasters and radios, and, importantly, he put in an area to stock and sell 78 rpm records. He set up small 'telephone booth' type rooms with record players in them so you could pick out a record and play it before deciding to buy it. The discs were made out of shellac, powdered minerals and cotton, and they scratched, chipped, and broke easily. Jerry had a job there, and Lee let him take home damaged records that could not be sold; he also gave Jerry a discount when he bought a record. Lee Horney was also notable for putting a private water well beside his house; I do not remember anyone else in town putting in a well.

Growing up, I never gave much thought to how people earned a living to pay the bills, and, although I was vaguely aware that some folks seemed to have more money than others, I didn't think of one 'job' being 'loftier' or more important than another. I did know what my Dad did for a living and what some of my friends' parents did: Pat Melroy's dad, Mickey, and her mother, Rose, both worked at Browne's clothing store; Mickey was a sales clerk and Rose did tailoring and altering for the store. Sandra's dad, Bill Isaac, had a furniture store; another furniture store was owned by Gordon Brantley, who also co-owned the Scott-Brantley Funeral Home.

Pat Harper's dad worked at the post office. Mail at that time was delivered twice a day, but a 'special delivery' letter would be delivered immediately when it arrived at the Post Office. Air Mail letters, written on onionskin paper and envelope to reduce the weight, were also special because they were deemed important enough to spend extra money to get them there quickly.

Bonnie Underwood's dad, Burchie, owned a Conoco gas station. Judy Rouse's dad was President of the First State Bank. I am not sure what Judy Brock's dad, Earl Brock, did, but her mother, Grace Brock, was a teacher and taught Latin when I was in high school. Claudine's dad worked for the Kansas highway; I think he was a civil engineer. John Hutcherson's dad had an electrical repair shop. Warren Bullock's dad was in real estate and owned gas properties and such. Lee Breckenridge's dad was a travelling salesman for Electrolux vacuums. Ronald and E. H. Allen's dad, Guy Allen, worked at the First State Bank, but I do not know in what capacity. Gene Reedy's dad was the maintenance man at the grade school. Carol Rhoades' father had died before she moved from a farm into Norton; her mother worked in an office or a bank in Norton. Carol Dieter's dad was a farmer, but I never met him and he died when Carol was young. Looking back, I wonder "How could I not have known more about my friends' families?!" Even though I have visual memories of my friends' mothers and fathers, I actually interacted with very few of them!

The Norton Country Club was a couple miles southeast of town. To get there, you drove past the post office and on east, past the Catholic Church, where you took a little jog to the right and went past the sewer plant to head down Country Club road. You could smell the sewer plant as you drove by and see the rotating long metal pipes spraying water onto the top of the large, round cement 'vat'...just one of the mental images I have retained. The Country Club was a stained wood structure that looked like a very large two-story house. The first floor was devoted to the golf club with the second floor used for the many Club parties and private parties held there through the years (at least from the 1930s to probably the mid-1960s when a new Country Club was built south of town). Beverly and Jerry co-hosted a party with Gloria Bee and Don Ward in December 1946. Being too young to participate, I watched the guests laugh and dance, the girls in long formal gowns and the boys in suits, looking forward to being old enough to attend such a fancy party. Later, I started learning to play bridge in college, and when I was home for spring break in 1953, I was invited to fill in at a bridge party at the Country Club. Avola Travis had long black hair pulled back into a sophisticated style; she was stately and distinguished looking and the wife of Gerald Travis, the esteemed principal at the high school. On top of all that, she was an excellent, and serious, bridge player. When she became my partner for one round, I was extremely nervous and intimidated, and I managed to commit the horrendous error of trumping her winning ace! I realized what I had done when I heard her gasp and saw the shock on her face. She was gracious about my goof and my embarrassment, but I was very glad when the afternoon ended.

There were several churches in Norton, but I remember only four of them. The Catholic church had a fairly large membership, and I noticed growing up that the Catholics seemed to party the most, get drunk often, and then go to confession and have all their sins forgiven. That sounded like a good plan. Dad was quite prejudiced against Catholics, and being a strong Mason, he disparaged the Knights of Columbus. When I was in high school, I started bristling when Dad berated those "*#* fisheaters", and I reacted by thinking that my marrying a Catholic would serve him right! (I did not find a Catholic to marry, however.) I was vaguely aware of the Episcopal Church because Marjorie Milz, a classmate of Mother's since grade school and also my piano teacher for several years, played the organ there. She would talk often of Father 'whoever' the current priest was, and I felt it was strange that the Episcopal priests wore a white collar and could marry and drink alcohol, but Catholic priests, though wearing a white collar, could not marry, although they could drink more than the holy wine.

We were members of the Methodist Church, which was a dark red brick building on the east side of State Street, half way down the hill from West Waverly to downtown Norton. Since Grandpa Drummond had been a minister in the Christian Church and Mother had grown up in that church, it seems odd that she chose the Methodist Church after marrying. I believe the reason is that the Christian Church required Baptism by immersion and the Methodist Church method was by sprinkling. Mother did not like the idea of immersion. In addition, many of Mother's friends were Methodists: the Isaacs, the Thomasons, the Hutchersons, the Underwoods, the Bullocks, the Jordans, and the Rouses. Wide concrete steps led up to the Sanctuary entrance of the church and smaller steps inside led down to the Sunday School rooms. There was a very large painting of Jesus in the Garden of Gethsemane in the foyer of the church and there were a few stained glass windows. Mother would tie a coin in the corner of my handkerchief to take to Sunday School. It felt good to untie it and put the coin in the collection plate. I liked going to Sunday School and hearing the Bible stories, but I enjoyed going to the church service more. I liked the music and opening the hymnal and singing the traditional hymns. I even paid attention and reflected on what the minister was saying.

The atmosphere of church was appealing to me. Growing up, Mother hung a picture above Beverly's and my bed of an Angel guarding two children as they walked across a bridge. It was always comforting to me, and I still have that picture hanging in the house.

Some of the kids in my class went to more Fundamentalist churches; I believe there was a Baptist Church and also a Church of God in Norton. I did not know much about those churches, but I did go on a church picnic with Lee Breckenridge, JoAnn Antrim, and Wanda Persell once while in junior high and was shocked that the kids were standing in a circle, holding hands, testifying, singing and praying aloud together. Methodists did not talk openly about what Jesus had done for them or how God had spoken to them. Methodists went to church, sang the Processional hymn "Holy, Holy, Holy", recited the Apostle's Creed, sang the Doxology, listened to the sermon, sang a few hymns, bowed our heads while the minister prayed, heard the Benediction, and went home to dinner. So, seeing this group of teenagers talk 'from their hearts' about Jesus was a new experience for me. Being this open about anything required being much more vulnerable than I wanted to be; I watched but did not say a word. However, I found something oddly appealing about the camaraderie of singing about Jesus on a quiet, October evening with a bon fire warming the body and the soul. I decided I needed to read the Bible. Every night before I turned off the light (and turned on the radio), I put Pond's hand cream on my hands and read a few chapters from the Bible. That was the first time I read all the way through the Bible. The smell of Pond's hand cream, still today, brings back those memories.

CHAPTER 8

Oh! The Things We Did!

I KEPT A DIARY FROM seventh grade to the first semester of my senior year of high school. Here are some of the things I wrote about doing during those five years: We made a lot of brownies, fudge, chocolate chip and oat-meal cookies, just for something to do. We played a lot of card games and board games such as Canasta, Pitch, Old Maid, Liverpool Rummy, Samba, Monopoly; and we worked jigsaw puzzles. I described many activities as being 'gobs of fun' or 'oodles of fun'!

Outdoor games (played until high school, when kids had cars) included Chalk the Corner where one team would set off and draw an arrow with chalk on the sidewalks, which the second team would follow to find the first team.

Andy, Andy Over was played by forming two teams who stood on oppo-site sides of a house, throwing a ball over a house, and calling out "Andy, Andy Over". When the person on the other side of the house caught it, they would run around to the other side of the house and tag someone, and the tagged person had to join the team on the other side of the house.

Kick the Can was played by finding an empty can and setting it up in the middle of the street. Someone was chosen to be "It" and then another person would kick the can down the street as far as possible. While the person who was "It" ran to get the can and bring it back to the spot from where it had been kicked, everyone ran and hid. The person who was "It" then tried to capture those who had run and hid, by spotting them or calling their name, tagging them, and then putting them in jail (usually a designated tree). If a person could run to the can and kick it before the person who was "It" physically tagged them, everyone in jail was set free, ran to hide again, and the game continued until everyone was captured and in jail and a new "It" was chosen. To end the game, the "It" person would call out "Olly, Olly, Oxen free"...at least that is what the words sounded like.

Games such as "Simon Says" were also popular. In Simon Says, one person becomes Simon and gives directions to the other players such as jump three times or take two steps forward. But, the directions must be preceded with the phrase "Simon Says". The tricky part is that it is easy to forget and impulsively act on the instructions without hearing the magic words: "Simon Says".

We rode our bikes with no helmet on our head, and we attached playing cards to the wheel spokes, thus making a noise like a machine gun as the wheels turned. Jacks, pick-up-sticks, crack-the-whip, roller skating, and rope jumping were also popular in grade school. At school, a 'turner' held a long rope (twelve to sixteen feet long) at each end and then swung the rope overhead as the jumpers ran in to jump the spinning rope. Rhymes were often recited as you jumped. You could also invite another person to run in and jump rope with you at the same time.

The playground at the grade school was an adventure! There were several swings hung on iron rods from a huge metal structure. This meant that we 'could' achieve one hundred and eighty degrees of swing! I do not think I ever made it that high, however. We would pump our legs with each swing to go higher and higher until we reached the apogee of swing, at which point we would jump out of the swing and go flying toward the ground. It could be a hard landing and did cause a few broken bones. The big teeter-totters were also fun. If you pushed off the ground with enough strength you could cause the person at the other end to hit the ground hard enough that it would cause you (on the high end now) to fly off the seat and bounce. It was necessary to hang on tight to the handles and try to bounce straight up rather than lean to the side and risk falling off. Another piece of equipment was the Octopus, consisting of a tall pole with long chains hanging from a 'wheel' at the top. You grabbed the metal handle at the end of a chain and ran around the pole until you would swing out and take off from the ground. The more kids running and hanging on to the chains, the higher you could fly. It was a bit like a maypole, except you would fly rather than dance around the pole. The Merry-go-round had metal looped poles attached to a large circular bottom plate, which was about a foot off the ground. After enough kids pushed it around to get it going fast, everyone would jump on and hang on to the metal bars. An extra feat was to hang on to the bar with one hand while stretching your body out and trying to pick up an object from the ground. There were 'high' slides and 'short' slides, which were hot to sit on in the summer time! We used waxed paper to make them true "slippery" slides, and then we whooshed down the slide and flew off the end of the slide because we were going so fast. The playground was actually a hands-on physics lesson. We experienced the meaning of g-force, centrifugal force, inertia, gravity, friction, momentum, to name just a few 'laws of physics'.

The schools in Norton were open for learning on January 1, unless it fell on Saturday or Sunday. Holidays were more 'noted' than celebrated in grade school. Halloween did not seem to be a big deal in Norton at that time, however; I made no entry of anything about Halloween in my five-year diary. May Day, however, was important during grade school; we would make baskets out of construction paper, glue on a paper handle, and fill them with some lilacs and a piece of candy. We would lay the baskets at the door of our friends, knock on the door, run away and hide, and watch them open the door and pick up the basket. Valentine's Day was exciting in grade school. In preparation, the class would cover a big box with red and white construction paper, decorate it with red paper hearts placed over white, lacey paper doilies, and cut a slit in the lid. We would buy or make Valentines and address one to each person in the class. On Valentine's Day, the teacher would open the box and read the names on the Valentines inside. Usually every student gave a Valentine to every other student, but sometimes there was writing on the card that made it 'extra special'. Memorial Day, or Decoration Day as we called it then, was important to all of the people of Norton. Each year Mother would cut some peonies, some lilacs, and any other flowers available and make bouquets to lay on the graves of Grandma and Grandpa Drummond. Peonies still today remind me of Memorial Day at the Norton Cemetery, the ceremony held there each year, and the many graves covered with large and small bouquets of flowers in remembrance of loved ones. July 4 and Armistice Day

(Veterans' Day since 1954) called for parades down State Street, and Easter meant new Easter outfits, including hats and even gloves, and, of course, dyed eggs, bunnies and baby chicks. Christmas decorations were not put up until after we sang "We Gather Together" at a church service and the Thanksgiving dinners were eaten. Wreaths were hung on front doors, stockings were hung inside, gifts were wrapped, and icicles were put on the Christmas tree one by one. Yet, we had only a few days off from school.

Music was an important and enjoyable subject taught in the schools at that time. Not only did it teach 'music', it taught teamwork, as the class sang together, and history. In grade school (kindergarten through sixth grade) we had a book with many American songs, and it also included folk songs from other nations for us to learn. These included Stephen Foster (the father of American music) songs such as "Beautiful Dreamer", "Camptown Races", "I Dream of Jeannie with the Light Brown Hair", "My Old Kentucky Home", "Oh, Susanna", "Old Black Joe", "Way Down Upon the Swanee River", and "Over the River and Through the Woods". There were Negro Spirituals such as "Swing Low, Sweet Chariot", "Nobody Knows the Trouble I've Seen", and "Massa's in the Cold, Cold Ground", plus folk songs like "Hand Me Down My Walkin' Cane", "When Johnny Comes Marchin' Home Again", "John Brown's Body", "Billy Boy", "Buffalo Gals", "A Hole in Her Stocking", "Clementine", "Long, Long Ago", "Dixie", "Tenting Tonight", "Tramp! Tramp! Tramp!", "My Grandfather's Clock", "I've Been Workin' On the Railroad", "Red River Valley", "My Wild Irish Rose", "When Irish Eyes are Smiling", "Blue Bells of Scotland", "Cielito Lindo" "Funiculi, Funicula", and "O Sole Mio". We learned about the history and cultures of many countries from the lyrics of songs. I suspect that many people who grew up in the 1930s and 1940s can still sing the words to most of these songs.

In junior high (seventh and eighth grades) and in high school, music was taught in band and choir, which most students joined. Sousa's marches became background music for the basketball games, and marching bands provided entertainment and spirit at the football games, as well as in town parades. Choirs, too, expanded our musical education with four part harmony of both classical compositions and popular favorites from Broadway musicals, such as "Carousel" (Rodgers and Hammerstein). For years, Beverly and I would cradle our hands in front of us, as we had in choir, and sing: "When you walk through a storm, hold your head up high and don't be afraid of the storm"...and end up giggling hysterically, because we were so bad. Those who played piano were called on to accompany the many choirs, soloists, and vocal ensembles. Claudine Priest, Pat Harper, Sonya Sleffel were classmates who joined me in accompanying groups and soloists. Pat Harper and Sonya Sleffel have continued accompanying many students on their solos through the years, as well as playing for many church services.

It was always exciting when the books for the next school year were delivered to Raney's Drug store in August. We must have rented the books each year and returned them at the end of the year, because I do not remember keeping any of them. The school year was filled with school activities. There was football in the fall, then basketball and wrestling in the winter, and track in the spring; team sports were only for boys at that time. Going to a relatively small high school has the very important advantage of giving everyone a chance to participate in extracurricular activities. Sports gave guys of every size and ability a chance to enjoy the camaraderie of being on a team. Dick McChesney was not big and muscular in high school, but he went out for (and did well in) wrestling in the 85 pound class. He signed my Norton Annual with his nickname, "Muscles". Norton competed in the Northwest Kansas Conference and the whole town supported the Blue Jays by attending all the home games and many out of town games. Going to the games felt like a town celebration with the businessmen and parents cheering wildly for the team and the individuals.

Being a cheerleader was as exciting (and attention grabbing) as it is today, and only five cheerleaders were selected for the high school teams. I could not be a first team cheerleader since I was a twirler in the marching band and played the French horn in the pep band. However, when I was a sophomore, someone felt the second teams deserved cheerleaders and these could serve also as backup cheerleaders, in case a regular cheerleader was ill or unable to be at a game. My chance had come! I practiced with the cheerleaders. Carol Deiter and Bonnie Underwood taught me all the cheers and the moves...when to jump up, how to wave the pompoms, how to crouch down on one knee and step the pompom down just a bit with each cry of "N! C! H! S!" and "2! 4! 6! 8! Who do we appreciate?!" It was exhilarating! However, the next day I could barely move! My muscles were in agony, I had lost my voice, and I was in pain!! I did get to be a cheerleader at a few games, and I learned how much energy and physical agility it takes to lead those yells. And that was before cheerleading became the gymnastic event it is today!

The band marched at all the football games as well as various parades and pep rallies. The high school uniforms were made out of blue wool with gold braid on the jackets, the shoulder epaulets, and around the sleeves; the high hats had gold braid on them, too, and a visor. The wool uniforms felt good when marching at the football games on a chilly, fall night, but they were very warm when marching in a parade on the Fourth of July! I was a twirler in junior high and all four years of high school; we wore large white furry hats with a gold braid across the front in junior high.

A few days before the Thanksgiving game with archrival, the Oberlin Red Devils, a Torch Parade and nighttime pep rally was held, with the band playing and marching all the way down State Street from the high school to the corner by Raney's Drug Store. In preparation for the big night, the Y-Teens made little 'red devils' out of red yarn and sold them to students and townspeople, so they could toss them into the giant bonfire at the intersection of Washington and State Streets. Just before the band began the march, the twirlers wrapped the ends of their batons in strips of cheesecloth to form a large ball at each end and dunked the ends into a bucket of kerosene. The touch of a match ignited the baton ends with a big swoosh, the drum major blew his whistle, and the parade began. The sound of the band playing and the flair of the twirling fire batons as we marched created an exhilarating atmosphere for everyone along the parade route. When the band, and all of the people who had followed the band down State Street, arrived at the pile of wood and tinder, everyone sang, "Cheer, Cheer for old Norton High", the twirlers touched their fire batons to the huge pile, and flames soared skywards. The football team and Coach Lefty Van Pelt and Coach Oran Burns were cheered on with more band music, and the cheerleaders led the crowd in chanting, "N. C. H. S..." After everyone threw their yarn red devils into the fire, the gathered crowd sang the Alma Mater, and we were ready for the big game.

I cannot imagine fire batons being allowed today, but it was an exciting and flashy thing to do! Another twirler, Shirley Rhoades, wrote in the back of my NCHS annual, "Remember the night of the Torch Parade. We were the torches." There was some concern about the safety of fire batons; Sandra Isaac's mother followed the band all along the parade route with a tube of burn ointment ready, just in case. Another ritual carried out in the week before this game was that girls could not wear anything red, including lipstick, since lipstick was red and Oberlin's colors were red and white. I felt that I looked terrible without lipstick, so I hated that ritual and would try to sneak on some pink-colored Chap Stick. Marilyn Sanderson noticed, however, called me on it, and I had to pay some kind of a fine, even though the embarrassment was the worst part.

The fight song, "Cheer, Cheer for old Norton High" had a parody version: "Beer, beer for old Norton high, Bring on the whiskey, bring on the rye, Send some freshman out for gin, Don't let a sober sophomore in, We never teeter, we never fall, We sober up on wood alcohol, As our loyal faculty lies drunk on the ballroom floor". So funny! So audacious!

Being a part of a small high school gave more people the opportunity to participate in music, drama, and a variety of special interest groups. There were many musical performances by the choirs and small singing groups (quartets, triple trios, etc.), as well as the band and the small instrumental ensembles (brass sextet, woodwind quintet, trios, quartets, etc.). Other student activities included the student council, Y-Teens, Hi-Y, 4-H, the student newspaper, the junior and the senior plays, and various school-sponsored parties, like Sadie Hawkins Day, picnics and bonfires, and hayrack rides. Many groups, such as Hi-Y and Y-Teens, went caroling every December, followed, of course, by a 'party'. There were school carnivals, lots of meetings of all the clubs, and lots of private lessons. There was work on the school annual and the school newspaper, "The Nugget", which meant going to the Norton Telegram office to set up the paper for printing. I wrote in my diary, "Messy!" And, we went to many banquets: Basketball, Wrestling, Football, Y-Teen, Hi-Y, 4-H, Father-Daughter, Mother-Daughter (both Teas and Banquets), Band, Choir, etc. Every organization seemed to celebrate with a Banquet! One of the memorable and favorite foods served at these banquets was ham loaf; it was much tastier than meat loaf, and I have never been able to duplicate the recipe!

I wrote in my diary that I went to Courtesy School, also called Girl's Interest Group, which was probably sponsored by a Norton women's club to bring etiquette and culture to the young ladies of the town. At one meeting at Mrs. Ruth Somer's house, after enjoying elegant appetizers and punch, a speaker showed slides and talked about Nicaragua. Our life wasn't "Downton Abbey", but the culture was similar in that it was important to know what was 'proper' and what was a 'no-no'. We learned how to set a table, for example…the correct location for the silverware, the salad plate, the bread plate, and the drinking glass. We also learned how to write notes and letters. It was considered polite and thoughtful to write letters to people who were away (as in the service or at college), who might be homesick, as well as write get well notes to people who had been in the hospital or were ill. Writing thank you notes was an absolute necessity, of course. Emily Post's Etiquette book was the guide for how to display culture, respect, and propriety.

Many individuals had parties at their houses at the least excuse. I remember parties at the homes of Pat Melroy, Carol Deiter, Judy Rouse (her family had built a 'rumpus room' for get-togethers), Pat Harper, Judy Brock, Leo and Rita Beckman (they had a barn with a hayloft!), Don Glenn, and Carol Rhoades, among others. Also, the First State Bank created a Blue Jay Nest at the bank that was filled with teenagers playing ping-pong, playing cards, and listening to music many nights a week.

Dad painted the basement floor of our house at 411 North. Grant a rust red color, bought a used ping-pong table from someone, and set up a record player downstairs; Beverly, Jerry, and I all hosted many parties in that basement through the years. Seated at the card tables are Pat Melroy, Nancy Vancura, and Darrell Baird. Standing are Leo Beckman, Pat Harper, Don Glenn, and Carol Rhoades. Dancing are Sandra Isaac and Don Conyac.

To my knowledge, bullying was never a problem when I was in school. Thinking that perhaps I was just not cognizant of such behavior, I asked classmates if they had been bullied. No one reported any problem except in a jesting manner. There was some teasing among some boys, apparently, but I do not believe it was intended to be mean or vicious. I do not pretend to understand male psychology, but locker room jokes seem to be a way that males bond. I will have to leave that to the psychologists! Most 'parties' were more like open houses and whoever wanted to come was welcome. I do not remember anyone making fun of or excluding another student. Drug use, such as marijuana, was nonexistent as far as I knew, but some older students did drink alcohol. Since Kansas was a dry state at that time, buying hard liquor required an eleven-mile trip to Nebraska. Even when beer did become legal in Kansas, the alcohol content was higher in the beer from Nebraska.

Those were the days when kids could go on hikes or wander the countryside without fearing any potential dangers; we went 'exploring'! On a hike somewhere in the country, our group of girls found a ramshackle house, walked in and wandered around inside, hanging out of the long-gone windows upstairs and imagining that a murder had taken place there, and now it was haunted.   We always had our Brownie Kodak cameras with us and took photos of each other in silly poses and, of course, photos of any boys we might see.   A favorite saying when we saw a cute boy was, "Hubba, Hubba, Ding, Ding, 'Click-Click' (sounded with tongue), Boing!"   One afternoon, we found some grapevines along a creek and imagined that we were smoking them like cigarettes.   Oddly enough, in all of these hikes and picnics in the country, I do not remember ever seeing a snake, no one stepped on or cut themselves on a rusty nail, and no one got poison ivy!   I think we were very lucky in that respect!

We would also go on bicycle rides together down Highway 36 until we got old enough to learn to drive. Claudine Priest and Sandra Isaac were sometimes able to drive their family car. On one such drive, Claudine was having trouble getting the car to go forward, and we all got the giggles when Sandra yelled out, "Goose it!" over and over. I did not get the use of our yellow Chevrolet very often, because Dad said he might need it "for an emergency".

Picnics at the old Mill Dam were also fun. Driving south out of Norton, you crossed the bridge over the Prairie Dog Creek and the first turn to the right would take you to the big rock dam which had been built years ago (probably in the 1920s or before). There was not much left of the dam, but it was a scenic spot with a small swimming hole. Guys sometimes would swim there, but I was brave enough only to dangle my feet in the water. Carol Rhoades remembers eight or more girls walked to the Mill Dam for a picnic when we were freshmen, and Rosemary Verdusco's parents furnished the hotdogs. There is a song, "Down by the Old Mill Stream", that we had to sing while we were there, of course. We would sing the song through slowly and dramatically once, followed by the faster version with the additional lyrics: "Down by the Old (not the new but the old) Mill Stream (not the river, but the stream), where I first (not last, but first) met you (not me, but you)." Parodies and 'take-offs' always brought laughs. There was also a Sand Pit in Jennings that was a good spot to go on a picnic.

Some hotdog buns and twigs for roasting marshmallows and wienies were all it took for a fun evening of singing and talking around a bonfire. And, on an occasion or two, a group of kids might ride by Mr. Rundell's amazing garden and swipe a couple watermelons. There were feelings of guilt in some of us. Bonnie Underwood said she went home and told her parents what she had done, but also said that this was the only and the last time it would happen. She found that "eating broken pieces of watermelon on the ground without forks, plates, and napkins, in the light of only the stars and car headlights, was not all that fun". Sonya Sleffel said many years later that Mr. Rundell did not mind losing a few watermelon or ears of corn to teenagers, but it did hurt when they just broke the watermelons and destroyed his garden.

Several groups such as Boy Scouts, Girl Scouts, Y-Teens, etc. collected money for charities each year. We made and sold poppies on Armistice Day (November 11) and collected money in small cans with a slot in the top for the March of Dimes. Polio was a serious concern before the Salk vaccine proved effective in 1955. There were periodic outbreaks of 'infantile paralysis' all over the world. This was brought home to Norton in the 1950s when Darrell

Webber and Kenny Kohfeld, two NCHS athletes developed polio. I remember Darrell in particular because we had been friends since junior high and sat beside each other in Constitution class when I was a junior and he was a senior. He became ill after an October football game in 1950, was diagnosed with polio, and was hospitalized in Hays. A group of students visited him there; seeing Darrell in the iron lung made all of us realize exactly what polio meant. Darrell missed a year of high school but did make a recovery, and, in spite of having a bad limp, returned to school the next year and graduated with the class of 1952. Kenny Kohfeld got polio a few years later; he was married to Mary Ann Amos and they lived in Salt Lake City. Mary Ann told me later how kind and helpful the people from the Mormon Church had been to them.

Elmwood Park was on the south side of town, at the bottom of a hill that started just south of the Rock Island railroad tracks, a block from Raney's drug store. There were two entrances. One was at the bottom of the hill on State Street, where the road curved into the park leading to the big, white-painted, wooden Grandstand, the animal barns, and the tennis courts. The other entrance was at the top of the hill, a block east of highway 283 (State Street). There were four red brick columns at the corner. One set of columns was the gateway to a walking path down the steep hill into the park, and the other set of columns stood on each side of the vehicle road into the park. There were many big old trees throughout the park, which helped keep it cool in the summer. About half way down the hill, at the edge of this driving road, was a huge, old elm tree leaning and stretching into space over the park below. A beautiful, long and strong branch held a goat swing, and a wooden platform served as a launching pad. We would climb onto the platform, reach for the big old rope, carefully secured to the tree by the previous user, and take a flying leap on to the small wooden seat on the end of the rope. It was exhilarating to fly out across empty space, feel the wind catch your hair, look down at the ground that seemed so far below, and swing way out before inertia stopped you and you came swooshing back to the platform. It took good hand-eye coordination to grab the rope with both hands, jump up and wrap your legs around the rope (which went through a hole in the wooden square of wood and was held there by a huge knot), and hang on for dear life for a great ride. I do not believe this goat swing would be allowed to be used without supervision today, as it would likely be considered much too dangerous to have young children play on it unattended. Looking back, it does seem a bit dangerous!

Elmwood Park would often flood because it was just north of the Prairie Dog Creek, and in heavy rains, the Creek would often rise and cover the highway and flood the park. This was a bad thing to happen during the County Fair! In the wintertime, if the weather got cold enough long enough, the fire truck would fill a small, low area of the park with water and we would have an ice rink for a few short weeks. It was bumpy ice and I never got my beautiful white ice skates, but I did have strap-on blades to attach to my shoes.

Before shoe roller skates became popular in the 1950s, most kids had metal roller skates that had an adjustable base, which was attached to regular shoes with metal clamps. A skate key was necessary to tighten the lug nuts used to lengthen or shorten the skate base, as well as to tighten the metal clamps holding the skate to the shoe. A leather strap at the back of the skate came around the top of the foot to hold the skate on securely. At least, the theory was that it would be secure. A common hazard was a bolt in the skate base or a clamp on the shoe coming loose while skating, which often caused a fall as the skate fell off. Also hazardous were the uneven sidewalks. One had to watch the level and cant of the individual cement squares that made up the sidewalks and be ready to jump over those danger spots of buckled cement. The streets in Norton were originally paved with bricks, which were very practical and lovely to look at...and rather tricky for street skating. Ann Browne was a year younger than I was and lived on North First Street just north of West Waverly. Her basement was large enough (and empty enough!) that a group of girls would often get together there for an afternoon of indoors roller-skating.

Sleepovers of one or two girls were common, and slumber parties of many girls were popular, especially when we got into junior and senior high school. Although all of the girls in our class were welcome, usually only the girls who lived in town were able to come, and there were usually around 15 or more girls at these parties. Judy Brock hosted many slumber parties. A group of us formed the "TLD" club...Two Legged Dears (I do not remember how we came up with that name!), and we all took cots up to Brock's basement for the many slumber parties. One night, we tried to find out how many girls could fit into the bathtub at the same time (yes, that is what I wrote in my diary!). Another night, on a Friday, the Catholic girls could not eat meat all evening, so when the clock struck midnight they eagerly ate up the meat sandwiches that were served. One Friday night, when we were at Brock's for a slumber party, Principal Gerald Travis called and said there were not many students at the high school dance and would we come over to the gym (Judy's house was across the street from the high school). Since we had come to the slumber party in jeans, and jeans for dances were a no-no, we went to Judy's closet and pulled out her clothes to wear to the dance; Judy finally looked into her closet and gulped, "What am I going to wear?!" Halfway through the dance, Carol Deiter and I decided to add some fun to the evening, and we went into the girl's bathroom at school and switched clothes. At another slumber party, the fifteen or so girls there got into an argument about something, split into 'sides', and the rift went on for a couple weeks. We also entertained ourselves by making 'prank calls'. We would dial someone we knew and ask, "Do you have Prince Albert in a can?" And, no matter what they answered, we would say, "Well, let him out. He can't breathe in there." Or, "Do you have your radio on?" "Well, take it off. You're going to break it." Soooo funny!

Summertime brought many activities. Every Thursday evening the band played a concert in front of the Courthouse, followed by an ice cream social. I hope crews of workers helped the band director, Lawrence "Spalsy" Spalsbury, get all those folding chairs and music racks set up! The local baseball team played games all summer at Elmwood Park, we played tennis on the courts in Elmwood Park, and we went swimming at the Burd Swimming Pool just south of town, open from Memorial Day through Labor Day. The Silvaire ballroom and skating rink, owned by the Sanderson family, opened on the southwest edge of town in the late 1940s. Big Bands played there on weekends and it was open as a skating rink in the evenings during the week. They also had a drive-in restaurant where I got a job as a 'carhop' during the school year. The pay was .25 cents an hour plus tips. My diary said I got $1.57 in tips one night! Joy Hutcherson, Marilyn Sanderson, Peg Long, and Judy Rouse also carhopped at the Silvaire. A specialty was fried chicken and curly fries served in a basket. The "Sunset" drive-in movie about a mile west on Highway 36 opened in 1952. Snuggling with your date in the car, eating popcorn, and listening to the movie through the gray metal speaker hung on the window was a fun, good-weather adventure. Carnivals and the Circus came to Norton every year, and in August was the week of the Norton County Fair.

CHAPTER 9

The Norton County Fair

DAD WAS ON THE FAIR Board for many years and helped set up many of the events to take place during fair week; these included horse races, car races, and a variety of special shows in the Grand Stand, as well as the carnival rides and game booths. There were various competitions for everyone to submit their work. As at all County Fairs, categories for homemakers and children covered entries such as pies, cakes, jams, home-canned fruits and vegetables, art projects, and sewing projects; 4-H members paraded their animal projects, such as steers, cows, bulls, sheep, rabbits, guinea pigs, and regular pigs. I do not remember entering much other than whatever embroidery or art project a teacher had encouraged the students to enter, and I won a few ribbons over the years for such projects. The Ladies Farm Guild (or some ladies group...the farm wives of Norton County?) always had a booth just outside the Grand Stand and served delicious hamburg-ers, with chopped lettuce and tomatoes and pickles. The Rotarians and Lions Club had a booth to sell sandwiches made from the barbecued hogs and steers, slow-cooked in a deep pit dug near the Grand Stand.

The Norton County Fair brought people from nearby towns in Kansas and Nebraska, and to get folks from other towns aware of and excited about the Fair, 'Booster Trips' were taken to surrounding towns. When I was in high school, I was among some band members recruited to go on booster trips for the Norton County Fair. We were in several cars driven by Norton busi-nessmen. On one trip, we left Norton mid-morning and headed to Nebraska. Before long, I realized that all of the men were drinking as we drove. In the 1920s, '30s, '40s, '50s, and '60s, smoking and drinking were the norm for adults. The movies reflected this, and the advertisements showed drinking and smoking as glamorous and as habits that enhanced your life. By the end of the day, after touring and playing in several towns, a 'pretty happy' group of adults, supported by a teenage pep band, was touting the Norton County Fair. I thought it was fun and exciting to play my French horn and see the Norton men acting silly, singing, and laughing. It never crossed my mind that drinking and driving could be a problem. Everybody did it! And, many people were killed in accidents. The very hilly, two-lane roads made passing another car hazardous whether sober or drinking.

The big, exciting events at the Fair were the shows in the Grand Stand and the carnival rides...especially at night. There were car races and horse races in the afternoons and musical and variety entertainment acts at night on the stage across the race track from the covered Grand Stand. There was also an uncovered Grand Stand, but we always tried to get there early enough to find a seat in the covered one. It was a white painted, all wooden structure with many levels (it seemed like at least twenty tiers to my child eyes) of deep, wooden bench seats rising into the sky, with space underneath which was used for storage. Even when we didn't go down to the Fair, we could sit on our back porch and hear the excitement of the Fair in Elmwood Park: the roar of the car races, the crowd cheering, the calliope playing, and the carnival 'music' floated from Elmwood Park through the town all the way up to North Grant.

The rides were exciting and scary. When I was younger, I loved the Merry-Go-Round, and I would imagine that I was riding a galloping horse over the hills or that I was a trick rider. One time when I was pretending to be a trick rider, I stood up on the Merry-Go-Round horse, then hung from its neck, and then jumped on and off (just like I had seen at the Grand Stand shows), as the Merry-Go-Round went round and round. The ride operator pulled me off at the end of the ride and properly scolded me. Then he told me that I could not ride the Merry-Go-Round anymore if I was going to act like that. I learned the meaning of chagrinned that day.

The Tilt-A-Whirl and the Octopus were two rides I loved. The cars spun this way and that with the G-force pulling you from one side to the other, as your hands clenched with a steely grip the security rail pushed against you. There was also the Spitfire, which consisted of 'cars' that looked like the body of a P-51 (my imagination saw it as that anyway), one on each end of a long metal shaft or rail, which was attached to a large rotator machine that revolved the long metal shaft around like a very fast Ferris wheel. The riders would get into the 'plane', which held just two people, and then the 'plane' would be slowly rotated upward until you were hanging upside down, while people got into the other car. Then, the metal arm would spin around and around, doing 360-degree loop-de-loops, with the riders being upside down, then right side up, faster and faster. The first summer it was at the fair, I loved the Spitfire and rode it again and again. The next summer I looked at it, and there was no way I was going to get into that tube!

The Fair was especially exciting at night with all the lights blinking on the rides, the game booth operators calling out their spiels luring you to come play, and all the sounds of riders screaming, the calliope playing, and people laughing. Then a big band would begin playing for a dance on the double tennis courts each night at nine o-clock. By midnight, everyone was heading home and looking forward to returning the next day.

CHAPTER 10

Burd's Swimming Pool

JUST SOUTH OF TOWN, ON a dirt road past the power plant, was Burd's swimming pool. There had been a dance pavilion on that site in the 1930s, but I have been told that there was a fire during World War II and the pavilion never reopened. When I was in grade school (1940-46), there was no swimming pool in Norton, and we would occasionally drive to Arapahoe, Nebraska where there was a public city pool. By the summer of 1947, however, the Burd swimming pool in Norton opened. The pool was three feet deep at the shallow end and sloped down to probably twelve feet deep at the diving end, with a heavy corded wire draped across the pool to show where the deeper water started. The wire must have been at about four and one half feet deep, because I could not walk to the wire without being on tiptoe to keep my head above the water.

The water was changed on Mondays (sometimes every week, sometimes every two weeks), and the water felt like ice water until Wednesday or Thursday. I do not think there were any filters, nor was chlorine used. By the time the water was changed, it was a pretty murky soup of old water and 'debris', and the sides of the pool had traces of green slime on them. Even so, this is where the Norton kids learned to swim. I took swimming lessons and lifeguard lessons, but never became a strong enough swimmer to become a lifeguard. I did learn enough, however, that one day when a person, who did not know how to swim, panicked just beyond the deep-end wire, grabbed for me, and started to pull me under, I somehow remembered I should pull the flailing person with one arm and do the sidestroke while swimming for the side of the pool. Fortunately, the side of the pool was not very far!

At the deep end of the pool was a two-level, white-painted, wooden diving platform. Narrow wood stairs led to the first diving level and then a straight ladder went on up to the highest diving level. John Hutcherson said that the diving boards were made from old bridge planks and he was so skinny he could not make them bounce even a little, let alone 'spring'! As with the Spitfire loop-de-loop ride at the Fair, one summer I was brave enough to find jumping off (not diving!) the high diving board fun, and the next summer I was not even brave enough to climb the wobbly, wooden steps to the high board. I could dive from the side of the pool, but jumping, while holding my nose, was my highest skill-set from the diving platforms. I did have a nose clamp, which helped while just swimming around, but it popped off when jumping in feet-first.

When I was 14, I inherited a hand-me-down swimsuit from my older sister, Beverly; she said her then-boyfriend and later husband, Alvin Hisey, had bought it for her at the PX in Alaska where he was stationed with the Air Force. It was a two-piece suit with a beautiful Caribbean scene on it...a beach, the ocean, and a palm tree...and the bra top had straps that tied around the neck. It looked like a suit from an Esther Williams movie! I felt quite sophisticated and so grown up in it! However, I did have an embarrassing event wearing that suit. One day, when I stood up in the pool after a splash fest with friends, the straps around my neck loosened and the top of the suit fell to my waist. I grabbed it so fast that I do not think anyone even noticed. However, I was aghast and embarrassed; I made sure things were secure after that!

The dressing rooms for the Burd pool were in the small cement building at the entrance to the pool. You walked in and paid the fee, got a numbered wire basket to put your clothes in, and went into the separate dressing area, which consisted of small cubicles with cement walls and fabric curtains across the 'doorways'. Some open wire at the top of the cement walls of the dressing room produced some ventilation, but it was a closed area and had a distinctive odor from the many bodies, the day-temperature shower water, and the heat and humidity. Next, you took off your street clothes, put them in the basket, put on your swimming suit, stepped into the small shower and pulled the cord for a quick 'rinse', before taking your basket to the counter where the attendant shoved it into the cubbyhole for the basket with your number on it. On the way to the pool was a small, cement basin, containing some water and a disinfectant to prevent athletes' foot, which you had to walk through.

In 1951 one of my first political-activist actions was to join a large group of high school students to petition the City Council to build a new pool. We made large posters and created a parade through town asking for a new pool; the Bond Bill did not pass. However, the next year a group of students went to the City Council meeting and presented the Council with the petition with the required number of signatures on it, and this time it worked. A new town pool (larger and with filters!) was built on the north side of town after I graduated from high school in 1952.

CHAPTER 11

Trains

THE SOUND OF A TRAIN whistle in the night brings a nostalgic memory to folks who lived in Norton. The Rock Island Rocket went through Norton at 4:30 AM every morning, and if you were at the station at that time while it was still dark, the headlight on the Rocket swinging back and forth in broad swaths across the tracks and the whistle blaring as it went through town was an exciting event. As a child, I always wondered what it must be like to be riding the train into a new adventure. Trains were important to Norton, as they were to every town that had a railroad track going through it. Both the Rock Island Line and the Burlington Railroad went through Norton. The depot for the Rock Island Line was just south of downtown, and the Burlington tracks were a block and a half north of the downtown area. The train brought the newspapers from Denver and Omaha, took large metal cans filled with fresh milk and cream to dairies to be processed, and brought the large bags of mail for the Post Office to sort and deliver. And, sometimes, people did get on the trains for personal or business travel.

An early fun train ride for me was when I was in junior high. A small train, only two cars as I remember, ran on the Burlington tracks between Norton and Oberlin; we called it the Doodlebug. On February 22, 1947, a large group of kids rode the Doodlebug to Oberlin for a game, and it was a wild and noisy ride with more than forty junior high age students talking (yelling) and running up and down the aisle. The Conductor tried to get us to be quiet, but we were all too excited and having too much fun to 'settle down'. At one point on the trip, one of the kids noticed that Mr. Hutcherson (John's father) was sitting on the train reading a newspaper. That put a damper on the noise level for a minute or so. It probably was not a good idea to have junior high age kids go on this kind of field trip! Other small, three-car (engine, utility car, and caboose) trains went to Almena, Calvert, and other nearby towns. These carried the milk and cream from small farms to the Ambrose Dairy in Norton or on to a large processor in Nebraska. Passengers could also ride in the caboose of these trains (eleven cents was a remembered price); names included Puddle Jumper, Pollywog, as well as Doodlebug. Sonya Sleffel said her dad called the train that went through Almena the "Tri-Weekly, because it tried every week to get to Norton".

Beverly, Jerry, and I took the Rocket to Phillipsburg when I was in grade school, and Aunt Edna met us at the station there. Mother and Dad came later and we rode back to Norton in the car. When Pamela was about two or three, my Mother and we took the train to visit Jerry and Lena in Clayton where Jerry was working at the time. On the way back, the train stopped and we sat on the tracks for a while. Soon, Pamela got impatient and called out loudly, "Giddy up!" She does have a commanding voice, and the train started moving again.

When we lived near Chicago, it was a sixteen-hour drive to Norton. When John and Pam were both away at college, I hesitated to drive there by myself. Then I had the brilliant thought, "Why don't I take the train from Chicago, rent a car in Holdrege, Nebraska and drive the short distance from there to Norton?" I arranged to have a private room in the sleeping car, thinking I'd be refreshed after sleeping in the secluded berth on the train...like in the movies (yes, those movies still had me at "Hello!"). Oddly, the continuous movement and rumble of the wheels turning did not lull me into a peaceful sleep! Many people think of trains as a nostalgic, romantic way to travel, and a case can be made for that! However, when Hank has suggested we should take that famous train ride across Canada, I have not fallen for those delightful advertising images.

CHAPTER 12

What Fun We Had!

THE RADIO WAS A GREAT source of entertainment for families. Gathered around the radio, we listened to programs such as "The Great Gildersleeve", Red Skelton, "Fibber McGee and Molly" (at the start of each show, Fibber would open the closet door just as Molly said "Don't open...", and the sound of everything falling out of the closet was heard; we would laugh every time), Jack Benny and Rochester, "Amos and Andy", Gracie Allen and George Burns, "Our Miss Brooks" (Eve Arden), Abbott and Costello, and "The Aldrich Family" (Henry! Henry Aldrich! Coming, Mother!). In addition, there were many music programs, such as the Lawrence Welk show, and Dad would conduct whatever orchestra was playing (he was quite good at conducting). Guy Lombardo played "the sweetest music this side of heaven", and every New Year's Eve, his distinct sound playing "Auld Lang Syne" would usher in the New Year. My favorite music show was the Hit Parade, sponsored by Lucky Strike cigarettes, with Frank Sinatra, Margaret Whiting, Bing Crosby, Doris Day, Dick Haymes, Martha Tilton, Dinah Shore, and many others. Every Saturday we would listen to hear what the number one song would be for the week. In 1948, the song, "There's A Tree in the Meadow", was number one, week after week. Richard Esslinger was in the Air Force stationed in Alaska at the time, and he wrote: "If they don't cut down that tree in the meadow this week, I'm going out and chop it down myself." At the end of the show, all the singers would sing, "So long for a while. That's all the songs for a while. So long to Your Hit Parade, and the songs that you picked to be played. So long!" Frank Sinatra was, not surprisingly, my favorite singer and, even though he was on and off the Hit Parade through the years, he also had his own radio show. He would end his show with "Put Your Dreams Away for Another Day", and we would...with a big sigh, "Ahhhhh."

We always had music in the house. Between Mother and Jerry playing the piano, I learned most of the songs written from the 1890s to the 1950s. There were some fun songs that were popular in the 1940s and 50s. One was "Mairzy doats and dozy doats And liddle lamzy divey, A kiddley divey too, Wouldn't you?" Other fun songs were: "A Tisket, A Tasket, a green and yellow basket", "One Meat Ball", "Open the Door, Richard", "Chickery Chick", and "I've got spurs that Jingle Jangle Jingle", to name a few. Mother got me some boots and a pair of fashion spurs at that time, and I wore them to school... once! Jess Vague, the grade school principal, called Mother and asked her to not send me to school wearing spurs because the 'jingle, jangle, jingle' was too distracting. Spike Jones was the master of parodies and 'cornball' silliness. This great music kept smiles on our faces from the 1930s to the 1960s.

I had a small, ivory-colored radio on the nightstand by my bed. After I went to bed, I would turn it on and listen to the wonderful orchestra music being broadcast "Live from the Aragon Ball Room" in Chicago or the Stork Club in New York City or the Coconut Grove in Los Angeles. Other 'ballrooms' that broadcast music were the Trocadero Ballroom at Elitch Gardens in Denver, and the Roseland Ballroom, the Copacabana, and the Latin Quarter in New York City. Eventually Mother would call up the stairs, "Turn off the radio, Marlyn, and go to sleep." So, I would turn down the volume and move my ear closer to the speaker and imagine myself someday dancing at one of those ballrooms. I finally did go to the Latin Quarter when Hank and I were on our way to Germany in 1955. I felt soooooo sophisticated!

Big Bands were a very important part of society at that time, and in much of the country young and old listened to the same music. We heard it in the movies, on the radio, and bought 78 rpm records to play on our turn tables, all in mono until the 1960s when Hi-Fi stereo records came out. Horney's Appliance store in Norton is where we bought records, and the records often got broken, chipped, and scratched. You could hear a click when the needle went over a scratch in the record, and a deep scratch could cause the record to stick, skip back, and repeat a couple grooves of the record over and over at that point. (A parody of "I'm in the Mood for Love" is based on a record getting stuck and repeating, as in: "I'm in the Mood for Love, simply because you're near me, Funny but, funny but, funny but...") If there was a chip broken out at the start of the record, you could just set the needle to begin playing after that. Judy Rouse had a 78 rpm record of Frank Sinatra singing "All or Nothing At All", and it had a chip broken out of the rim. However, I loved that song and Frank's singing and traded Judy something for it anyway.

Saturday was Farmer's Day in Norton, so all the stores stayed opened until nine o'clock. Then it was time to dance. The American Legion Hall was located about three blocks east of downtown. It was a large, two-story red brick building with broad steps leading up to a wide porch. A large black cast iron canon stood outside the Hall until it was donated for scrap metal during World War II. After climbing the cement steps and crossing the porch, wide white double-doors opened to a large hall where many community dances took place. School dances in junior high and high school were held there, and the boys would stand on one side of the room and the girls would sit on the other side, waiting and hoping for a boy to be brave enough to cross the room and ask for a dance. At a more formal party, there would be 'dance cards' to fill out in advance, telling you with whom you would be dancing. Parents helped sponsor school events and tried to think up ways to get the boys and girls to dance and mingle; my mother, Dorothy Butler, gave dance lessons at many dances.

After the war, in the late 1940s, the Sanderson family opened the "Silvaire", a big Quonset hut building, on the southeast side of town. You could go skating and eat at the drive-in on weeknights, but on Saturday nights the Silvaire became a ballroom. Norton was about half way between Kansas City and Denver on Highway 36 and made a perfect spot for a one-night gig for the many bands that were touring at the time and going from the Pla-Mor Ballroom in Kansas City to Elitch Gardens in Denver. Among the many bands that played in Norton, and which I mentioned in my diary, were Gene Krupa (7/21/50), Stan Kenton (9/26/50), Jimmy Dorsey (5/2/51), Charlie Spivack (6/21/51), Jan Garber (7/28/51), and Claude Thornhill (8/28/51).

Other big bands included Benny Goodman, Harry James, Kay Kayser, Vaughn Monroe, Guy Lombardo, and Dick Jurgens. There were also 'territory bands' that played, including Freddy Joe, Bobby Mills, The Rhythmaires, a "Negro Orchestra" (2/4/50), and the Jack Everett band that recruited Jerry when they played in Norton. If you did not go to the dance inside, you could drive up and sit in your car to listen to the music. The Silvaire always drew a large crowd of dancers and 'the joint was always jumping'. The dances started at 9 PM and ended at 1 AM, with a long intermission around 11 PM. During intermission, most people would go out to their cars and spike their Cokes or 7-UPs from a bottle of liquor wrapped in a brown paper sack. I had a date with Jimmy to the Silvaire dance one night, and he brought a bottle of Peppermint Schnaps. That night I had my first (very small) sip of hard liquor. I do not know where he found this strange choice of liquor, especially since he was too young to buy it himself. Bonnie Underwood lived about a mile from the Silvaire and, on Sundays, she would ride her bike to the Silvaire to pick up all the pop bottles that had been tossed from cars the night before. She said the redemption value made it worth the trip down the hill and back.

CHAPTER 13

The Shows We Saw And Loved

UNTIL I WAS IN JUNIOR high, the Cozy Theater was on West Main Street, about half a block west of State Street, the north-south main drag of Norton. Although musicals were in Technicolor by the 1940s, most of the dramas were in black and white until the late 1950s. Going to 'the show' (we did not say 'the movies') was something we did at least three times a week, and was a form of socializing. The shows were exciting to see, and we always saw friends there, too.

I loved the dancing and singing in the movies and would try to imitate the steps I saw on the screen. I was not crazy about Fred Astaire and Ginger Rogers; he seemed very old and their dancing style was pretentious to me, but I loved Gene Kelly. He was smooth, sexy, a good singer, and a fantastic dancer; he wore white socks with loafers and jeans or black pants. I so wanted to tap dance! I would go down the basement at 411 North Grant and try to imitate Gene Kelly's tap steps and to act out and sing "Mammy", "Swanee", and "California, Here I Come", as performed in "The Jolson Story" in 1946 with Larry Parks and Evelyn Keyes. I wrote in my diary that I went to that movie Sunday afternoon and again Sunday evening, and "it was the best show I've ever seen." I was enthralled! I dreamed of dancing and singing on stage one day.

There was no one in Norton who taught tap, but Mrs. McClure gave ballet lessons, so I had some ballet lessons when I was in junior high. It was not tap, but at least it was dance. One day during the class, there was a loud, explosive sound. Mrs. McClure did not know what it was, of course, but stuck her head out the door to look. What she saw looked like a fireball streaking across the sky. She thought whatever it was could be dangerous so she would not let any of us out the door to see it. This was soon after the war ended and, at the time, the Cold War was starting; fear of a Russian invasion was a worry. Mrs. McClure's immediate thoughts were that it could be a bomb, or maybe a UFO. What it turned out to be was a meteor.

I also received 'elocution' lessons. It was obvious to my teachers that I had a lisp, and it was suggested to Mother that I get help for the problem. Mother tried to make it sound fun and exciting..."like acting lessons!" However, elocution lessons sounded more like 'remedial' lessons before 'remedial' became a familiar epitaph. It was embarrassing to have to take lessons to learn to speak! The woman who gave me the lessons was an elderly person (Mrs. Elliot, I believe), very sweet and very proper, with snowy white hair which she wore piled on top of her head like a crown. She would have me do tongue exercises and lip exercises and show me where to place my tongue so the 'ess' sound would not be a lisping sound. "Over the rolling waters go, Over the rolling waters blow, As my little one, As my pretty one sleeps." Every syllable was enunciated with exaggerated movements of my lips. Trying to make it more fun for me, she found 'clever' recitations, and I even had to perform at various functions such as ladies meetings, just for the practice. One such recitation was about having the measles: "I've got 'em. I've got 'em on my belly, I've got 'em in my hair, I've got 'em on my toes. I've got 'em everywhere!" I did work very hard to speak without a lisp so I would not have to endure the torture of more lessons.

In addition to wanting to dance, I wanted to be able to sing well. Hopeless as it was, Mother let me take singing lessons when I was a freshman in high school from Miss Cleo Burroughs, the high school choir director. Miss Burroughs decided I was a soprano, and assigned the song, "From the Land of the Sky Blue Waters, I heard a maiden cry", for me to sing. To adequately describe how bad my thin, squeaky voice sounded would be difficult. I will just tell you that when I stood by the piano in the living room to practice, Mother had to run from the room to keep from bursting out laughing in front of me. We soon decided that expecting singing lessons to help was hopeless and I should discontinue them. At this same time, Miss Burroughs scheduled a recital date to present her students, as is the usual practice for piano and vocal teachers. Mother mercifully called her the night of the recital and told her that I had been called in to work that night at the Silvaire, where I had a job as a carhop, and I would not be able to sing at the recital. Mother did not believe in recitals; she felt that student recitals were difficult for most students and painful for the listeners, and she never made me play piano, or sing, in one. Bless her heart!

Because of my love of dance and music, the movie musicals were my favorites, and they were what played on Sunday afternoon, evening, and again on Monday night. There was "State Fair", "Singin' in the Rain", "Easter Parade", "Show Boat", "Meet Me In St. Louis"...so many wonderful songs, so much wonderful dancing! "Thousands Cheer" in 1943, with the amazing Gene Kelly, made me want to be a dancer even more. I absolutely loved "The Greatest Show on Earth". It was such an exciting movie that I begged and begged until Mother relented and let me go back and see it again!

Tuesday nights at the Cozy Theater, the 'show' was a 'B movie'; these were the low-cost movies, with second tier actors and actresses (yes, there were still 'actresses' then), usually crime dramas or romantic scandal dramas. These movies did not draw the crowds that the musicals or the big dramas did, so the movie owners tried various incentives to get people to come to the movies on Tuesday nights. One lure was to have a drawing for one hundred and fifty dollars on Tuesdays at the end of the movie, and Mother was the winner one night! One hundred and fifty dollars was a lot of money! This was very exciting, of course, and she decided to spend the money on a long, black, sealskin fur coat, bought from The Alaskan Fur Man. Every year the Alaskan Fur Man would come to the Cottage Shop to show the beautiful fur coats that were luxurious and the ultimate desired coats, and he would sell a few coats on each visit. This was long before animal rights groups brought attention to the horrors and cruelty of the fur trade. When I was in college, Mother bought me a deep brown, hip-length mouton fur coat. I wore it to Germany in 1955, of course, and it kept me warm when we went to the 1956 World Ice Skating Championship, held outdoors in Garmisch that year, as well as visiting Linderhof Castle near Garmisch. It was very, very cold in the Alps in March!

On Wednesday, Thursday, and Friday nights the shows were the large production dramas. These were movies with the top dramatic actors and actresses, such as Jimmy Stewart, Humphrey Bogart, Henry Fonda, Ingrid Bergman, Barbara Stanwyck, Tyrone Powers, Spencer Tracy, Katherine Hepburn, etc. These movies were often rather frightening to me as a child. "Life Boat", "The Best Years of Our Lives", "The Treasure of the Sierra Madre", even "It's a Wonderful Life"…all of these were very disturbing to me, not so much because of the dramatic plots but because of the meanness and human ugliness of the characters. I remember "Life Boat" and "The Treasure of the Sierra Madre" as being full of grizzled, angry men cursing and yelling; "The Best Years of Our Lives" had the father of the returning Veteran yell at him, "Who do you think you are? God?" I winced. Any movie in which the characters screamed violently at each other bothered me. "It's a Wonderful Life" had the scene when Jimmy Stewart gets drunk and angry and yells at his family. This made me want to run out of the theater. I wrote in my diary my critique of the movie: "Not good." Since these films were either Academy Award winners or nominees, it is clear that I was not destined to be a film critic.

On Saturday, the matinee and the evening movie was a western (Roy Rogers, Gene Autry, the Cisco Kid), plus a serial (Captain America, Captain Marvel, Superman, etc.). No wonder I wanted a horse to ride and thought I could fly! Young kids filled the theater every Saturday afternoon, so not only were the movies exciting, it was also fun to see and meet your friends there. The kids my age always sat on the right side of the theater with the older kids and adults on the left side and in the middle section.

Going to the 'shows' was how we were educated about life outside of Norton. For example, there were no African-Americans in Norton, so my whole awareness of the Black community, referred to as Negroes or Colored at that time, came through movies. Movie roles for Blacks in 'White movies' were generally as domestics or in servile positions, and they were depicted as living in run-down areas, having to walk or ride a bus to their jobs, and being powerless. The 'White' roles were the businessmen and bankers who lived in nice homes with manicured lawns and often had servants. There were some 'Black' movies, like "Cabin in the Sky" with Lena Horne. In spite of Lena Horne looking beautiful and singing wonderfully, this movie was very frightening to me as a child, because it showed dark stormy skies, lots of physical and verbal violence, and 'the devil' was an important character.

Indians, stereotypically, were dressed in the movies in deerskin, with decorative beadwork and either feathers on a leather headband or many feathers on the large headdress; footwear consisted of deerskin leather moccasins. And, of course, they rode bareback on beautiful pinto horses and lived in colorfully painted deerskin teepees.

There were three Hispanic families in Norton. Although I was vaguely aware that they were of Mexican descent, I did not think of them as having a different ethnicity; they were just my friends. However, in the movies, there was typecasting. The Mexican heritage roles in movies, especially when about Texas, showed men wearing black pants with silver disks down the legs and on their black bolero jackets, plus a large sombrero. The women were dressed in colorful skirts and peasant blouses. The movie also generally included some flamenco guitar and exciting dancing. I was so impressed with the flashy and tap-dance-like foot work of Flamenco dancing that I tried to imitate it at home in the basement; I really wanted some castanets to hold and play the delightful clicking rhythms.

I do not remember any movies about Germans nor Japanese, except as the enemies in war movies. Many movies during the war years, and after, were about the heroism of American soldiers and sailors, of course. "The March of Time" newsreels brought home the visual reality of war and helped keep us informed about the world events. The scenes of ship battles on the roiling Pacific and Atlantic oceans, scenes of tanks rolling across Europe, scenes of British civilians running for air raid shelters as the sirens blared, scenes of destruction and bombed out buildings, and the sound of planes coming closer followed by the whirr of bombs spiraling down and the explosions when they hit the ground left lasting impressions on my mind. Even though the newsreel had been produced weeks before it was shown, and it was never current news, it brought the devastation of war to our awed senses. "The March of Time" was shown in theaters from 1935 to 1951 with the monthly episodes running from 15 to 20 minutes long. With the rise of national television by 1951, 'the nightly news' then became our visual exposure to the world, and in the 1960s and 1970s the Vietnam War was served with dinner and again before going to bed on the Six 0'Clock and Ten 0'Clock news.

The movies also served as a form of 'sex education', teaching us from a young age how to flirt, how to kiss, and when and how to say "No!" I was so young, unworldly, and naïve that, until I was in junior high, I did not know what it was I should say "No!" to. I thought that women got pregnant by going on a 'special diet', and it was my fear that I would accidentally get on that diet and become pregnant. I was shocked when I first heard what 'intercourse' was. I could not believe that God would design us to do such a weird-sounding thing. In junior high, we were shown 'sex education' films, and one that I remember well was about the dangers of going out with a good-looking musician with curly black hair, dressed in blue jeans, a white t-shirt and loafers, and seductively singing, "Rock it! Everybody does it! Rock it!" "Oh, yes!" I thought, "I want to rock it!" Maybe I did not understand the moral of the story very well.

Before 'the Pill' was available in the 1960s, getting pregnant out-of-wedlock was a worry, because getting pregnant came with labels (loose, tramp, hussy, promiscuous) and could cause an extended visit with an aunt in a far-away state or even 'studying abroad' for a year. Movies reflected this with 'good girls' stopping the romantic moments and the transgressions of 'bad girls' leading to disaster. The Hollywood Production Code spelled out exactly what was and was not acceptable content for motion pictures and was applied to TV, too, from the 1930s to 1968. It covered more than sex, but rules like "no more than three second kisses" or "married couples must be shown only in twin beds" reveal the sexual repression that was the norm. I was well indoctrinated in the 'no-no' mindset.

The "Omaha World Herald" and the "Denver Post" were two city newspapers delivered to many people in Norton; being from Nebraska, Dad chose the Omaha paper for delivery to our house every morning. The local daily newspaper, "The Norton Telegram", came in the afternoon, with the front page briefly covering world, state, and local news. However, the 'real', important, news was about the people we knew...the obituaries, who had been on a trip, who had a baby, who was in the hospital, etc. Each bit of news appeared as a separate four or five line squib, with a space before the next 'item' of interest. In addition, the local school news was reported: football, basketball, wrestling, honor roll, and school events and programs.

Community Theater was popular in Norton, as it is in most communities where the local residents can fulfill some of their fantasies of acting, singing and dancing...aspirations put aside for the realities of daily living. About 1950, when I was in high school, a production about Americana and politics was staged in Norton. I do not remember who sponsored it, but the high school drama teacher, Mr. James Deay, was a director and Miss Cleo Burroughs, the high school vocal teacher, directed the singing; I was asked to play the piano and accompany the performance. I remember playing "Smile! Darn Ya' Smile" and "Happy Days Are Here Again", which had been played at the 1932 Democratic Convention and was the Democratic Party's theme song for many years. It was not a sensational show, but it is always fun and exciting to participate in a theatrical production!

Earlier in Norton, in the 1930s and 1940s, a "Minstrel Show" was staged almost every year, sponsored by the Lions Club and the Rotary Club. This form of entertainment had been popular from the mid-1800s, and the tradition continued in many towns all across America, such as the Chautauqua shows that flourished in the early 1900s, which Mother talks about in her writings. These were basically town talent shows of the vaudeville variety type...singing, dancing, comedy skits, wisecracks, jokes. I assume that a standard script was obtained from somewhere for the local groups to use. The formula had a Master of Ceremonies, called the Interlocutor, who acted as the 'straight man' and talked with the row of characters sitting on chairs across the stage behind him. The jokes came from misunderstood banter between the Interlocutor and the 'end men' of the line. The whole cast would sing standard Minstrel songs such as "Camptown Races", "Dixie", or "Oh, Susanna", songs that everyone knew. A highlight of the show was the Cakewalk, when everybody 'strutted their stuff' and the best dancer won the big prize...a cake, of course! By the 1950s, the popularity was fading, but I remember many Minstrel Shows being put on in Norton, and Dad was the Interlocutor many times. One of the traditions was for the actors to be in Blackface for the performance. Red and white striped vests, tall black hats, and canes were traditional costuming for the participants. This kind of performance seems shocking today, but even when I was in grade school, my fourth grade teacher, Miss Rumsey, taught me a tap dance routine to "Dinah", and I, along with other kids in my class, put on Blackface to perform at the grade school assembly program. I wrote in my diary that I "Blacked up" to dance "Rosie" in a Y-Teen program in 1949, and "I had to Black up" to accompany a group singing "Porgy and Bess" for the Father-Daughter Banquet in 1950. It seems strange today to realize that such performances were standard fare at that time! Since there were no Blacks (Negroes at that time) in Norton, no one that I know of thought a thing about it. I was completely unaware of the concept of racism and do not remember anyone ever commenting on any racial issue. However, I was shocked to learn years later that there was an active KKK group in Norton during those years, and any Blacks who came through town knew it would be best not to be in Norton after sundown. There was an all-Black town, Nicodemus, about fifty miles southeast of Norton on Highway 24; I was not aware of Nicodemus when I was growing up in Norton, but I did visit Nicodemus many years later when I had the opportunity to see Dr. and Mrs. Kraft perform at the St. Francis Hotel in Nicodemus.

CHAPTER 14

Dinner's On!

MOTHER ALWAYS BOUGHT JUST A few groceries at a time. One reason was that Dad would complain about the bill if she bought too much at a time. However, this worked out well since there was no pantry, and the small cabinet above the sink was the only storage area in the kitchen. The Fiesta dishes sat in the left upper cabinet, glasses and coffee cups in the middle cabinet above the sink, leaving the right cabinet for storage of a few cans of vegetables (corn, green beans, peas, lima beans), a can of Clabber Girl baking powder, a small box of Arm & Hammer baking soda, a container of Morton's Iodized salt, and a small can of McCormick black pepper. Larger and heavier items, such as a 3 lb. can of Crisco, a 5 lb. bag of Pillsbury flour and a 5 lb. bag of C&H sugar, were stored in the lower cabinet. Every morning, Mother would decide what to fix for the noon dinner and for supper and call in the order to the grocery store. They would deliver the groceries within 30 minutes and put it on our bill, which Dad would pay monthly. The order would usually be for a couple cans of vegetables, bread, butter, white potatoes, and a meat of some kind.

Meal portions in the 1930s, '40s, and '50s were not large, even in restaurants. Generally, there was a small portion of meat, boiled potatoes, a vegetable, bread and butter, and dessert. Dessert could be cake, cookies, tapioca, or pie (apple, cherry, chocolate, lemon, banana cream were popular choices). The noon dinner entrée was usually chicken-fried steak, baked ham, meatloaf, baked heart, chuck roast with potatoes, carrots, and onions baked with it, or fried chicken. When Spam became available after World War II, Mother would sometimes use that instead of fresh ham and 'fancy it up' with sliced pineapple and some brown sugar on top. I loved it when, walking home from school at noon, I would smell chicken fried steak wafting from the house. What a wonderful aroma! To make chicken fried steak, Mother would buy a full round steak, about a twelve by eight-inch oval. Then she would mix some salt and pepper into a cup of flour, get a small plate out of the cupboard and the large wooden cutting board from the bottom cabinet. She sprinkled some of the flour onto the board, laid the meat down on it with more flour on top and then pounded it and pounded it with the edge of the plate, turning the plate this way and that and adding more flour as she proceeded. Next, she cut the pounded and flour-dredged steak into pieces and heated a good glob of Crisco in the iron skillet. When the Crisco splattered when she dropped a bit of water in it, it was hot enough and she would lay the steak pieces into the skillet. The sound of the sizzling steak and the aroma was intoxicating!

On Sundays, we might have catfish that Dad caught in a local farm pond or pheasant, in hunting season. Norton is in prime pheasant country and every fall hunters come from all over to go pheasant hunting. Dad went every year, too. He had a shotgun or two that he kept in the basement, and he would usually bring home a few pheasants each year. He loved to fish all spring, summer, and fall; many of his patients lived on farms and would invite him to fish at their farm ponds. In addition, Dr. Stevenson had a farm with a small lake, Steve's Lake, and he invited Dad to fish there at any time. I would not be able to find the way to any of the ponds. I just remember sitting in the back seat and riding over unpaved, bumpy roads at top speed with the car windows down and the dust flying. Dad mostly caught bullheads, a type of catfish that is mild flavored and delectable. Sometimes the fish would have bulges on their bellies that held many fish eggs sacs. Mother would roll the one-inch diameter fish egg sacs in seasoned flour and fry them until they were crisp. I loved them! The catfish sold in grocery stores and in restaurants today always have a fishier taste and the meat is less flaky than the bullheads from a country pond. Often in the summer times, Mother would pack a picnic supper, usually consisting of bologna sandwiches and potato salad, and we would go to Steve's Lake or to the new Johnson Lake just across the Nebraska state line, north on Highway 283. We would leave in the afternoon on a Saturday, after Dad closed his office, and stay all night, sleeping (if we could) in the car; evidently the fish would bite best in the late evening and early morning. Mother was an excellent cook and the baked pheasants and fried fish were delicious and special treats. When eating the pheasants, you needed to watch for any buckshot still lodged in the meat. I think Jerry and maybe Dad went squirrel hunting a few times, but fortunately, I do not remember eating any squirrel!

On Sunday evenings, we would often have oyster soup, usually made with canned oysters, but sometimes the grocery store would have fresh oysters when they were in season (in months with an 'r' in the name). We had boiled potatoes most days, which we would mash on our plates, add butter, salt and pepper, and then cut into little squares before eating them. Alongside, there would be a vegetable, usually canned corn, green beans, Campbell's pork'n beans, beets, peas, or stewed tomatoes with chunks of white bread added. Suppers were usually leftovers or cold meats. 'Boiled ham' was considered a special treat; minced ham (bologna) had great flavor and was used in sandwiches and also ground for ham salad sandwiches. We would get out the hand-turned meat grinder, attach it to the table, and grind bulk bologna, then add hard-boiled eggs, hand-chopped sweet gherkins, and Miracle Whip for sandwiches. Liverwurst came in slices with a narrow strip of white fat around the slice, which we carefully removed before eating. This was slightly different in taste from Braunschweiger, which came in a tube with no white fat around it. Ham and beans with cornbread was a standard dish also. If we got hungry between meals, Mother would make a bread and butter and sugar sandwich for us. It tasted great and filled 'the spot'. Bread and butter sandwiches with sliced icicle radishes were also yummy!

In addition to the usual things we all ate, Dad had a few favorite foods (some of which no one else would eat!): 'head cheese' and other cold meats that looked inedible, limburger cheese, raw hamburger sandwiches with a big slice of raw onion, lamb fries, sardines, and horseradish (which he called 'horse', as in "pass the horse"). Every year the Lion's Club put on a 'Lamb Fry Dinner', which was a big deal in Norton. I suppose the kids from the farms knew what they were, but I did not know what a lamb fry was nor did I ask. Everyone seemed to look forward to this big dinner and enjoy them, so, I grew up eating lamb fries. Many years later on our way to visit Beverly in Kimball, Nebraska, we stopped in Holyoke, Colorado for lunch, and Mountain Oysters were on the menu. My daughter, Pamela, was about 10 at the time and asked the waitress what Mountain Oysters were. That waitress got so flustered she could not speak trying to evade that question from a child.

Liver with onions was a popular dish and thought to be good for you because of the vitamin A and iron in it. The consistency of liver was a bit mushy, but the sautéed onions gave it a decent flavor. Occasionally Mother would bake a beef heart or boil a beef tongue. The beef heart would be prepared with stuffing, had a firm but tender texture, and tasted 'okay'. The tongue had a strange texture and looked unappetizing. It had globule-looking edges where it had been separated from the carcass plus all the bumpy and coarse taste buds on it. White foam collected on the surface of the boiling water in the pot, but it was tolerable to eat with enough mustard. Eggs scrambled with beef brains was also a dish that people fixed in the 1930s and 1940s; Mother fixed it once to please Dad, but no one but Dad would eat it. Mother also boiled kidney once, but the smell was so bad that she never fixed it again. I boiled kidneys many years later to give to our cat, Sparky, but eating it was out of the question.

At that time, fresh vegetables, other than white potatoes, onions, and carrots, were not plentiful in the stores all year. Mother loved it when the first spring onions came into the grocery stores. These were the long, thin white sweet onions with a very small bulb and long green fronds on them. Fresh tomatoes, watermelons, corn on the cob were available only in the summer months, when we could also get fresh snap green beans and peas in the pods. We placed the beans and peas in the blue and white metal colander, which had been in the family for years, and rinsed under the faucet in running water. Then we pinched the edges of the pods open to pop out the peas. It took lots of pea pods to make enough peas for a family. After rinsing the green beans, you snapped off each end of the bean and then snapped it into two pieces... they were called snap beans for a reason! You knew the beans would be tough and stringy if they did not make a snapping sound when you broke them. Mother liked to cook these for a long time with white potatoes and a piece of ham with the fat on it for flavor. Mother prepared pickled beets by adding vinegar and sugar to the juice from the can; then she added hard-boiled eggs to the beets. The eggs would turn a deep purplish red and the sweet-sour beet juice made the eggs taste delicious.

I associate two treats with summer: lemonade and strawberry shortcake. Lemonade was special because of the preparation: we rolled the lemons back and forth a few times to 'loosen the juice', got out the glass juicing dish, cut the lemons in half and pressed them on to the top of the dome that rose from the catch basin of the juicer. The juicer had a small spout on it to pour the juice into the large, pressed-glass pitcher. Then we filled the pitcher halfway with water, added sugar, stirred, tested, and added more sugar until it was just sweet enough. Next, we got the metal ice cube tray from the freezer section of the refrigerator, turned the tray upside down and ran water from the tap over the bottom of the tray to loosen the ice cubes, pulled up the lever to change position of the dividers and popped out the ice cubes. So sweet and cool on a hot summer day!

Strawberry shortcake was a special treat because it was available only in the summer. Mother would prepare the strawberries by rinsing them well, removing the stems, slicing the berries into a bowl and spreading sugar over the top. After a short time, the sliced berries would absorb the sugar to form a perfect blend of pulp, juice, and sugar. Sugar was added to Bisquick to make a sweet dough that was shaped into three-inch diameter shortcakes. While they were still a bit warm from the oven, the sweet berries would be spooned over the split shortcakes and real whipped cream dolloped on top for this delicious summer indulgence.

Jell-o was a popular dish even before I was born, but after electric refrigeration became standard in homes, it became easy to prepare and serve. Mother prepared lime Jell-o in an oblong Pyrex dish, added pear halves, and then sliced green olives (with pimento) all over the top. Another Jell-o dessert was made with Vanilla wafers, crushed pineapple, and cottage cheese in lemon Jell-o. Jell-o creations were, and still are, brought to potluck dinners everywhere.

Mother did not make cakes often, but when she did, she assured us they were good for us because they contained wheat, milk, eggs, and butter (which was high in Vitamin A). Pies, however, were the favorite dessert at our house. Mother made apple pie, cherry pie, rhubarb pie, gooseberry pie, chocolate pie, and banana cream pie often. Making the pie crust was an art that Mother taught to Beverly and me. Mother used Crisco for frying and for making pie crust. She used lard, which came in pound packages just like butter, for a long time, but Crisco became her favorite shortening. To make piecrust you first cut the Crisco into the flour using two dinner knives until the texture was like coarse sand, then added iced water and kneaded the dough with your hands until the batter just stuck together. Knowing when to stop adding water was the tricky part, because a tough crust could result if the texture and consistency were not 'just right'. After letting the dough rest in the refrigerator for a short time, Mother would get out her mother's wooden cutting board and wooden rolling pin. Next a handful of flour would be spread around on the board, and half of the divided dough would be put on the board and pressed down with her hands to get a large enough circle to start rolling it out. Starting in the center and rolling one way then another, she gently spread the dough into a circle slightly larger than the pie pan. When the circle had been rolled to about 1/8 inch thickness, she would gently lift it off the board and place it in the pie pan. The process was repeated with the second half of the dough and, after putting the fruit filling in the lower crust, the top crust was placed over the pie. She would crimp the edges between her index fingers and thumbs to seal the crusts. Designs could be cut in the top crust, but Mother generally just pricked the top with a fork in several places to let the steam escape as the pie was baking. If there were any leftover dough, Mother would sprinkle it with cinnamon and sugar and bake it, too. Ummmm good!

One summer when we were living at 411 North Grant, Mother decided to bake bread. It was such an unusual and, I felt, exciting thing for her to do that I got my camera and took her picture. She got it all mixed and then kneaded it carefully, folding the dough over itself and kneading it again and again. Then she put it into a greased and floured pan and put the dough into the warmed oven to rise. After a while, she peeked in the oven, and the bread had risen so much that it was overflowing the oven and almost attacked her when she opened the oven door. She screamed, jumped back, and managed to pull the huge blob from the oven. We both started laughing hysterically at the sight of the giant, wobbly mass of dough! Her solution? She wrapped the whole batch of dough in a large kitchen towel and, laughing and giggling all the way, carried it out the kitchen door, down the porch steps, across the backyard, and dumped it in the trash barrel in the alley at the back of the house. I do not remember her making bread ever again.

Around that time, pressure cookers became popular and Dad gave Mother one as a gift. I do not know what she was cooking in it, but I do remember seeing the top of it rising, steam coming out, hearing the loud whistling and seeing the pressure rise on the dial. Mother was afraid it was going to blow up...I was, too! She never used it again. Those pressure cookers did frequently blow the lid off and spatter the contents all over the ceiling.

Mother loved to sit around the kitchen table, talk, and laugh...we all did. If any company dropped in, Mother would fix a pot of coffee, open the lid on the red Fiesta ware cookie jar, full of Hydrox cookies, and we would gather around the table for some good conversation. Fun times!

Coffee was made, by the way, by putting water in a pan, adding one table-spoon of coffee for each cup of water, bringing it just to the boiling point, and letting it sit for a few minutes so the grounds would settle to the bottom. Then we would pour it through a strainer to catch the coffee grounds. Since filters were not used for making boiled coffee, the coffee beans had to be coarse ground to get the flavor from the coffee without having coffee bean 'sludge' in it. One trick was to drop an egg shell into the boiled coffee, or even a whole egg, in order to get the sludge to drop to the bottom of the pot. The 'milkman' delivered milk in glass quart bottles to the house at that time, and since it was not homogenized, the cream would rise to the top of the glass bottle. There were usually 3 or 4 inches of cream at the top, which we would carefully pour off into the cream pitcher to use in our coffee. In the winter, it was important to bring in the milk soon after it was delivered in the morning, because the cream would freeze and lift the milk cap off the bottle.

CHAPTER 15

The Products We Used

THE SELECTION OF PERSONAL PRODUCTS was much smaller than it is to-day, of course, and we used what was available at the drug stores in town. Mother used a lanolin oil, Lanicare, on her face for many years. The cloudy-looking, grayish-white liquid came in a frosted glass bottle about the shape of today's Olay moisturizer. When Oil of Olay came on the market in 1952, Mother switched to that. She had beautiful skin so maybe one of those products made a difference. She also used Lady Esther cold cream to remove her makeup; she would dip her fingers into the jar, spread the thick white cream over her face, and then wipe it off with Kleenex. Oddly, the cold cream always felt cold to the touch. Max Factor and Revlon were popular brands of makeup, but Mother used DuBarry foun-dation (called Sophisti-creme), a smidgeon of lipstick or a powdered rouge on her cheeks, and loose face powder. Mascara came in a small red plastic container with a small brush; you wet the brush, rubbed it against the dry, black mascara powder, and then applied it to your eyelashes and eyebrows. If it rained or if you cried, black mascara would streak down your face. Most women carried a decorative compact in their purse that held a mirror and some loose powder for touchups during the day or evening.

Dad had a shaving brush that he would wet with water, swirl around the bowl of shaving soap, and then brush the white lather on to his face; the razor held a double-edged razor blade; any nick on his face caused by a dull blade was covered with a small piece of toilet tissue to stop any bleeding. Dad used Old Spice Aftershave; I did not like the smell of it. It is still popular today and I still turn up my nose when a man wearing it goes by me! Lava soap was a popular soap for men; it was dark gray in color with a course, gritty texture.

A nightly ritual for girls was setting our hair with bobby pins. Mother did have a curling iron from the 1930s that was heated by holding it over the flame of a gas stove; this could be used if hair needed to be curled quickly, but it was awkward to use and risked a burn on your face. After I lost the curl on top of head that I was born with, my hair was straight straight straight. A beauty operator in town got a new permanent wave machine in 1939 and Mother, always fashion conscious, decided I should get a permanent. First, the hair was rolled around metal curling rods, and then big, heated metal clips hanging down from a permanent wave machine were clamped over the rods on your head. Unfortunately, the operator touched my scalp with a hot clip and burned my head. Mother was furious and I was traumatized; I did not get another permanent for a long time (I still do not like spending time at a 'beauty' salon!). When I was a teenager, Mother gave me the new-on-the-market Toni home permanents. Even then being beautiful took time as the curling product needed to be on the hair about an hour before rinsing out and putting on the neutralizer.

When I was in high school, hair gel came on the market which helped the curls last longer. Guys used Brylcreem, which was advertised with the jingle, "A Little Dab'll Do Ya!" I shaved my legs with a razor for the first time in June 1947, just before my fourteenth birthday. When Nair, the hair remover lotion, came on the market, I tried that on my legs. I then looked at my arms and thought, "Oh! They are so hairy!" The solution: put some Nair on my hairy arms. It worked amazingly well, but my arms looked amazingly weird without hair! I wore long sleeves until the hair grew back and I no longer looked like a freak.

Other products that were popular in the 1940s and 1950s were Ipana toothpaste (also good for hiding small holes in the wall because of its neutral beige color), Camay, Lux, and Cashmere Bouquet bar soaps, butch wax, Burma-Shave, scented talcum powder, and fragrances such as Taboo, Evening in Paris, and Yardley lavender cologne. Grandmother Idy thought Vicks VapoRub was a cure-all for sore throats and colds; Mother leaned more toward Mentholatum. Memorable radio commercials include "D-U-Z, D-U-Z, D-U-Z does everything!", "I'd walk a mile for a Camel", and Dinah Shore singing, "See the USA, in your Chevrolet, America is asking you to call..."

Tennis shoes or sneakers were not widely worn as an everyday shoe until the 1950s, so when I was growing up, we wore leather shoes. I had a pair of wonderful, soft-leather brown shoes when I was in fourth grade, which I felt helped me run really fast. When I outgrew them in fifth grade, I had to get a new pair of shoes and Mother took me to Brown's Clothing Store to look for them. Lanny Davis tried so hard to help me and brought out every pair

he had, but there were none that looked or felt like my old pair. I remember feeling so disappointed and frustrated when I had to buy a pair of brown leather shoes that I thought were ugly and made me feel awkward. (Fifth grade insecurities were setting in!) I am wearing the ugly shoes in this photo and Beverly is wearing cute sandals.

When I was in seventh grade, I started wearing loafers. Penny loafers had the slot on the top of the shoe where we would slip in a coin...true 'penny' loafers. Saddle shoes and white buck shoes were popular when I was in high school and college. And, of course, bobby socks (white anklets) were worn by girls and boys. Boys generally wore white t-shirts with rolled up blue jeans to school. Girls always wore skirts to school, never jeans or slacks. Sweater sets were popular when I was in high school and college, especially with a scarf tied around the neck.

Gathered skirts with a wide belt were very chic, too. This was at a time when it was embarrassing to let a bra strap show or to have a slip hanging below the skirt hem. Having a run in your hose was another no-no. Girls wore their hair in pony tails or had a poodle cut (short!); boys had crew cuts or sometimes a Mohawk.

I always loved jeans and started wearing boy's jeans when I was in grade school and junior high, but only on weekends. Jeans for girls (Missy sizes) were not available until 1960 or so, and then they had the zipper on the side rather than the front; they were designed to sit at the waist and be loose and baggy in the seat and legs. I never had much 'rear end' and I liked jeans to sit on my hips rather than waist, so I continued wearing mostly boy's jeans until 1980, when Calvin Klein made tight-fitting jeans for women. Brooke Shields' TV ad saying, "Nothing comes between me and my Calvin's", caused an uproar, but the jeans fit great! Beverly and I laughed because women had 'stand-up' jeans, which were so tight that you had to lie down on the bed and inch them on, and 'sit-down' jeans that were loose enough that you could sit down in them.

CHAPTER 16

World War II

"THE MARCH OF TIME" NEWSREELS at the movies started showing stories of war in Europe and England in the late 1930s, but it seemed like a movie to me, not reality. I was too young to realize any threat to Norton. However, when Pearl Harbor was attacked on December 7, 1941, even I became aware that something terrible had happened. Everyone in town was alarmed, and young men and older men raced to enlist in the Army or Navy. The "Home Front" activities consisted of everyone pitching in any way they could. We saved paper, string, and anything metal for the war effort. We formed balls of tinfoil from our gum wrappers for the scrap metal effort and collected newspapers for the paper drives. We helped plant Victory gardens for our use at home so commercial food resources could go to our soldiers. There were cards with images of planes on them for civilians to learn to recognize enemy planes in case any flew over. War Bonds, purchased for a certain amount, would be worth more at maturity. Since kids, and many adults, generally could not afford to buy a full War Bond, stamps were bought at the Post Office and pasted into a little booklet, which would be worth a War Bond when filled.

Shortages of meat, sugar, butter, lard, cheese, tires, gasoline and other commodities brought rationing books into our home to insure that everyone had a fair share of what was available. Instead of butter, white margarine came with a little capsule that we crushed and stirred into the margarine to make it look yellow, like butter (it did not taste like butter!). Fabric for clothing was also in short supply, so our mothers made clothing and curtains by repurposing old clothes as well as using feed and flour sacks. Sonya Sleffel remembers that her mother felt that chicken feed sacks had the prettiest fabric, and JoAnn Antrim remembers having clothes made from flour sacks. Every family received rationing books with stamps inside, which were torn out when you bought rationed items. I remember the rationing books, but I do not remember ever feeling that there was not 'enough' of whatever we needed.

There were posters on swinging metal stands outside the Post Office saying, "Uncle Sam wants YOU!" and "Loose Lips Sink Ships". A very large white, wooden sign stood on the courthouse lawn with the names of every Norton County person who was in the military; we felt sad when we saw a gold star beside their name, because that meant they had been killed. Flags with a gold star hung in the windows of families who had lost a husband or son. William Muir and two of Mary Wieland's brothers were killed in the war, so flags with gold stars hung in the front windows of the Wieland and the Muir homes. Seeing these gold star flags in the windows was a reminder of the horrors of war. There were others from the Norton area who lost their lives, I am sure, but I did not know them personally.

Some other people from Norton who served included my cousin, Margo Butler, who was a nurse in the Red Cross. My Cousin Helen Drummond Heaton's husband, Robert Heaton, served in Europe, and when he returned to Norton after the war, he showed me a German helmet, knife, and boots that he had brought back. Bus and Junior Sanderson were in the military during the war, as well as the fathers of Dolan McDaniel and Willard and Rex Welch. Willard said his father fought in the Pacific and then Italy and Germany. A German officer shot him, but the round hit his belt buckle and he was able to shoot back. He brought home the German officer's German Luger. My classmate, JoAnn Antrim, had two brothers in the military: Bill was in the Navy and Seth was in the Seabees. Neil Johnson was an Army Air Force navigator. We learned that the Army Air Force practiced along local highways when, on our way to visit Aunt Blanche in Geneva, Nebraska, we were stopped and told to get in the ditch because they were practicing bombing runs on that road.

Troop trains and military convoys frequently passed through Norton. Carol and Shirley Rhoades lived on a farm east of Norton and remembered waving at the soldiers in the truck convoys as they passed by on Highway 36. Carol said that sometimes the soldiers would throw pennies and candy to them. JoAnn Antrim talked about going to McMahon's grocery store and getting treats to throw to the soldiers on troop trains on the Rock Island Line when they stopped in Norton. Willard and Rex Welch also remembered throwing candy to the soldiers on the troop trains.

War time songs became standards: "Comin' in on a Wing and a Prayer", "White Cliffs of Dover", "Boogie-Woogie Bugle Boy", "I'll Be Seeing You," "Sentimental Journey", and many more. "Bell Bottom Trousers" was another popular song, and when someone gave me a pair of real Navy bell-bottomed trousers with the buttons around the front flap, plus a white navy cap, I thought I was stylish and so chic.

With so many men away to fight, women stepped in to fill the many jobs formerly held by men; and many women stayed in the work force after the war. The idea that a woman's place was in the home was supplanted with the knowledge that women could have real careers. Women flowed into the work force and many became doctors, lawyers, and business owners...roles that men had dominated prior to the war.

We thought, after VE Day (Victory in Europe) and VJ Day (Victory in Japan), that there would be no more war, even though the Cold War was an ever-present threat to world stability. When the Korean War, and then the Viet Nam War, came along, more Norton young men went to war. Beverly's future husband, Alvin Hisey, and his friends, Richard Esslinger and Jimmy Maddy, joined the Air Force and went to Alaska. My brother, Jerry, was drafted into the Army and left on January 2, 1951 for basic training; he was fortunate enough to go to Germany rather than Korea. Verle Ritter and Lawrence Harold Williams went to Korea. Verle made it home, but the Williams boy was killed in Korea, posthumously receiving a Purple Heart. This was a time when writing letters to friends who were away was a normal, friendly and thoughtful thing to do; I wrote in my diary about writing and receiving many letters from people I knew who were away from home. I saved a letter from Verle that he wrote from Korea. I am putting his letter into this book to honor Verle and all Veterans for their service and because it describes succinctly what happens in war. We did not yet have a TV at home, so we did not get constant reporting about the Korean War. Verle's letter opened my eyes to the reality of what was going on so far away from my safe haven of Norton:

Friday, June 6, 1952
Korea

Dear Marlyn,

Hi! It's been a long time since I've heard from you, but I was think-ing of Old 'Doc' Butler just now and thought I might as well write. I haven't much to do for the next hour or so.

Tonight everyone in our Battalion is a little restless. There are three hills out in front of us that the Chinese use as outposts and our Battalion is going to attack them tonight and then try to hold them. Two of them won't be too hard to hold, but the third may be different. The infantry will take it tonight and then shortly after they've secured the hill the engi-neers, with 150 Korean laborers, will come on the hill. The engineers will dynamite holes for bunkers and the Korean workers will set up pre-fabri-cated bunkers in the hole. This is all supposed to be done before day light tomorrow. Then if they get the job done the Chinese will come after it the next night. Our Company is lucky again. It was our turn to make the at-tack but "I" Company's Company Commander volunteered his company. The boys in that company swear if they got the chance they'd shoot him. Many of us are about 15 to 45 days away from rotation and then to have a man volunteer you to take a hill makes you pretty mad.

The first of we U.S.'s will leave between the 15th and 25th of June. That will be married men. I'll leave about the middle of July. What a day that will be.

We've been having air strikes all day on the Chinese hills. Our tanks have been firing and so has the artillery. Just before the attack starts our artillery will blast the devil out of those hills again. Still they (the reds) are dug in so deep that we won't be able to get them out with artillery. We are supposed to leave this hill about June 15th. It is supposed to be our last time.

Tell 'Doc' hello for me. I miss the ol' <u>cuss</u>. He'd better start practic-ing up on his billiards because I'm gunning for him.

Bye Now.

Love,
Verle

PART III

Houses and Schools

We start life as blank slates, ready to be written on and sculpted by the world around us. Every event, every person we meet, every love or loss, every decision we make transforms our souls into works of art.

CHAPTER 17

1935-1939: Toddling Around On North Wabash

THE HOUSE AT 211 NORTH Wabash faced west with a small front porch that led to the front door of the house. A formal parlor was at the front of the house, and three or four bedrooms ran along the north side of the house, with doors off the parlor and the great room. Walking straight on into the house was the great room, where there was a large, pot-bellied stove, the only heat source in the house other than the coal-burning stove in the kitchen. This is where I remember my Grandfather sitting in the rocking chair. On the north wall of the great room stood an upright console radio and Victrola, which had a wooden grill in the front and a ramp behind the grill that sloped up to the back of the unit. I used to peek through the grill expecting little people to march down the ramp, especially when the record, "Big Rock Candy Mountain", played. Nothing ever came down that ramp. Jerry recalls the Victrola being in the front formal parlor rather than the great room, and he could be right since Mother loved to decorate and often rearranged the furniture! Jerry also remembers that we all liked the record, "Two Black Crows in Hades", a recording by Moran and Mack, the well-known minstrel, radio, and vaudeville blackface team. Obviously this was published at a time before any thought of racial sensitivity evolved. There were many such songs with blatant racial lyrics from the 1800s through the early 1960s. I was given a collection of sheet music from the early 1900s and I was shocked at the words and pictures of many pieces of music. At the time, these flagrant comments and depictions were so prevalent that no one...at least no white person...thought of them as being degrading. Derogatory labels and perjorative words were the language of the day.

For an anniversary present early in their marriage Dad had given Mother a black spinet piano, and it sat in the parlor, across from the front door. It was always a focal point of wherever we were living. Mother played the piano often and Beverly and Jerry took piano lessons, and I listened as they played. When I was four years old, I sat down at the upright piano in the parlor and started playing what I had heard them play: "Country Gardens", "Minuet in G", and some boogie-woogie. Mother was in the kitchen and she wondered who was playing, since Beverly and Jerry were in school; she was surprised to find me sitting at the piano. I do not know why she was so surprised, since she and Jerry both played by ear. I do not know how I knew what to play, but I just 'knew' without 'consciously knowing' what keys needed to be pressed to make the music I heard in my head. It was just 'there'. I gave my debut concert with a public performance at the high school soon after that. How well I remember walking up the three or four steps at the side of the stage, climbing up on the piano bench and playing my three 'pieces'. Mrs. Eloise Ryan, Beverly and Jerry's piano teacher, was so impressed that she told Mother she would give me free lessons because it was such an unusual thing to have a child play with no training. Surprisingly, that was a bit unfortunate, because instead of developing playing by ear, I was pressed into reading and playing notes. Playing the piano became more complicated and less fun, and I did not play much by ear until I was in third grade. Sonya Sleffel told me she could play "When I Grow Too Old to Dream", and I thought, "Well, I can do that! Big deal!" So, I sat down and started playing by ear again, which was a lot more fun than taking lessons and practicing things out of the red John Thompson piano books! Even though piano playing came easily to me, I did take piano lessons for many years. However, I never worked at learning technique and practicing those monotonous scales, and as a result, my technical skills limited my ability to play classical music. That was okay with me at the time, because I much preferred playing popular songs, boogie-woogie, and old standards. However, I have wished many times that I had worked harder to acquire keyboard dexterity when I was young.

Beyond the great room, at the back of the house, was the kitchen with a big, black stove, which used coal or wood, and on which Mother managed to cook all our meals. At the very back of the house was the bathroom, which was added after I was born. I do not remember not having it, but Jerry said there was just an outhouse when we first moved there. There was a covered porch on the south side of the house, outside the great room. One time when we were bored, Mother gave us some old Edison records to play with (these were flat like the later 78 rpm records but thicker). We laid them in the sun until the heat had softened them enough to bend, and then we formed them into 'pottery'. What was she thinking?!

Dad had his office in a duplex that was north of the Methodist Church on State Street; Grandma Ida Butler lived in the other side of the duplex. This is a picture of me sitting on the steps at the duplex in front of Dad's office ("Office Walk In") pretending to play Mother's Banjo-Uke, which she had taken to Kansas State and was autographed by her college friends.

A GE refrigerator, which stood on twelve inch legs and had the big round motor on top, sat in front of a small opening near the floor of the wall between Grandma's living area and Dad's office. I made the exciting discovery that if I crawled under the refrigerator, I could peek at Dad in his office and watch him treat patients. I do not know if Dad knew I was there, but it was very interesting to me.

I was afraid of bugs. One day when I was about three years old, I was in the bathtub and saw a little tiny black bug on the floor. I was so scared! I yelled for help as I peered frantically over the rim of the bathtub watching the little black speck get closer. Finally, Mother came in to rescue me. However, her idea of a rescue was to put me, bare naked, into a tiny little bucket, carry me outside to the porch and take my picture!

Items that I had and loved included a very large stuffed bunny, a German girl doll wearing a kerchief that I named Gretchen, and an outfit of furry chaps, holster and gun, cowboy vest, hat, and mask. I loved the Raggedy Ann and Andy dolls that Mother made for me, the Mammy doll that 'Aunt' Emma Butler gave me, and a stuffed panda bear.

My brother, Jerry, had a bad accident when we lived at 211 North Wabash. He had been at the Norton County Fair and watched the "Jimmie Lynch Death Dodgers" drive cars off ramps, through burning walls, etc. He thought that looked exciting, so when he got home, he tried to be a 'Dare Devil" on his bike. He built a ramp and pedaled as fast as he could up and off the ramp. Unfortunately, his bike's front wheel was not secured, dropped off as he flew through the air, and he made a crash landing. He nose-dived into the ground, getting a bad gash on his forehead and top of his head and a bad concussion. He had to stay in bed for a while in the back bedroom, which was off the northeast end of the great room. Someone brought him a Pepsi-Cola, which came in a big, tall bottle (twice the size of a Coca-Cola bottle!), and it sat on the table next to his bed. When I peeked in and saw what to my four-year old eyes looked like a huge bottle, I really wished I could have some of that Pepsi-Cola. That was the first time I coveted someone else's possessions. Speaking of Pepsi, we rarely had bottled pop in our house...that was something you ordered at the drug store, called a 'fountain cola'. Later, when we lived in the Hale house at 109 West Waverly, the Rouses, who lived across the street, would buy Coca-Cola by the case! That must have been the second time I coveted something. My cousins, Helen and Robert Heaton, owned the Coca-Cola bottling company in Norton, so they always had Coke in the refrigerator. When I was a teen, I was not comfortable babysitting (I was intimidated by tiny bundles of joy and afraid I would drop them), but there was a big reward for conquering my fear and babysitting for Judy and Jean Heaton. Going to the Heaton's refrigerator, reaching for a Coke and feeling that wonderfully fizzy and sweet taste sliding down my throat made it all worth it. It WAS a big deal!!

Wabash Street divided just south of the Burlington railroad tracks, which ran in the deep ravine, or the 'draw', just north of our house; there was an added right lane forming a U-turn under the viaduct, with the two lanes of Wabash going up and over the viaduct. The viaduct was constructed of large, creosote-soaked, dark-brown wooden beams, which made it a very strong and sturdy bridge. To continue walking north on Wabash street, it was necessary to go under the viaduct on the south side of the tracks, climb the big, wide wooden steps up to a landing, turn and climb another flight of steps to the top of the viaduct, then walk over the arched top of the viaduct above the tracks and end up walking north on the sidewalk on the west side of Wabash. I hated to have my hair brushed, combed and put into braids because it was painful when my long hair tangled. For some reason, Mother referred to the tangle as a 'rat's nest'. Jerry told me that there were rats living in the wooden supports of the viaduct and, when I went under it, they would come down and make nests in my hair. So, I would cover my head with my hands or books and run as fast as I could under the viaduct. Well, I was only five, and I believed everything my brother said.

These pictures of the viaduct stairs and bracing were taken in 1949. Every Norton kid must have memories of playing and climbing on the viaduct.

CHAPTER 18

1940-1941: First Grade at The Garrett House

WE WERE STILL LIVING IN the house on North Wabash when I started kindergarten in 1939. Miss Edith Deister was my kindergarten teacher, as she was for many, many Norton kids through the years. She had upswept, whitish-gray hair, was very petite, very kind and gentle, and everyone loved her. We had the usual graham crackers and milk break and nap time on the small braided rugs. There were two kindergarten classes…one in the morning and one in the afternoon. I went in the afternoon; evidently I did not like getting up early even at that age.

While most of the kids in my class were normal, average kids, there were a few who had some learning disabilities. For example, two boys in kindergarten had difficulty understanding or accomplishing what Miss Deister asked of them, and one girl's entire family was cognitively impaired. There was another family that lived a few blocks north of us on North Grant. One day Mother was looking out the upstairs bedroom window and saw the couple walking down the sidewalk pulling their little girl in a wagon. The mother needed to urinate so just pulled up her skirt and squatted in the grass. Mother told me later that, when the woman had the little girl, the attending physician tied her fallopian tubes so that she would not get pregnant again. Although this was legal at that time (Supreme Court ruling in 1927), in a small town and at that time (early 1940s) no one would call foul. Even though these folks had mental difficulties, the people of Norton for the most part accepted them as they were and often tried to help them when they could.

When I was six, we moved to 'the Garrett house', which was catty-corner from the southeast side of the grade school and owned by Noah Garrett. The big thing I remember about that house is choking on a piece of hard candy and Dad picking me up by my heels, dangling me upside down, and slapping me on the back to dislodge the candy. Maybe that is why I still have a fear of choking!

I do not remember much about first or second grade...just mental images of the classrooms and the hall. My first grade teacher was Mrs. Lona Bower, who seemed (to me) to be a stern, serious woman; when I was older and she was not my teacher, I realized she was quite nice. Miss Brenner was my third grade teacher. She was young, had long blond hair that she wore in a page-boy with a pompadour in front. Miss Brenner married Lawrence Spalsbury, the high school band instructor. Remarkably, Mr. Spalsbury's brother, Clark Spalsbury, would become a relative of mine because he married my future husband's aunt! Who would have guessed that I would marry the nephew of my high school band teacher's brother! Small world!

The grade school had a basement and two upper floors. Replicas of famous paintings lined the walls on the first and second floors. A contest tested the students each year to see who could name all of the paintings and the artists. I have an award certificate saying that I got them all right (at least one time).

When I was in Brownie Scouts during the war, the leader decided it would be nice if we knitted washcloths for the soldiers. As I started knitting, I imag-ined how happy the soldier would be when he opened the package and found the beautiful, hand knit washcloth. I and the other Brownies happily knit row after row, and before long strangely shaped washcloths appeared (mine was about six inches wide and eighteen inches long). I imagine the soldiers got quite a laugh when they opened the package of 'artistic' washcloths and read the little notes that we had written to go with them! Another Brownie Scout project was embroidering tea towels to enter at the County Fair. I re-ceived a ribbon for my gorgeous entry!

For Mother's Day, we painted a tall catsup bottle red, with a white area at the top, and stuck a perforated metal sprinkling head with a cork bottom into the top of the bottle. At that time, most clothing was either cotton or wool, and if it was cotton, it had to be ironed. Therefore, the sprinkler-top catsup bottle was quite useful. The method was to lay out the shirt or blouse or cotton skirt on the ironing board, sprinkle them generously with water, roll them up, put them into a plastic bag (or a pillowslip) and then place in the refrigerator overnight. This made them evenly damp and much easier to iron. If you wanted shirts and blouses starched, it was necessary to mix up a batch of powdered starch and water in a pail, dip the clothes in it and wring them out, hang them up to dry, and then spray them with the catsup-bottle sprinkler. Canned spray starch was introduced when I was in high school; you just sprayed the liquid starch onto the clothes before ironing. That was much easier.

CHAPTER 19

1941-1944: Second to Fourth Grades in the Hale (Hell) House

WHEN I WAS IN SECOND grade, in 1941, we moved to 109 West Waverly, the 'Hale house', so called because we rented it from the Hale family. Sometime during those years, I was in a store with Mother and someone asked me, "Where do you live, little girl?" I answered, "The Hale House", except the way I pronounced it was "The Hell House." Mother got all flustered for some reason.

This was a one-story house that seemed huge compared to the Garret house, and it sat on a double lot. The Hale house faced south and had a very large great-room/dining room combination in the center of the house, which was entered from a porch running along the front of the house on the south. The front door was on the east side of the great room, and a triple bay window on the south was on the left when you entered.

There was a large parlor to the west of the great room with big sliding wooden doors separating the rooms. Mother and Dad's bedroom was to the north of that parlor. Since the house did not have central heat, the parlor doors were always closed, and it was cold on the other side of those doors in the winter. In the large central room sat a large, gas 'base burner' that provided heat for the whole house. I do not know how Mother kept warm sleeping in an unheated room, quite a distance from the central heater. Maybe there was another small heater in the bedroom? I do not remember much about being in the west parlor...it was hot in the summertime and cold in the wintertime, and we 'lived' mostly in the great room. I do remember Mother having lumbago and having to stay in bed in that front bedroom, but that part of the house was 'off limits', except at Christmas.

At Christmas, the tree would be set up in the parlor where it would last longer because of the coolness there. On Christmas morning, the sliding doors would be opened and we would rush in there to open our presents. There was always an orange and some shelled nuts in the stockings plus toys such as some jacks and a ball or a deck of cards. Gifts were often placed on the branches of the tree, which worked well since many of the gifts were small in size and helped decorate the tree. It was exciting to find a pretty package addressed to me on a branch! Pajamas, socks, scarves, or maybe pretty sweaters were popular gifts. Another exciting Christmas tradition to me was Dad bringing home a white box of Stover's chocolates or maybe a yellow box of Whitman's chocolates, gifts from the pharmacists at the drug stores because Dad was a doctor and his patients filled prescriptions at the drug stores.

I shared a bedroom with Beverly on the east side of the great room, and there was a walk-through bathroom from that bedroom into the kitchen. Jerry had his own room, which was off the great room to the north. The kitchen was on the northeast side of the house and had a large butler's pantry. The cooking range was a large, green-colored unit that stood on four shiny metal legs, with a large oven below the four burners on top. That stove, as well as the Roper Range that was later in the house on North Grant, used gas, but neither stove had an automatic pilot light. To light a burner you struck a match, then turned the knob on the front of the range to get the flow of gas, and held the match close to the burner, which would light with a whoosh. The oven also was lit with a lighted match held close to the little hole near the front of the bottom of the oven. Whoosh! It was on!

The burning of the open gas burners and the oven, left a sticky residue on the tops and burner plates of the stove. Cleaning the oven before the self-cleaning type came on the market (I think my first one was in Libertyville in 1974) was a challenge! There were special, strong oven cleansers that required big thick rubber gloves to use. The cleanser was sprayed or brushed on all the surfaces of the oven, and then it had to 'sit' for a while to dissolve all of the gunk. Next, wearing those big, yellow rubber gloves, you wiped off all the goop using old newspapers (this was before paper towels were common). You ended up with a sack full of gooey black, crumpled paper and a lingering chemical smell when the oven was turned on again.

The Hale house was large and comfortable, and Mother decorated it with the antique furniture from her folks and put up white crisscross and tieback curtains and valances in the parlor and the great room. These were called 'Priscilla' curtains, and Mother used them in every house we lived in. Roll-up shades were used with them, rolled up in the daytime and down when the sun was too hot in the summertime or for privacy in the bedrooms.

This was during World War II and we had a Victory Garden on the large, double lot. Dad planted tomatoes, potatoes, peppers, carrots, corn... even watermelon and cantaloupe. Tomatoes picked fresh off the vine and eaten from your hand tasted wonderful. We did not worry about washing it in those days since pesticides were not used until after the war. I do remember Dad later using a small, metal hand sprayer for bugs on non-edible plants. There was a small 'can' at one end attached to a long metal tube with a hand pump screwed onto the tube, and Dad would pull and push the handle to distribute the pesticide.

One day I went into the long, narrow bathroom from the bedroom, sat down on the toilet and then looked up to see giant bugs crawling on the towel at the other end of the room. I was petrified and yelled for help. Mother came running in. When she realized what I was screaming about, she showed me that the 'bugs' were walnut halves. Jerry had been playing with them in the sink, pretending they were boats, and then stuck them to the towel to dry. Mother was kind and did not burst out laughing at me, but I felt pretty foolish!

When I was in third grade, Dad bought an old, used blue bicycle for Beverly and me to share. It was a very solid bike, weighed a ton, and had a single speed: slow. It had been painted so many times that the blue paint was thick and probably added a pound of weight. It was almost impossible to pedal! A popular activity was to get a few friends together and go for a bike ride. I envied Sandra Isaac, because she had a new, and lightweight, boy's bike. I wanted a boy's bike...one that I could step on the left pedal, push away and swing my leg over the top of the bike to ride. But, the heavy old blue bike had to suffice. As a result, neither Beverly nor I went on many bike rides.

I felt that taking vitamins was important, even at that age. Mother got a bottle of vitamins for me, and I tried to learn how to swallow them. I stood at the big kitchen sink with a glass of water and a vitamin pill, trying to get it down. Before long there were little brown pills all over the sink that I was unable to swallow and spit out before I choked on them. Dad was not happy that I had wasted all of those vitamins!

I had been told that milk was good for a body and would make you strong. I did not particularly like milk, but, again trying to be healthy, one summer day I decided I needed to drink more milk. Therefore, I sat at the kitchen table with a quart bottle of milk and a glass. I filled the glass and drank the milk, one glass after another, until I had gotten the whole quart down. Then I decided to walk down to the library, which was about three blocks away. By the time I got to the Burlington railroad tracks on the north side of the library, all the milk I had drunk overflowed and ended up on the tracks. I was not nauseous...just too full. Having solved that problem, I walked on to the library.

The library had that distinct 'library' smell...old books and glue, I suppose. I still remember where the Nancy Drew mysteries were in the library, as well as the science books. A book about Trilobites and a book on Egypt were two books I found interesting. Nancy Drew mysteries and books about Clara Barton were also favorites.

Somewhere along the way, I must have seen a movie or read a book about the Chinese way of mind-over-matter thinking. I remember walking down that State Street hill on a very hot summer day and telling myself that it was really a chilly and cold day and imagining myself as comfortable and cool rather than hot and sweaty. I seemed to feel much more comfortable!

The Hale house was just a block west of the grade school, so we walked to and from school, which ran from 9 AM to noon, with an hour lunch break, and then 1 to 4 PM. When the noon whistle blew, it was lunchtime for everyone in town, and I would walk home to have lunch. Mother did let me eat at the school cafeteria once after my begging to do so, but it was not as good as what Mother cooked, and I never wanted to do that again. At the east end of the block, between our house and the school, was a large house with a black wrought iron fence in front, which I had to pass to get to school. I dreaded going by there because a big, red Chow dog lived there and, if he were outside, he would come charging down to the fence growling and barking at me. It really scared me! I was so relieved when the dog was inside when I walked by.

In those days children wore 'snowsuits' in the winter (a heavy wool coat and matching, loose-fitting, heavy wool pants with suspenders), helmets with a strap under the chin, galoshes in snow and in rain, and mittens to protect us from the elements. To keep from losing the mittens, Mother would attach the end of a long string or piece of yarn to each mitten and run the string from the sleeve opening across the shoulders and down the other sleeve. When the weather was not freezing and snowy, long stockings were considered warm enough. One winter day, Mother insisted it was too cold for just long stockings and I would have to wear a snowsuit to school. We lived only a block from school and, even though there was snow on the ground, I did not think it was that cold out; I threw a fit and cried and cried. As always, Mother did win the argument and I did wear the snowsuit to school, but my eyes were red and puffy from crying. When my teacher asked me why I had been crying, I told her I had fallen and hurt my elbow. She said she was so sorry! I had learned how to tell a white lie...or, maybe just lie.

When I was in fourth or fifth grade, I had a black flutophone, which I loved. When I went back to school after lunch one snowy day, I had it in the pocket of my heavy wool coat. There was a big rock wall, about five feet high, across the corner of the school grounds, and a deep snowdrift had accumulated below it. I joined a group of kids who were jumping off the wall into the snowdrift and having a wonderful time. Then I discovered that my flutophone was gone from my pocket. All the kids helped me look for it; we dug in the snow until the bell rang, but I never found my flutophone. And, I never got another one. I was very, very upset!

'Boyfriends/girlfriends' were a part of life even at that young age. My first 'boyfriend' was Jimmy Sargent, who lived across the street on North Wabash.

There was a big, old mulberry tree in his front yard and we would gather the sweet, juicy, messy mulberries and eat them fresh off the tree from our purple-stained hands. So good!

When I was in third grade, I was going up the big wide stairs from the basement floor to the first floor of the school, and Lee Breckenridge ran up the stairs after me and asked me if I would marry him when we grew up. I was surprised, but I said, "Uh...okay." By the time I reached the top of the stairs, however, I realized what that might mean; I stopped and turned around, and said, "Well...maybe." My fear of commitment started at a young age! On Valentine's Day when I was in third grade, Lee's older sister had received several boxes of candy in heart-shaped boxes from her boyfriends, and she gave one to Lee. He got on his bike to bring the box to me for Valentine's Day, but ate several chocolates on the way. Mother and I laughed about that then and many times later.

In fourth grade, my boyfriends were John Hutcherson and Warren (Butch) Bullock. They would put pennies and nickels on my desk, either as a male rivalry or (maybe) to impress me. Also in fourth grade, Carol Deiter and I chased Roger Raske around the school grounds one day, threatening to kiss him. I do not know why he ran! In fifth grade, Darrell Winder and Darrell Webber were potential boyfriends. The way it was decided who would be boyfriend/girlfriend was to make a list of potentials that we liked, then compare lists, and see whose lists coincided. Negotiating 'love'? Where did we learn that? There was no actual 'dating', but the idea of boy/girl pairings, the sexual attraction, and the flirtations did start at a young age; and one's self-confidence was affected by this. In junior high, liking or not liking someone was important enough for me to put in my diary: "I don't know who I like", or "I like no one". I was so insecure about whether any boy liked me that one entry in eighth grade was: "Guess I like Darrell, if he likes me". Everyone seemed much more confident about himself or herself than I felt about myself. Incidentally, I (and probably most of my classmates) was unaware of any lesbian or gay identification. Maybe I was just uninformed, but I never heard the terms until I was in college. If any classmates were lesbian, gay, or had any gender identity issues, I suspect it was very confusing and difficult for them. There was nothing in the movies or the books that we read that gave any clue that romance could be anything but between a man and a woman.

Miss Loraine Rumsey was my fourth grade teacher, and a favorite. For one school assembly she taught a couple of us to do a tap dance to "Any Bonds Today". I loved it, and I still remember most of the steps. For another program, she taught me a dance to "Dinah"...I loved it! Another time, she had me do a skit with John Hutcherson. I was to impersonate Dad and give John a 'treatment' by pulling on his arm and pushing on his back to 'make him better'. I loved it! She found my inner 'ham'. Everyone in the class loved Miss Rumsey, so when April Fools' Day came around, we thought it would be fun to play an April Fools' prank on her. We went into the classroom early one day, turned over all the desks, and wrote on the blackboard, "Miss Rumsey loves Mr. Wolfe". We thought she would be so pleased and understand that we did it because we liked her so much. We waited in giddy anticipation for her to have a big laugh when she came in and saw what we had done, but when she saw it...she cried! I was completely surprised and only then did I realize that doing those things was not funny. She called all of our parents and told them why we would all be required to stay after school for a month... well-deserved punishment, no doubt! Since then, I have felt that April Fools' pranks are neither fun nor funny.

That same year, Miss Joanie Johnson was our music teacher. She was young, had long, dark hair, was so nice, and she made music such fun. About half way through the school year, she was called into the Army...it was 1943. I was heartbroken and burst into tears when she told us. She took me out of the classroom and sat on the steps with me for a long time while I sobbed.

One day Rita Aitken came to my house to play after school, and her mother called later that night to let us know that she had broken out in a rash and had a high fever. Scarlet fever was a feared disease at that time, because the infection could spread to other parts of the body causing organ damage as well as rheumatic fever, which often caused permanent heart damage. It is known now that strep bacteria cause it, but before antibiotics were available, it was a serious disease. We held our breath for the four days incubation period and somehow I did not get it. Measles, mumps, chickenpox, whooping cough, and diphtheria were other dreaded childhood diseases. Orange cards were placed in windows when someone inside had a contagious disease to warn people to stay away. I'd had chickenpox when I was a baby, and somehow dodged getting mumps, whooping cough, and diphtheria, but I did get the 'red' measles (as opposed to the three-day German measles) when I was in sixth grade. We were living on North Grant then and Mother put curtains on the window to keep the room dark, because it was believed that bright lights and using your eyes while you had measles could damage one's eyesight. The only treatment was bed rest and aspirin; I remember feeling ill enough that I did not mind staying in bed.

One Saturday on the way home from a movie, after seeing the serial "Captain Marvel", I wanted to fly like he did. Coming uphill on State Street, the sidewalk in front of one house had a two and a half-foot high cement retaining wall running along it with a level top about eight inches wide. I was walking along on top of the wall, when I came to the pyramid-shaped top on the large posts on each side of steps leading up to the house. I pretended to be Captain Marvel and made a big leap trying to fly from one top piece to the next, but I missed. I landed face down on the cement post smashing my nose. I cried. I bled. I sat on the street curb crying and bleeding until Mrs. (Winifred) Rouse heard me and came across the street to help. She picked me up and carried me home, and Mother called Dad. He came into the bedroom, where Mother had put me to bed, and tried to put splints up my nose. They looked like Popsicle sticks...maybe they were? Anyway, having the sticks poked up my nose did not help the pain, and I yelled and cried. Dad decided to just stuff my nose with cotton and put tape over my nose. As a result, my nose has a bit of a bend in it.

The Rouses (Bill, Winifred, Ann, and Judy) lived across the street from us on the corner of State and West Waverly. Ann was in Beverly's class and Judy and I were in the same class. Winifred was a good-hearted person, but, if mother asked her how she was, it always seemed something unpleasant or frustrating had just happened. Guess we have all had those kinds of days!

Sonja Heine was an Olympic Medal winning ice skater who appeared in several movies when I was in grade school. She looked so beautiful in her white satin and fur short dresses and white ice skates. I asked Santa for ice skates every Christmas, but never got them. I suppose this had something to do with the facts that they were quite expensive and that the only place to skate in Norton was that small patch of ground in Elmwood Park, which the city would flood if the weather got cold enough for the water to freeze. However, Judy Rouse had beautiful, white ice skates; I was envious. I found three letters 'among my souvenirs' which I'd written to Santa, the first asking for ice skates. Mother obviously taught me how to be polite...even to Santa.

Dear Santa Claus, I know that you don't have many dolls, but I would like a Baby doll if you have them, and I'd like some ice skates too, there hard to get here, and I don't know if you have them. And a drum. I don't know where I'd keep this, but if I had a place to keep it I'd like a pony to ride. I would like a Book, a BB gun and a knife like Jerry's. And give mommy a fur coat. I would like a Brownie Scout Uniform. I liked the letter you sent me and wish you would send me another one. I guess that's all. Marlyn Butler Thank you. P.S. I would like a bike, too, and a 6 power telescope and a boxing bag please. I would like a big picture of you. Pick 1 or 2 things out of these things.

I became less greedy (or less hopeful) in a later letter. I also added my address in case he had not known where to leave all the things I had asked for previously.

Dear Santa Claus, I want a slate blackboard and anything else that you would think I would like and Not to Much. Marlyn Butler, W. Waverly Street, Norton, Kansas

One day, when I was in third or fourth grade, I went to Pat Harper's birthday party. Pat lived several blocks away, up the hill toward the junior high, but living in a small town it was safe enough to let nine-year olds walk that far, and Pat Melroy, Judy Rouse, Sandra Isaac and I walked together since they lived on the way. On the way home, we came across several young boys who were torturing newborn kittens! It was horrible to see, so I picked up one that was still living, wrapped it in the party napkin I had wrapped a piece of cake in, and carried the baby kitten home. I am not sure that Mother was thrilled, but she understood that the kitten needed to be rescued. The kitten's eyes were not open yet, but Mother made a little box for her and found enough food and milk to feed her, and it lived. We named the black and white kitten Snoopy. She grew up to be a very sweet cat. I remember the first time she had kittens right on the front porch. Watching the birthing process was interesting and, of course, educational. Snoopy was an outside cat and had several litters of kittens before we moved again.

The only other pet I remember having was Rusty, a red, wavy-coated water spaniel. He was given to Dad as payment for osteopathic treatments. I liked Rusty and wrote in my diary "played with Rusty" about every day when I was in junior high. I do remember coming home and lying in the hammock on the back porch and petting Rusty. We did not have him very long, however, because he got distemper and Dad 'took him to the country', a euphemism for shooting him. I do not know if Dad shot him or had someone else do it. I remember seeing dogs who had distemper being unable to walk straight, having muscles spasms, and coughing. Distemper claimed many lives before the vaccination was developed.

CHAPTER 20

1944–1945: Fifth Grade and Two More Quick Moves

WE WERE STILL RENTING THE Hale house at 109 West Waverly in early 1944 and wanted to buy it, but the owners decided they wanted to move back in. Therefore, we needed a place to live quickly, and in Norton at that time during the war, the 'pickins' were slim. We ended up living in a small 'apartment' above the First State Bank for a short time. (I presume that Bill Rouse allowed us to stay in an empty area above the bank, since we were virtually 'homeless' at the time.) Much of our furniture was stored in an empty space on the first floor; the area upstairs was very small…my memory of it is a wood-floored room with open rafters for a ceiling and a window that overlooked Main Street. I remember looking out that window and watching the people below…and dreaming of the future. The piano was stored on the first floor, and Jerry and I would go downstairs to play the piano. We both loved to play and, whenever we would get home from school or from a ride, before we even got out of the car, we would yell "dibs on the piano". Sometimes I would win the dibs, but usually Jerry did.

I do not remember being upset about the upheaval in our living arrangements, but I do remember having less self-confidence in fifth grade, and even my grades reflected this. Looking back, I now wonder if such disruptions in a child's routine causes more trauma and insecurity than is recognized at the time.

After a few months, we found a house to rent on North Second, just a block west of the Hale house. Shortly after we moved in, we discovered that Snoopy (who had decided to stay at the Hale house, as cats are prone to do) had borne another litter of kittens. We tried to move them with us to the new location on North Second, but Snoopy didn't like that idea and carried her kittens, one by one, back to 109 West Waverly. One of the litter was a beautiful, longhaired black kitten, and Mother thought it would be nice to bring that one to the new house and have as a pet. She went to the Hale house, caught and wrapped the black kitten in a big towel, and carried it to the new house. Unfortunately, by that time, the kittens had become feral, and when Mother released the beautiful black ball of fur on the screened-in porch, it was so frightened that it raced wildly from side to side of the porch, clinging to the screens and completely unapproachable. No amount of soft talking and bowls of milk could calm the kitten, and Mother realized it was too late to have it for a pet. Catching it again was a challenge, but Mother finally caught it in the towel and carried it back to our old house.

Our newly rented house had a screened-in porch on the front, facing east on North Second, and a large room between the porch and kitchen area. There were three bedrooms along the north side of the house. Beverly and I slept in the center bedroom. Mother and Dad's bedroom was at the front of the house, and Jerry's room was at the back. We lived there about a year. We were there for Christmas of 1944, and Dad bought a record player and each of us received a record album for Christmas. My album was "Red Nickels and his 5 Pennies", Beverly got Bing Crosby's "Blue Skies" album, and Jerry got...I do not remember!

Mother and Dad had a bridge party while we were there and set up card tables all over the large living area. It was probably the last bridge party that they hosted because, according to Mother, Dad did not like to lose. Having a couple drinks did not make him a happy guy, and this night he threw his cards across the room when he lost. Mother said they did not go to many bridge parties after that. Chick Tillotson, a lawyer in town, once said, "Doc is his own worst enemy".

In July of 1945, I had my 11th birthday while in that house, and Mother took a picture of all the girls that came. The one birthday present that I remember was from Jo Ann Antrim...a fresh, cleaned, ready to fry chicken. Normally, Dad got the breast and Jerry, Beverly and I took turns getting the wishbone or the wings. However, this time, I got to eat the breast because it was my birthday present. Mother said she liked the legs and thighs, but maybe she was just a good mother and ate them because all the rest of us liked the white meat. Jo Ann, by the way, was a good athlete and would have been a star if there had been any girl sports teams then. Most of our games were just on the playground at school or in gym class, and everyone wanted Jo Ann on their team because she could run faster, hit the baseball farther, and put the basketball through the hoop. The photo shows in the front row: Rita Aitken, "me", Jo Ann Antrim, Judy Brock; second row: Jeannine Goodman, Sandra Isaac, Judy Rouse, Pat Harper, Pat Melroy.

1945   11th Birthday

Speaking of birthdays, since my birthday was just before the Fourth of July, I usually got some firecrackers, which I did again on my next birthday when the Rouses (Winifred, Bill, Judy, and Ann) came to our house on North Grant to celebrate the Fourth in 1946. Judy and I were sitting on the back porch steps lighting firecrackers with wooden matches from the big box with the sandpaper on one side for striking the matches. After striking a match to light a firecracker, it fell into the open box of matches causing a big whoosh of flames to flare near Judy's skirt. Fortunately, I saw what happened and was able to knock the flaming matchbox off the steps before Judy's skirt caught fire. We were lucky that we did not become a Fourth of July accident statistic!

In the early summer of 1945 while still at the house on North Second, I found an old, bamboo-fishing pole and decided to learn to pole vault with it. A strip of yard on the north side of the house had no trees or bushes, so there was a place for me to run. I held the fishing pole as I had seen local athletes hold the pole to vault and ran forward as fast as I could. I stuck the pole into the ground to take the flying leap over the imaginary bar, but, as my feet flew up, the pole broke and I landed with a thud on my back. It knocked the wind out of me and hurt a lot! Mother came to my rescue (I was crying loudly) and brought me in to lie on a cot on the screened-in porch. I started having chills and she brought blankets out to cover me, even though it was over eighty degrees outside. Dad came home and examined me, and he decided I would be okay, so I did not have an x-ray. Years later, an MRI showed an abnormality on the ninth rib. When a follow-up CT scan verified a growth of some kind, Dr. Barbosa was sure I had bone cancer. I remember her quietly saying, "I'm sorry". After having a bone biopsy that was not definitive, the doctors decided that it probably was not a sarcoma and they would just 'observe it'. I suspect that I broke a rib in the fall and the scar tissue is what the scan showed; maybe that is the cause of the back pain I have today.

Next door to us to the west lived Mike Bridges with her two young children. Her husband, Dwight Bridges, was a Colonel in the army. He had been home on leave and Mike was pregnant with her third child. We all loved Mike. She had long blond hair and a beautiful smile. She was always cheerful and so nice to us. When the war ended in August of 1945, Mother and Mike sat on our screened-in porch and drank a beer to celebrate. Mike hoped that Dwight would be home before too long since the war was over. Shortly after we moved into the house on North Grant in September of 1945, the phone rang while we were home at noon. Mike had had her baby at the Norton hospital, had gotten an infection and died. I was broken hearted and burst into tears. Although penicillin had been developed during the war and was used for the military, it was not yet available for the general population. It would have saved her; it became available to the public a few months after Mike died. Dwight had not made it home yet, so the doctors did not reveal that she had died, because they feared the Army would not let him take leave quickly unless they said she was very ill and he needed to get home as soon as possible. Mike's body was held in the morgue for a couple weeks until he got home for the funeral.

Another antibiotic, sulfa, had become available in the early 1940s. While we were in the Hale house, I was sick and Dad brought this new wonder drug for me to take. The sulfa was in a chocolate syrup base and tasted awful. It was obvious that I was allergic to it when I broke out in a rash. Later, when I was a senior in high school, I got bronchitis right at the time that Norton was set to play in the state basketball championship. I really wanted to go, so Dad brought me the new, improved form of sulfa, in pills. However, the method of delivery did not stop my allergic reaction. This time I broke out in hives from stem to stern, inside and out. As if a bad cold was not enough, itching all over...even down my throat...was horrible. So, Dad brought me another new medicine...an antihistamine. I did recover, but not in time to go to the game; I listened on the radio. I did get to go, however, the year before when Norton won the state championship in 1951. Many people from Norton rented rooms at a hotel, and it seemed like the whole town was there. We high school kids had a great time running up and down the halls of the hotel. I think I was allowed to go because I was in the pep band, and I rode with Judy in the Rouse's car. After an exciting back and forth battle, when the whistle blew, Norton was the winner! A couple hundred cars, full of Norton folks, drove to the fourteen-mile corner south of town to greet the team when they came home the next day. A long stream of cars escorted the team, with the car horns honking and police sirens blaring, all the way to the high school where a big celebration honored the team.

CHAPTER 21

1945: The Move to 411 North Grant

DURING AND AFTER THE WAR, the housing shortage was severe, both because the materials for building were in short supply and because the soldiers were returning and setting up new households. Since there were no houses to buy or rent in Norton, Mother and Dad bought a lot at 411 North Grant and a house in Oronoque, a town about eight miles southwest of Norton. Oronoque, like many small, farm-based towns in the area, had been an active town with a bank, two churches, a grain elevator, a general store, an implement business and a creamery, as well as a depot for the Burlington Railroad. However, the Dust Bowl years and the Great Depression took their toll on many small towns, and Oronoque was almost a ghost town by 1946. The owner of the house was the Post Master as well as the operator for the Consolidated Telephone exchange and had managed both businesses from the house my parents bought. By the spring of 1945, the hole was dug for the foundation, a cement block basement was built, and then the day came to move the house from Oronoque. The house movers raised it off the old foundation, rolled it onto a huge trailer bed, and slowly moved down the road. The truck brought it into Norton on the shortcut of Highway 383 that came into town on the south side of Norton and slowly turned on to North Grant by the tall grain silos, which were a couple blocks south. When the truck with the house on it came into view just south of 411 North Grant, there was Dad standing at the top of the house with his body sticking up through the chimney, so he could lift any wires hanging across the streets up and over the house. It was an exciting sight to see! As I recall, the lot cost four hundred dollars, but I have no record of what the house cost.

I was in sixth grade, eleven years old, when we moved into the house at 411 North Grant. It was September of 1945, just after World War II ended. This is the house where my folks lived until the early 1980s. That is when Dad's health became so bad that he agreed to go to a nursing home in Kimball, and Mother moved first to a senior citizen home in Goodland before going to the Andbe Home in Norton. This is the house that all their grandchildren remember visiting when they grew up.

Of course, the house had to be remodeled on the inside, and Mother had many ideas for how she wanted it decorated. There had been big, wooden doors that would slide into the walls between the living room and dining room, and Mother was torn whether to leave them in place or take them out. Even though the paneled doors were solid walnut, she decided that she wanted the living room and dining room to be open with a wide arch between the two rooms. Another decision was the stairway, which had been behind the living room wall with a door at the bottom, closing off the stairs from the living room. Mother wanted a more open feel, however, so part of the wall was removed and the bottom six steps were open to the living room, with a white painted wooden stair rail and a Newell post at the bottom. The construction of the walls was plaster over lath strips. When we first moved in, Mother had wallpaper in all of the rooms. The kitchen had green ivy on a white background; the living and dining rooms had a soft blue, damask-like pattern with wide silvery stripes and large fleur-de-lis between the stripes. That wallpaper went on up the stairs. Mother and Dad's room was downstairs and she looked for a long time to find wallpaper with large, red roses in an all-over pattern; it was very pretty. I do not remember the wallpaper that was in Jerry's room, but Beverly's and my room had a soft blue pattern. Many years later, Mother painted over all of the wallpaper, using a colonial blue paint in the living and dining room, yellow in the kitchen, and white in the bathroom.

Mother wanted an antique hanging lamp for the dining room and searched until she found a beautiful globe lamp with crystal prisms. It became a ritual to periodically climb up and take off all of the prisms and the china globe, wash them very carefully, and then lovingly rehang all of them. This was a ritual handed down through the years and it was something like a rite of passage for the grandchildren to be trusted to wash the dining room hanging lamp.

In the dining room stood the corner cupboard holding English Blue Flow china. This cupboard was hand-built by my Great-grandfather Corfman, and the Blue Flow dishes had been an anniversary present from Grandfather Abraham Lincoln Drummond to Grandmother Minnie Corfman Drummond, so their historical and family importance made them very special. Another important piece of furniture was the walnut secretary desk, which had belonged to Grandmother Drummond. This piece had a drop-down front to make a desk and three drawers with teardrop handles below, plus a top decorative shelf on which sat the Seth Thomas pendulum clock. A new, mahogany Duncan Phyfe drop-leaf dining table with additional leafs that would extend the table to seat twelve with matching Duncan Phyfe chairs sat in the middle of the dining room on an oval braided rug.

When we first moved in, the floors in the entire house, except the bathroom and kitchen, were four-inch wide yellow pine. The many family pieces of handed-down antique furniture fit in beautifully with the Early American look that Mother wanted. Oval braided rugs covered the floors in the living room and dining room. We used an oil mop to polish all of the wooden floors using a red-colored liquid, the odor of which I would recognize still today. We also had a 'sweeper' that we pushed back and forth all over the floors to pick up the dust and lint. It had brushes on the bottoms that picked up and deposited the dust and debris into a rather small compartment, which needed to be emptied frequently by shaking it outside.

Coming in the west-facing front door you stepped into the living room, with the dining room to the right through the open archway. The kitchen was east of the dining room, and Mother and Dad's bedroom was east of the living room. With the six open steps of the stairs between the living room and bedroom, the entrance to the house was attractive and inviting. Mother hung the large walnut mirror she inherited from her parents at the bottom of the stairs. The piano always sat on the east wall of the living room, directly across from the front door, and was a focal point of our lives. The "Gone with the Wind" lamp was another important fixture in the house. The large globe top and the smaller globe base were hand-painted with large roses in soft tones of red. Mother had it wired for electricity, and it was beautiful to look at when the light was on. It held a place of honor in the living room all the time I was growing up, sitting on top of the marble top table that had belonged to her parents. During a threatening storm, Mother would move it away from the window to protect it in case hail broke the window. Each time, when we moved from the Garrett house to the Hale house, then to the house on North Second, and then on to 411 North Grant, it was carefully packed and slowly rolled in a wagon to its next location. I am now the 'keeper of the GWTW lamp' and I am too intimidated by its history to risk displaying it. It is a symbol of what is precious and meaningful in life. Every time I think, "I really should put it somewhere for everyone to enjoy", I think about the possibility of a tornado or a hailstorm. Therefore, it sits protected in a safe place, unseen but very much appreciated.

A landing at the top of the stairs had a door to a balcony porch on the original house, but Mother decided that a balcony could be a problem, so it was removed and a window was installed instead of the door. An antique rocker that my Great-Grandfather Corfman made sat in front of a window, and a small table, which Dad had made for Mother as an early anniversary present, was beside it, holding a second telephone. I now have that table by my bed. There was even enough room to set up an ironing board when needed.

A white painted banister ran along the hall from the landing to the bathroom. This was handy to hang hand washing on overnight. We hand washed a lot of our clothing (panties, bras, slips, blouses, sweaters) and hung them over the banister or, in the summertime, on an outside clothesline. We never had a washing machine or dryer...most people did not in the 1940s. The early washing machines had no spin cycle, so there was a 'wringer' device above the tub to wring out the clothes, with the water dropping back into the tub. At first, these were manually operated, and when they became powered, it was not unusual for people to get their hands caught between the rollers of the wringer. Also, the early machines had to be bolted to the floor because the action of the agitator often caused the machines to 'walk' from the vibration. The Rouses were one of the first people in town to own a new 'automatic' washer, around 1947. Dryers were not available until the early 1950s.

So, Dad's shirts and underwear and the sheets and towels were sent out to Mrs. Antrim. Seth Antrim would pick up the laundry at the house in a basket, Mrs. Sie Antrim would wash it in her washing machine at her house, hang it out to dry, iron whatever needed ironing, and then Seth would deliver it to our house. This sounds extravagant, but this was standard practice before washers and dryers were available. The Antrims were patients of Dad, so the charges due for the laundry service were deducted from the charges for Dad's medical services.

Mother wanted a washing machine and dryer, but Dad did not feel that was a good idea. Since we always had only one car, when a Launderia opened in Norton and Mrs. Antrim stopped taking in laundry, Dad insisted on taking the laundry to the Launderia on Sunday, rather than have a machine at the house. We take for granted having a washer and dryer in our houses today, but when one's income is based on how many patients appear and whether the patients actually pay (as opposed to knowing the dollar amount a regular paycheck would be), it made more sense financially for Dad to spend a couple of dollars each week at the Launderia than to pay several hundred dollars all at once to buy a washer and a dryer.

Woolen clothing and things that could not be washed (wool skirts, sweaters, velvet dresses, coats and Dad's trousers) were sent to the cleaners. There were two dry cleaners in Norton: Roark's and the Norton Cleaners. Jerry applied for his first job at the Roark Cleaners, and Mr. Roark asked him if he could drive. Jerry said, "No." Mr. Roark tossed him the keys to the truck and said, "Go teach yourself." Jerry took the truck and practiced driving it for a few hours, got the job, and started picking up clothing at houses all over town, taking them to Roark's cleaning facility, and then delivering the clothes back to the houses in a day or two.

The only bathroom in the house was upstairs and had a large walk-in closet in it, which Mother used. A recessed area in the bathroom served as a 'vanity' area. Because the house was rebuilt as World War II was ending in 1945, copper and brass were in short supply. Noah Garrett was the Norton plumber contracted to put in the plumbing, but either he couldn't get the faucet fixtures for the tub and sink or he let someone else in town have the ones he could get. After waiting and waiting to get the fixtures from Noah, Dad gave up and ordered the fixtures for the tub and sinks from Sears. Noah

Garrett was so angry with him that he refused to install them, so Dad had to find another plumber to get the tub and sink installed in time for us to move in. At that time, incidentally, Dad was doing so well financially that he was able to pay for most of the things done on the reconstruction of the house out of his pocket. Therefore, the loan from the First State Bank was for the house and the renovation. The cost of the lot, $400, sounds like a bargain now, but at that time $5,000 was a high income for anyone, even in the large cities, to earn in a year; Dad's income was closer to $2000 a year.

At that time, the telephone numbers in Norton had three numbers. Our house number was 485, Dad's office number was 385, Pat Melroy was 618, Sandra Isaac was 608, and Judy Rouse was 125. Our phone hung on the west wall of the kitchen. To make a call, you took the earpiece off the hanger clip, the operator at the switchboard in the telephone office would see our line's light go on, plug in a connector and ask, "Number, please." You would say "385", she would take the cord and put the other end of it into the matching plug, and Dad's phone would ring in his office. Many people, especially those who lived in the country, had 'party lines' where two or three people would share the same number and calls for each would be signaled by one, two, or three rings. Of course, it was possible for everyone sharing the line to hear the conversation, but, of course, no one would be so rude! In reality, when people heard the phone ring, they would often join the conversation, so they were using a forerunner of today's conference calls.

Beverly and I shared the upstairs bedroom on the west front of the house. The closet was on the south side of the room and had a narrow six-panel door with a heavy black metal doorknob on it. A pull chain turned on the bare light bulb in the closet. A chest of drawers was on the east wall of the bedroom, and an antique, pine 'school marm's' desk was on the north wall. This is where I sat to study at night. Beverly and I slept together in a double bed all the time we were growing up and, in the house on North Grant, I slept on the side of the bed next to the wall. For some reason (I hate to admit this!), I liked to scratch designs, words, or symbols (such as M.B. + H.C.) into the soft wallpaper. I do not remember that Mother ever scolded me for doing this; she was always a tolerant and forgiving mother and felt it better to 'let things go' rather than attack her children with yelling or criticism. That was certainly one of Mother's most wonderful attributes!

Jerry's room was at the back (east side) of the house. Since he was the oldest and the only boy, he always had his own room. There were closets at both ends of his room, with the entrance to the attic in one of them. Dad used one closet and Jerry used the other one. Jerry was a sophomore in high school when we moved in.

The basement held a very large furnace with the many pipes and vents running from it. There were 'basement windows' on the north and south sides which let a little light in and could be opened for ventilation. After a few years, a shower was installed in the northwest corner, but Dad was the only one who used it. Jerry was on his own by that time, and the open shower seemed very 'exposed' to the modest ladies in the household.

There was a door on the east side of the basement that led to a dirt-floored (and unlit) storage area under the back porch. I never had the nerve to do anything but peek in when Dad would put something in there; I imagined all sorts of bugs, and centipedes, and spiders (oh my!) in there.

The backyard was deep, running all the way to the alley in back and had a plush lawn of buffalo grass. Dad built a corral-type fence across the back of the yard, about 20 feet in front of the alley, and painted it white. One day many years later when Pam, John, and I were visiting Mother and Dad, Pam was playing on the fence and imagining she was a cowgirl with a horse corral. Mother called to her to come inside and Pam ignored her, continuing to play. After Mother had called her many times, Pam turned and looked at her and said, "I don't hear you."

Ona and Roy Wingfield lived to the north of us, and Irene and Oren Hollinger and their children, LuAnn and Gary, to the south of us. The night we moved into the house, I woke up about four-thirty in the morning hearing a dog howling mournfully. I looked out the window and saw this poor little doggy sitting on the sidewalk in the moonlight; I thought he was probably lost and lonely and I felt so sorry for him. Later, I found out that he was not a lost, lonely doggie, but that he was the Wingfield's dog, Prince, and he howled at the train whistle of the Rock Island Line

Rocket every morning as it went through town. I also discovered that Prince, a blonde Cocker Spaniel, was not a sweet little doggy and would growl and snap at me every time I went outside! There were no fences around lots at that time, so Mrs. Wingfield tried to control him by tying him to their clothesline with a long leash; this resulted in his running back and forth along the clothesline growling and snarling at me. I was as afraid of that dog as I had been of the Chow on West Waverly.

Just before Christmas in 1947, we had gone to the 'show', and when we came home, there was an odd odor in the house, like something burning. Dad discovered that the wall in the upstairs bathroom was "hotter than the dickens" (to quote my diary), so he called the fire department. Mother, Beverly, and I carried outside all the packages from under the Christmas tree...just in case. The problem was a blower fan that was not working, so heat was accumulating in the flue; there was no fire...yet. However, the people of Norton were there to help. I wrote in my diary, "The whole town was up here!"

Homes did not have central air conditioning when I grew up. Some people bought fans that they would turn on in the area where they might be working. Dad did have a fan in his office, but we did not have a fan at home. Roll-up shades were in each window; these had a half-inch wide wooden slat slipped through a small hem at the bottom of each blind that you would pull down slightly, causing the blind to roll up. These needed to be replaced often, because the spring that allowed them to roll up did not last long. In the summer, Mother would shut the front door and pull down the blinds on the windows after the noon meal, before the sun hit the west side of the house. This helped keep the house from heating up more than necessary.

There were screens on all the windows and screened doors for the front and back doors. In the summer after the sun went down or was behind the trees and houses across the street, Mother opened the front and back doors to let any breeze move through the house. Beverly's and my bedroom was upstairs on the west side, and the sun kept shining directly on our room until sunset. In the summer, it was hot upstairs! We would pull the bed in front of the window and pray for a breeze. An old iron bed with a very old mattress was in the basement, and sometimes Dad would go down there to sleep. No one else wanted to sleep on that old bed, although the cooler air was tempting. There was an old army cot on the back porch and a woven hammock stretched from the house to the post at the east side of the porch. On hot summer evenings, we liked to sit on the back porch where it was cooler, lying in the hammock or sometimes sleeping on the cot, and sing "Goodnight, Irene" to our neighbor, Irene Hollinger, as well as a lot of the old songs like "Let Me Call You Sweetheart" or "When Irish Eyes are Smiling". That was much nicer after the porch was screened in so that the mosquitoes did not eat us alive. In August when the County Fair was on, we could hear the sound of the cars racing around the track and the sounds of the calliope playing in the distance. Moreover, the singing of the "Katydids" (okay...cicadas) was always so relaxing to hear. Ah, the sounds of a summer night.

CHAPTER 22

1945-1948: Sixth Grade and Junior High

IN SIXTH GRADE, MR. WILTFONG and Miss Heilman each had a homeroom class, with Mr. Wiltfong teaching geography for one hour a day and Miss Heilman teaching English one hour a day to the other class. I was in Miss Heilman's homeroom. She had a stern presence, was tall, wore her black hair pulled back into a tight bun, did not smile much, and she was strict. Jess Vague was principal of the grade school.

My breakfast (usually toast or cereal) never lasted long, and I always got hungry mid-morning. Mother's solution was to give me a candy bar to take to school, which I then hid in my desk and would sneak a bite when Miss Heilman was not looking.

The room was arranged with the rows of desks running from front to back. I sat in the front of one row. Carol Deiter sat near the back in the next row. We were good friends and one day we were passing notes back and forth, until Miss Heilman caught us. Our punishment was to write a twelve-page report on the Civil War. That seemed like a huge and impossible task! I still remember the challenge of writing twelve pages in cursive!

Claudine Priest moved with her Mother and Dad from Topeka to Norton that year and joined our sixth grade class. When I met her, I felt she was arrogant and 'stuck up'. For one thing, she had on a fashionable cardigan sweater set with the sleeves pushed up on her arms to her elbows, and, with her elbows bent, she held her arms out in front of her with her hands hanging down at the wrists in what I perceived as a haughty stance. She was pretty and smart and, to make things worse, she played the piano! Well! I realize now that I felt threatened by her talent and sophistication; I at least pretended to be friendly. But, one day as we were leaving the classroom, something happened and we got into a hair-pulling, fall-down, wrestling fight. I do not know how such a thing happened when I was such a sweet young girl! We did become good friends after that encounter, and I wrote in my diary many, many times about things that Claudine and I did together.

The junior high was about four blocks north and a block west of our house on North Grant. It seemed like a very long walk…and all uphill! In seventh grade, different teachers taught different subjects. Miss Spring taught math. Adding, subtracting, multiplication, and division were not difficult, but math was boring, and Miss Spring's stern and unsmiling face did not help to make math fun. Miss Mustoe taught home economics; I took cooking one semester and sewing another semester. We made a peasant blouse, gathered at the top with elastic or a cord to tighten it, and I ran the needle through my finger while trying to stitch it on the sewing machine. Surprisingly, it did not hurt. The thing that did hurt was Miss Mustoe's habit of using the thimble on her finger to thump you on the chest or your head to get your attention. The cooking class learned by helping prepare lunch for the school cafeteria; no one enjoyed the days that required boiling and then slicing the big, mushy cow's tongue. I was happy to be able to go home for lunch!

The English teacher was Miss Conkey. Harlan Conkey was from Edmond, but he came to Norton to go to school that year, and he was definitely a "Hubba! Hubba!" guy. He became my 'boyfriend' that year. "There once was a boy named Harlan who went with a girl named Marlyn…." A 'fad' at that time was to cause yourself to pass out by taking a deep breath and quickly bending over. Often at recess a group of students would gather on the playground and do this, but one time when we got back to the classroom, Miss Conkey had to leave the room and warned us that "no one had better be passed out" when she got back. As soon as she left, the kids in the class dared me…"Do it! Do it! Do it!", and, wanting to impress Harlan, I acted on the dare. I took the deep breath, bent over, and woke up to find Miss Conkey bending over me and yelling, "Wake up!" I have no explanation of why and how I could have been so stupid!!

Lyman Rowh was the school superintendent; he and Mr. Conroy were basketball and football coaches. Another teacher was a tall, nervous woman, Miss Sebelius. The boys in the class would bring mirrors to school and, when she would be in the aisle between the rows of desks helping a student, the boys would hold the mirror under her skirt. She ran crying from the room many times. Mr. Lindsley was the history teacher and had a nervous tic, supposedly from trauma in the war. The boys teased, imitated, and laughed at him, and the girls joined in with nervous giggling. Junior high...the cruel age!

The band teacher was Mr. Harris, whom we called Mr. Hairy Ass.

This nickname was not because we disliked him, but just because we thought we were so grown up and clever to turn Harris into Hairy Ass! I had started playing drums in grade school, then switched to cornet (because Jerry had a cornet), and then switched again to the French horn, using the school's mellophone. I was also a twirler in junior high. When the band was scheduled to march in a city parade, the twirlers did not have the typical white, majorette boots and none could be found to buy, so we were told to wear white, low-cut shoes. Mother, however, thought that was a terrible idea: "A twirler needs white, majorette boots!" Therefore, she called everyone who had ever been a twirler and found a pair of used white majorette boots for me to wear! Mr. Harris was no match for my Mother! I felt pretty special wearing those boots!

At this time, I saw no reason why I could not get my friends together and have a jazz band. Sandra Isaac played clarinet, Judy Rouse played cornet, and Pat Melroy played drums in the school band. I wrote out parts to "Strike Up the Band" for them, with me playing the piano, and they came to our house to practice. I could not understand why they were unable to read the notes I had written for them and play the way I wanted them to play!

A box supper on Sadie Hawkins Day was held each year in the school gym. The girls would decorate a big box, put a picnic supper in it, and bring it covered, so no one could see it, to the school. The girls placed their boxes on a big table and the boys would then bid on the boxes. The girl would claim the box she had made and eat supper with the boy. Of course, the girls planned ahead and told the boys they wanted to have supper with how their box was decorated. Sandra Isaac and I went together on decorating a box for the Sadie Hawkins Day party in seventh grade. Yes, Harlan Conkey and LeRoy Ciboski managed to buy the box for $3.75!

After basketball and football games, there was a dance in the gym. Junior high games were not always high scoring. I wrote in my diary that Norton won 22-1 in basketball, and a football game score was 0-0. Ronald Allen was my boyfriend for a while in eighth grade, and we had a 'date' for the dance after one game. He walked me home afterward but asked me if he could wait on the corner northwest of our house while I walked on home. Jerry and Beverly were having a party at our house that night and the number of kids going in and out of my house looked pretty intimidating to an eighth grader.

Gladys Hazlett was in an auto accident that year and broke her back. She was able to return to school wearing a large back brace that seemed to run from her hips up to her neck. I suspect it was uncomfortable, and I remember how straight it made her sit and walk. After she healed and was able to stop wearing the brace, she had beautiful posture.

When Mother could not find the right dress for me to wear to my eighth grade graduation, we drove to Kearny, Nebraska and found the perfect dress. It was made of white cotton pique, with a circle skirt and a fitted jacket top that had a red plaid yoke around the shoulders and a bow at the waist in the back. I kept that dress for years and wore it many times!

I had a date with Ken Deeter to the graduation dance; he gave me my first corsage. His dad ran the Norton theatre, so after the dance, he asked if I'd like to go to the movie (which he got into free, of course). I said, "Sure", not thinking at all that my folks might be expecting me home when the dance ended. We walked downtown and went to the movie, "The Outlaw" with Jane Russell, which was a very risqué movie at the time. Mother became worried when I did not come home when she expected me and sent Dad to hunt for me. He drove all over town looking and finally saw us innocently coming out of the movie about midnight. I do not remember either of them reprimanding me or being angry with me, which seems very strange looking back. However, there was not an atmosphere of constant surveillance at that time, and it never occurred to me that they might be worried about me or that I should have let them know where I was. The only reason I think they were not upset was because they felt that Ken Deeter was a nice boy and not 'dangerous'.

CHAPTER 23

1948-1952: High School

CAROL COUSINS WAS A YEAR older than I was and, when she had a birthday party the summer before I started junior high, she invited me as well as others in my class...sort of a 'welcome to junior high' courtesy. At the party, we played spin the bottle. This is played with everyone sitting in a circle and the person who is 'it' spins a milk bottle (quart sized and made out of glass). Whomever the neck of the bottle is pointing at when it stops has to kiss the person spinning the bottle. And, this is how I received my first kiss...from Warren Bullock. Ooooh! So grown up!

Just before my freshman year of high school in 1948, Marilyn Sanderson invited some incoming freshman girls to her birthday party at the Silvaire. Everyone skated for a while and then, later in the evening, a group of girls gathered in a circle outside the entrance of the building. They were passing around a cigarette and Marilyn asked me if I wanted to take a puff of it. Always eager to please, I said, "Sure!", and they handed me the cigarette. Wanting to appear sophisticated and to be part of this older and influential group of girls, I took a big drag on the cigarette...and immediately choked and started coughing my head off. An embarrassing moment! Many high school students smoked at that time, but I never became 'hooked' for some reason. Maybe all the second-hand smoke I had inhaled for years gave me an immunity, like a vaccination.

Marilyn Sanderson and Mary Wieland were my idols and role models. I really wanted to be like them. Mary, Marilyn, and I all played French horn in the high school band, which was enjoyable for me. Mary was such a cheerful, positive, always-smiling person and was so encouraging to me. Marilyn had a flair for honesty and openness. She was going steady with Walter Wolf, a star basketball player, and I saw her throw a kiss to him at a basketball game and whisper, "I love you, Walter Wolf!" I was so impressed, because I could never be so honest about my feelings; it was dangerous to be so vulnerable. Marilyn waved at me one day on the way to school and I shyly waved a little wave back. Later she came up to me and said, "Marlyn Butler, when I wave at you, I want you to give me a big wave back and act like you're glad to see me!" I was so surprised and so joyful that my idol wanted me to be more outgoing with her; I was always glad to see her!

The Norton County Fair was a big event in Norton, and the whole County looked forward to and went to the Fair! Shortly after Mother and I got back from Albuquerque in 1948 (talked about in the chapter about vacations), Jimmy called and asked me to go to the Norton County Fair and the dance with him. I'd had my first date with him earlier in the summer (I had worn my new white eighth grade graduation dress) when we went to a movie, and we continued dating through the year. Jimmy had a green Pontiac with an outside visor across the windshield, and he would drive past my house and honk to let me know that he had gone by. I was crazy about him, but Mother felt he was a bit too suave and mature for me and did not always let me go out with him when he called for a date. She probably sensed that this was a strong attraction and felt I was too young to get involved in a serious romance. However, Mother did let me go to the dance at the Fair with Jimmy, and the date was magical. The Bobby Mills orchestra was playing that night and we danced cheek to cheek as "Little White Lies" played; that became 'our song'.

There was quite a bit of drinking done by high schoolers then, and smoking was common. Between music sets that the band played, people would go to their cars and spike Coca-Cola or 7-Up with the bottles of hard liquor that they had stashed in their cars. By the end of the evening, many people were 'under the influence'. As Jimmy and I danced at the Fair that night, I took notice when a high school student, with his date beside him, roared his car in reverse all the way up the hill from Elmwood Park to the street above. That same night another young man was killed in a car wreck on Highway 36.

When we were in high school and kids had access to cars, we dragged Main a lot hoping to see who was out and with whom we might talk (flirt). Everyone knew who drove what cars, of course. Even I could recognize the make and model of a car if it belonged to someone I knew. A fun game to play when cruising Main was "Padiddle". When you saw a car with one headlight out, you cried out, "Padiddle!", and got a kiss from your date. When I was a fresh-man, Bonnie Underwood and I dressed up in high heels and 'Sunday' dresses and walked all over town taking photos of each other. My feet were suffering by the time we stopped! Bonnie was hoping to see Bill Lathrop, and I was hop-ing to see Jimmy... which we did manage to do, making walking all over town in high heels worth it! Success!! The top photo shows Bonnie standing outside Jimmy's Pontiac and me in the driver's seat on that memorable photo-shoot day; the bottom photo shows Jimmy, Bill Laws, and Roger Dietrich standing by Roger's Ford, which was full of kids at noon or after school.

Jimmy was a senior when I was a freshman. During school, I would sit on the front row in Latin class and Jimmy would sit by the door of the library across the hall. Then we could see each other and flirt. It is a wonder I learned any Latin from Mrs. Grace Brock. After football or basketball games, a dance was held in the gymnasium, and the last record played was always "Twelfth Street Rag", a great Dixieland tune. Jimmy was a wonderful dancer and it was great fun to jitterbug to that with Jimmy! For Christmas he gave me blue topaz earrings...I still have them (some mementos you just cannot discard). I dated Jimmy for at least two years. We had gone to a movie on the Sunday night that the Korean War started. I remember hearing the news come over the radio as we drove east along Highway 36 that night. Both of us were stunned by the news; the world was in another war.

Don Strevey was in Beverly's senior class, too. His grandparents had raised him on a farm near Norton. He was a football player and a heavy-weight wrestler in high school; he won the state wrestling championship his senior year and earned a scholarship to Oklahoma State University, as did Bill Lathrop who was a lightweight wrestler. I dated Don occasionally my freshman year (I was not going steady with Jimmy) and occasionally when he came home from Enid, Oklahoma when I was a sophomore. One Sunday night, we went to the movies and afterwards were riding around in his grandfather's old car. We turned north off of Highway 36 and went up and over the railroad tracks where Don turned into a country road to turn around. Then the car stalled, and he could not get it started again. We had to walk to a nearby farmhouse to call his grandfather to come and get us. Even though I was late getting home, Mother was not upset, because she trusted Don and felt that he was a nice young man.

Sometime around 1950, the BERKS came into being. Bill Krehbiel's parents let Bill and his friends create a BERK house in their freestanding garage, and the BERKS were born. B was for Joe Ballinger, E for Stanley Elsea, R for Gary Rowley, K for Bill Krehbiel and Bob Kline. Gayle "Harpo" Griffith was also a member. They built bunks in the garage and set up a place where they could be guys. Joe said they set it up as a teen hangout and had rigid rules: "no alcohol and no taking girls there for sexual purposes, so parents would feel okay with their daughters there. Of course most of us didn't know what to do with a girl anyway." Another no-no, he added, was "...we were gentlemen and didn't talk about women/girls even among ourselves." They slept there about every weekend and had many get-togethers. All of them served in the military, and the camaraderie of these men has lasted through the years.

I thought all the BERKS were great guys, as indicated by what I wrote in my diary, "They're all spooks!" They found an old car, painted it silver and named it the BERKMOBILE. The photo shows Harpo Griffith on the hood, me, Rita Aitkin, and Bill Krehbiel on top of the car, and Bonnie Underwood in the driver's seat.

I knew Joe Ballinger better than any of the other BERKS, and he led me on a few 'adventures'. He graduated in 1950, two years ahead of me, went to Kansas State, and joined a fraternity. He invited me to go to his fraternity's Christmas ball and Mother, surprisingly, said I could go. Narvelle Oglevie was in Manhattan at the time, so Mrs. Oglevie asked if she could ride to Manhattan with us to visit Narvelle. The three of us set off in Joe's 1939 Terraplane on a December day just as it was starting to snow. I was in the middle of the front seat (it was a coupe so there was no back seat) between Joe and Mrs. Oglevie as the snow and wind continued to turn into an old-fashioned blizzard. The further away from Norton we got, the deeper the snow got on the road; yes, I was a little anxious! Nevertheless, we made it. The Christmas party at the Manhattan Country Club was exciting and elegant and Mrs. Oglevie got to visit Narvelle, but the snow was piled along the highway in deep drifts with many cars in the ditch when we drove back to Norton the next day. Mother was anxiously peering out the window when we drove into the driveway late Sunday night. Weather forecasting was a bit limited at that time; perhaps if we had known how bad the weather was going to be, we might have stayed in Norton.

Another escapade with Joe took place when I was home from the University of Kansas one summer. A couple cars, full of kids, were 'cruising Main' looking for something exciting to do. Someone (Joe?) had a bright idea and led everyone out to the airport and onto the field where the airport tower stood. "Come on! Let's climb the tower and ride the beacon light!" someone suggested. No one had a thought such as, "Hmm...That could be dangerous!" No, we all just climbed those skinny little metal stair rungs, crawled through the opening to the platform, and took turns climbing up on and straddling the big metal beacon light and riding it around and around. I am afraid of heights, but it was night, it was dark, I could not see the ground, and group-think can be hazardous to one's health. Groupthink also led many teenagers to climb the water tower in Norton, a real test of one's ability to handle heights. Today, when people (myself included) wonder how teenagers could do some of the dumb things we read about them doing, I reflect and know exactly how they could be so dumb.

In Cuba in the 1940s, political unrest caused many doctors to leave Cuba and come to the United States, and several came to Norton to work at the Norton Sanatorium, a tuberculosis hospital. Raul Cuadrado was the son of one of the doctors. He was very charming...the tall, dark, handsome type...and he had a wonderful accent. I had a few dates with him and one night after going to a movie, we were standing on the front porch talking before saying goodnight. I thought he said, "I want to leave." I was surprised and rather insulted. I said,

"Okay, leave!" What he was saying, however, was "I want to live" in his Cuban accent. Oh, okay! Communication can be such a problem!

Darrell Webber was in the class ahead of me, but when he got polio his senior year, he lost a year of school and was then in my graduating class. Early in my senior year, he asked me to go to the senior prom with him and I said yes. By May, however, he was dating Carol Depew, and she was a bit upset that he had a date with me rather than with her. I offered to let him take Carol, but he said no, he had asked me, and he would keep the date. A true gentleman!

I had not earned particularly wonderful grades in elementary school or junior high nor had I thought much about grades then. However, when the grades came out at the end of the first six weeks of high school, I was shocked that I had all 'I's (A's) and was at the top of all my classes. (In the Norton schools at that time the grades were given as: I, II, III, IV, and F, rather than A, B, C, D, and F.) I was amazed and liked the feeling of having done well; from then on, I wanted to make all 'I's. Throughout high school, I did that except for a 'II' in driver's education. I blame this on the fact that the driver's education teacher, Mr. Casper (who was also the wrestling coach with a 52-inch chest), was drafted into the Army a few weeks after school started (this was during the Korean War in 1951). He had given one test, I missed one question, and received a 'II' on the test. When the principal, Mr. Gerald Travis, took over the class, he never gave another test, and whatever the student had received on that first test was their final grade! We learned to drive in a car with manual transmission, no radio, and no turn signals. To signal a turn you had to roll down the window with the manual handle, stick your left arm out the window and put your arm up for a right turn, straight out for a left turn, and down to signal slowing or a stop. I may have 'gotten even' with Mr. Travis for giving me a 'II' when I accidentally stepped on the brakes too hard and threw Mr. Travis into the front windshield.

After not liking math in grade school and junior high, I loved algebra, geometry, and trigonometry and analytical geometry taught by Miss Mary Norris. I thought she was an excellent teacher, although Jerry had a different opinion. Miss Norris always drove a Ford, which she called Henry, and had a fondness for reassuring the class by saying, "Don't worry, we're not going to have a test…(long pause)…yet". I did learn from her and got first in the state in algebra and third in the state in trigonometry, and I quizzed out of the first year math class at KU. Every year before Christmas the geometry class would design a 'stained glass' window using all the geometric figures we were learning about, cut out the shapes using different colored paper according to the design, and attach them to the front high window of the school to create a large 'stained glass' window.

Miss Mary Farrell and Miss Emma Smika taught typing and stenography; both classes were difficult at the start of the semester, but after a few weeks, the finger dexterity and the brain patterns suddenly clicked, and I became quite adept at both. Typing was considered a basic skill for boys and girls, and stenography, or Gregg shorthand, was considered important for girls, since it was expected that many would become secretaries. Both skills were helpful in college, steno for taking notes and typing for all the required essays. I still take notes in shorthand today.

Journalism was another class I enjoyed. Miss Doris Ballard, who also taught English and Speech, taught journalism. I worked on the school newspaper, "The Nugget", and the yearbook, "The Blue Jay", my junior and senior years. I was editor of the school newspaper my senior year so Miss Ballard asked me to interview Nelson Eddy when he came to Norton to perform in concert. She taught us the basics of writing a news story: the five Ws…Who? What? Where? When? Why? plus, the additional How? If you wrote an article that was not your best writing, she would ask oh-so-kindly, "What would you think if we said…instead of…? Good! I think so, too!"

Oran Burns taught biology. Like every biology room, there were jars with all sorts of gross-looking 'things' preserved in formaldehyde sitting on shelves around the room. In one gallon-size glass jar was a loosely wound long, pale yellow-colored tapeworm bobbing in the jar. Each year he threatened the class that this was the year the tapeworm had to be rewound, and this would be a project that the class would soon undertake. We were all relieved to have the year end with the tapeworm still bobbing loosely in the jar. One project that every class did was killing, mounting, and identifying insects. We brought a pint-size, glass Mason jar to school, into which Mr. Burns put some cyanide. There was not a lot of cyanide in the jar, just enough to emit a distinct odor whenever the jar was opened and to kill a bug when it was closed. Our assignment was to catch insects in the jar, watch them die, remove them, pin them to a board, and label them. Unfortunately, I dropped my jar the first day on my first insect hunt; it broke all over the sidewalk, leaving me no way to catch insects. In spite of my pleading, Mr. Burns would not give me another jar! Judy Brock was nice enough to lend me her jar to catch the required insects. Oran Burns was one of my favorite teachers and when he was recalled into the Army as a Major in 1951, soon after the Korean War started, I was heartbroken. The class got together and gave him a sock shower before he left; several girls, including me, embroidered loving thoughts on socks for him.

During the junior or senior year of high school, everyone took Constitution for one semester. I found it challenging to understand and remember all of the Articles and Amendments and background of what was going on in the United States at that time, and I wrote in my diary, "I studied Constitution all evening and still don't know a thing!" We had excellent teachers, obviously, because I got second place in the State Contest in Constitution that year.

I was a member of Y-Teens, on the student council several years and was elected to National Honor Society my sophomore year. I sang in the choir and the girl's triple trio and accompanied many vocal soloists and groups on the piano. I also played the piano for the weekly luncheon meetings of the Rotary Club and Lions Club, held at the Kent Hotel. I accompanied the men as they sang a few popular songs before lunch was served, as well as the boys' quartet or some other high school group that sometimes performed during lunch. I enjoyed a lovely lunch as my reward. A member of the Rotary or Lions Club picked me up at the high school and took me back after the meeting. I also played piano in the swing band, what is now called jazz band. When there were programs at the high school, many students were in several performing groups, either as a singer, an instrumentalist, or as an accompanist. This is a good thing about being in a small school...students have the opportunity to play multiple roles.

The band director for my first three years of high school was Mr. Lawrence Spalsbury, or "Spalsy". Spalsy was rather rotund and played the violin. I can still see him sitting in the band office, sprawled and leaning back in his large, springy chair, his feet up on the desk, and playing the violin. He was a happy person, friendly and smiling. The band played and marched at all the home football games, and a smaller group became the 'Pep Band', which played at all of the basketball games and sometimes went to out of town games.

I played French horn solos at the yearly contests, played in the brass quintet, and accompanied on the piano many of the other soloists. One memorable soloist that I accompanied was Lee Breckenridge. He played the sousaphone but did not have a great 'ear' for music. The end of the piece called for him to play a long, loud, sustained note while the accompaniment finished playing the passage to the end. Unfortunately, he missed and blared out the wrong note while I tried to play quickly, and loudly, to end the misery. The yearly contests were a big deal (they still are!). Everyone practiced for months to be ready, and everyone dressed up for the contests. For one contest held in Colby Mother bought me a red and white polka dot suit. It had a fitted jacket, buttoned down the front with a peplum in back, over a knee length tight skirt; I wore white, high heels all of a very long day. I looked good anyway!

I had been a baton twirler since junior high. Between my sophomore and junior years of high school, Carolyn Eppinger and I attended a music camp in Gunnison, Colorado, and Mother and Dad drove us there. At the Continental Divide, there is a large sign announcing this and, oddly enough, it reminded me of my parents because they had opposite opinions often. I insisted that we stop, so I could take a picture of them in front of the sign. I do not think they were aware of the innuendo I sought, as I posed them on opposite sides of the Continental Divide, but I thought it was clever, funny, and ironic imagery.

The camp took place at Western State University, and we stayed in a dorm on the campus, which was my kind of camp...indoor plumbing and no tents! When we were not practicing or going to classes or rehearsals, we had time to explore the countryside. One time we waded across a mountain stream and climbed the "W" mountain. It was not a high peak, but I did huff and puff, and we decided we did not need to make it to the top! Music camp was a great experience. I loved the feeling of being in a dorm and on a college campus, and the classes and the students energized me. We both took twirling lessons, as well as band and private lessons on our instruments.

David Schneider had been the drum major for the Norton high school band and, when he graduated, that position came open. I felt like a shoo-in for the job because of the twirling camp I had just attended, my years of experience as a twirler, and being the back-up drum major for two years. However, Spalsy chose a girl a year younger than me! Although the rationalization was that Joan could be the drum major for two years and I would have to be replaced after one year, I was hurt and shocked that he would give the position to someone else. I felt somewhat betrayed...like some of my identity was taken away.

Spalsy stopped teaching mid-semester that fall; he seemed to be having some health problems and went to work at the Texaco gas station in town. He died within a few years of pancreatic cancer. A temporary band instructor, an Italian, Vincent Tumolo, was hired until a permanent band instructor could be found. The second instructor, Charles Callahan, came in before the end of the year and stayed several years after I had graduated.

Every year the student body elected a Senior King and Queen and Senior Prince and Princess. Beverly was elected Senior Princess when she was a senior in 1949, with Joy Hutcherson as Senior Queen, Don Strevey as King, and John Travis as Prince. In 1952, I was Senior Princess, with Bonnie Underwood as Senior Queen, John Hutcherson as King, and Ronnie Allen as Prince. Bonnie and John deserved their election to be Senior Queen and King, and they have done an excellent job keeping up with all their classmates since high school.

In May of 1952, it was time to graduate from high school. Lee Breckenridge was quite smart and we were in competition for the Valedictorian spot. I had had all I's except for that II in Drivers Education, but evidently he had received one more II than I had (maybe in band because of that missed note), so I was named Valedictorian and he was Salutatorian. We both gave speeches at the graduation ceremony, so the only difference was the title.

Aunt Ruby wrote a lovely letter to me when I graduated from high school; I have treasured her words of encouragement:

"Dear Little Marlyn,

I'll start this-a-way—I love you! And I'm so proud of you, for so many reasons. I see in you, my Sweet, all that is good, all the fine ideals and strength of character it takes to produce a wonderful woman; and that is exactly what you are going to be, for out of the perfect rosebud blooms the perfect rose!! You couldn't be otherwise: Your training, Your home with Daddy and Mother, Brother and Sister, Your many friends, both old and young, have all helped to give you what is now 'You'. You have tossed aside, as undesirable, many things; and you have kept within yourself, those ideals you have found to be good. There is still a bit of "Rocky Road" ahead, but with your brains and good judgment, you'll ride along smoothly in the places that "matter". And try, Darling, to smile and not let the "hurty" things mean too much, because mostly those kind of things are said in anger or impatience or ignorance, and they cannot hurt you, not really, unless you keep them in your memory. I say toss them away as you would drive a stinging wasp or a bee out of the house, and forget. You can, but it takes a bit of doing, and you, my Dear, can do!

Again, I'll say it, I love you Marlyn. XOXOXO

Your Aunt Ruby"

PART IV

Expanding Horizons

*Look! Listen! There is a world out there waiting to give you
knowledge, insight, understanding, tolerance, love, grace,
hope. Open your heart and senses; absorb the wonders.*

CHAPTER 24

Vacations and Trips

WE TOOK ONLY ONE REAL 'vacation' trip. Dad rarely took a day off because, as a Doctor, if you were not in the office and available to your patients, not only did you not get paid, but it left your patients at some risk. As a result, it was difficult for Dad to be away from Norton any length of time. However, in 1944, a patient told Dad about a Dude ranch in Platora, Colorado (I know now that the town is Platoro, but my 10 year-old ears heard Platora and that is what is in my memory). He said it was "beautiful", with wonderful accommodations and scenery, and there were "horses to ride", which I was excited about since I had always wanted a horse. Over the years, I had begged anyone who had a horse in Norton to let me ride. Amazingly, some folks did let me and my friends ride their horses. One horse I borrowed was blind in one eye, so you could turn him only in the direction of his good eye, making for an interesting and circuitous route. Another horse was the "Brown Bomber", named for Joe Louis, the world boxing champion at that time. Another borrowed ride was a Shetland pony, which I rode without a saddle and ended up sitting on its ears by the time it had stopped running away with me. Robert Heaton had a pony that he kept out in the country and one lovely day in May, he took me to the farm to ride the pony. However, it had not been ridden all winter and promptly bucked me off, which did instill fear in me and took away some of my desire for a horse for a long time. However, the bucking off came after the trip to Platora, so I was still eager to ride the horses when we went on the vacation to the dude ranch.

The car we took to Platora was a 1937 Plymouth two door sedan. The back had a slope from the fender to the top of the back window, which had two small panes instead of one. I liked to stand on the back fender and lean against the back of the car.

Beverly, Jerry and I sat in the back seat with Mother and Dad in front. It was at least a two-day drive from Norton to Platora, which is in the San Juan Wilderness Mountains in south central Colorado. Even today, it is referred to as a 'remote retreat'. The mountain roads going up to Platora were narrow, graveled and unpaved, and the switchbacks slowly climbed the mountain. On one of the curves, there was a big truck coming toward us and Dad had to get as far over as possible. Unfortunately, far over meant that we were on the outside edge of the road, with no guardrails to keep us from sliding down the plummeting drop a few feet from the car. Beverly was sitting on that side of the car and she still hates to drive in the mountains.

When we got to the Dude ranch in Platora, it was obvious that it had deteriorated since Dad's patient had been there. The 'horses' amounted to one old mule in a corral, which I got to ride around in circles for about an hour, and the log cabin we were in had a sign over the door, "The Black

Gnat". Inside the one room cabin, which had no electricity, were feather beds, a wood burning stove for heat, and kerosene lanterns for light. Mother was not pleased. Throughout the night, we heard coyotes, wolves, and mountain lions howling. The next morning Mother decided that was enough. She was not going to spend one more night in that awful place...we were going home.

By the time we got to Colorado Springs, it was a "dark and stormy night". And, we could not find anywhere to stay; motels were not widely available in the 1940s. Dad stopped at a gas station to see if they could help guide us, and they told him there was a woman who took in boarders sometimes and "she might let us stay overnight." As the rain poured down, Dad found the address; I remember it as an old, Victorian-looking house. The electricity had gone out because of the storm and, when the old woman cracked the door open to see who was knocking on her door on such a night, she was carrying a kerosene lantern, wore dark clothing, squinted at us and asked, "What do you want?" It was scary! She agreed to let us come in, and we followed her kerosene lamp as she led us down the long, dark hall to a room where we could sleep. I was so relieved when morning came and we left for Norton!

We would occasionally drive to Geneva, Nebraska where Dad's sister, Blanch, and her husband, Dr. Harold Rosenau, lived. He was also an osteopath and they lived in a large, two-story home. They had three children (Harold, Ronald, and Beth) who were all older than I was, so I was the little kid tagging along with them. Aunt Blanch could act a bit pretentious. She always referred to her husband as 'the Doctor', took pride in her singing voice, and performed for us songs that she had recently performed somewhere. Her voice was pseudo-operatic, and one of the songs she sang was "Indian Love Call": "When I'm calling you-oo-oo-oo-oo-oo-oo..." We sat on the big sofa in the living room and listened politely, with Mother stifling a snicker under her breath. Applause and praise followed the performance, but I understood the innuendos and learned 'smile and be kind' tact. Dr. Harold Rosenau made homemade root beer that he bottled and let 'ripen' in the attic. Sometimes it fermented too much and exploded from the bottle with a big bang; whenever we visited, I waited in anticipation, hoping to hear the bang. One afternoon when we were there, all six of the 'kids' walked downtown, and I had a nickel to spend on candy. I bought a Mars bar...white nougat covered in milk chocolate with a whole almond on each end. I opened the wrapping at one end and started to eat with the wrapper covering the candy bar as we walked home. Suddenly, bird poop landed on the wrapper. I looked at it for a moment, weighing the loss of a candy bar against the possibility of eating bird poop. I decided the solution was to remove the wrapper (that's where the poop was!) and continue eating the candy bar. Maslow's hierarchy of needs!

Mother, Beverly, and I took a bus to Geneva during the war. The bus was so packed with soldiers that there were not enough seats, and I ended up sitting on my suitcase in the aisle. An elderly man noticed me, took a necklace with an agate stone out of his pocket, and gave it to me. I was surprised and awed by his kindness, and I have treasured that necklace. On another visit to Geneva, we drove to the big city of Lincoln, Nebraska where there was a large department store. I had never seen an escalator and was having a marvelous time playing on it...running up the down escalator and then riding down on the rail...until the store manager came over and told me, "Don't do that, little girl." I was embarrassed, chagrined, humiliated; but, I learned how not to behave. On this same trip, I lost a 'gold tooth' that I'd found earlier. I thought it was worth a lot of money and put it in my pocket when we went to Lincoln; and then it was gone! I probably lost it on the escalator!

We also visited Dad's other sister, Aunt Edna and her family on their farm outside of Phillipsburg, about thirty-five miles east of Norton. Dad usually drove us to Aunt Edna's, but at least one time we took the train from Norton to Phillipsburg. Aunt Edna and Uncle Les had three children (Phyllis, Maxine, Bud); they were all quite a bit older than I was so I never interacted with them. The house was an old, two-story farmhouse, with no indoor plumbing. The stairway leading up to the second floor where we slept was very narrow and steep, as well as very dark. I remember scooting on my bottom up and down the stairs step by step, because I was afraid I was going to tumble down the stairs. A slop jar sat under the bed for use at night, so we would not have to go to the outhouse in the dark. The farm scared me a bit, and I do not remember much about it except that there was a large barn with big farm machinery in it, a tall silo, and a big round storage pit for grain. It was scary to peek over the edge and see some grain far below; I was afraid to get too close to the edge lest I fall in! Aunt Edna was a sweet, loving woman who worked hard, as all farmers' wives did. Mother didn't like for us to be alone with Uncle Les, however, because he liked to hold little girls on his lap and hug them a bit too much. So, Mother would insist that she hold me on her lap whenever he was around.

When I was fourteen, between eighth grade and high school, Mother and I took a trip to Albuquerque. Mother had been having a medical problem and Aunt Ruby (who was living in Albuquerque then) knew a doctor there who she thought might help. Since Beverly had just started a job for the summer, she stayed home to "take care of Dad". Dad drove Mother and me to Dodge City to catch the California Limited train to Albuquerque. While in Dodge City, we took time to visit the old graveyard named "Boot Hill", so named because the graves had cement boots sticking out of the ground. When we got to Ordway, Colorado, a real cowboy got on. My eyes grew large when he walked past me, and I knew he was real because he wore boots, spurs, chaps, a vest, a big hat, and a gun in a holster on each hip! The train car was colorful, too. It was very 'old west', with gas lanterns and red velvet seats, and looked like something out of an old movie. It was a long trip and we slept in the train seats. The next morning, we went to the elegantly decorated dining car for breakfast. The table had a white tablecloth with white linen napkins. The waiter took our order of French toast and coffee. I had never had French toast made from thick, real French bread and served with butter and powdered sugar. It was delicious, and the way I have eaten French toast since that time. Eating in the dining car and watching the end of the train curl around the mountain while sipping a cup of coffee was enthralling. The experience seemed sophisticated and charming, just like I had seen in the movies.

When we got to Albuquerque, my cousin Dixie (Ruby's daughter) and husband, Eddie, and their two children Bobbie and Barbara (who was my age), met us at the train station. It was a historic adobe building, southwestern in style, and they took all of us to dinner at a Mexican restaurant that night...the first time I had eaten a tortilla. Aunt Ruby worked in a photography studio and lived in an apartment. We stayed with Aunt Ruby but visited Dixie several times at her home while there. Dixie fixed a Mexican dinner for us. This was the first time I ate tacos, enchiladas, or guacamole; I had never seen a fresh avocado. Aunt Ruby's boyfriend, George Twomey (whom she later married) took us to see "Gone with the Wind" at the richly decorated, historic movie house in Albuquerque. He also took us to see the Indian Reservation, Isleta, in his old black car. It was a dusty ride and I was shocked at the primitive conditions in which the Indians lived. George had been wounded in the war and had a metal plate in his head. That made an impression on me and, as I sat in the back seat staring at his head, I pondered what that must look like and feel like.

The trip to Albuquerque was a fun and educational trip. Other than visits to Geneva, Nebraska and the trip to Platora, Colorado, I had not traveled outside of Norton, and this was the first time I had a glimpse of how people lived in another area of the United States. After being away from home for about three weeks, I heard the "Sword Dance" from the Gayne Ballet Suite coming from a distant record player. Jerry had brought that album home not long before we left Norton, and hearing the music softly wafting through the air made me homesick. We took the train back to Dodge City soon after that, where Dad met us to drive us home to Norton.

CHAPTER 25

The Unexpected Things We Learn On The Job

Oren Hollinger and Tommy Thomason were pharmacists at Stapleton's drugstore. Since Oren lived next door, Mother asked him if there was a job opening for me when I was fifteen, in 1949, and he was kind enough to give me a chance. My salary was $15 a week, around fifty cents an hour. I was proud and happy to earn a salary! When I talked with former classmates, I learned that John Hutcherson earned $25 a week at Bower's Hardware for a sixty-six hour week; Bonnie Underwood and Pat Harper both earned between ten and twenty-five cents an hour for babysitting. Willard Welch beat all of us shining shoes at Jake's barbershop in the basement below the Safeway Store on State Street. He shined so many shoes that even charging just twenty to thirty-five cents per shine, he earned over $20 every Saturday (tips must have been good!). Willard and his brother, Rex, also helped their dad in the house moving business. Willard told the story of the day he was guiding wires over the roof of a house as they drove down a highway, and an overhead wire caught on a nail on the roof. When Willard pushed the wire off the nail, the wire jerked quickly backward pulling Willard off the roof and leaving him hanging from the wire above the highway. He said he could see people in the cars with their hands over their mouth wondering if he would fall or hang on. His dad, realizing what had happened, managed to back up several hundred feet so that Willard could drop back onto the roof. To quote Willard, "I was extremely lucky that day."

Stapleton's Drug Store went through the middle section of the block with the west door opening on State Street and the east door opening on Kansas Street; it was a long store. My job was as a 'soda jerk'. A long counter with stools formed one side of the 'soda fountain' area where the food was prepared, and there were two rows of booths adjacent to the fountain area. We served handmade ham salad sandwiches, egg salad sandwiches, and pimento cheese sandwiches, all served with potato chips. White, square 'sandwich' bread was used so that the sandwiches could be cut diagonally one way and then cut again diagonally the other way to form triangles, which were set on the plate with the points up; potato chips were then scattered on top. I often went to the meat shop at the Safeway down the street to get the three-pound roll of bologna, which we would grind in the manual meat grinder attached to the counter. Then we added ground sweet pickles, chopped hardboiled eggs, and mayo. We washed piles of dishes at all the drug stores I worked in since disposable dishware, cutlery, and glasses were not yet available.

Supplies, like napkins and straws, were stored in the basement. Whenever we needed anything, Tommy or Oren would go down to get it; they did not want any of the counter help going to the basement, because there were large rats there. Deliveries to all the store basements were made via underground passages that ran beneath the sidewalks on both sides of State Street, with access by stairs at both ends of the block. There was also at least one elevator in the middle of the east side of the block to provide delivery of heavier items to the basement; I remember the metal hatches in the sidewalks but did not realize their purpose at the time. Some east to west tunnels ran under State Street and along Main Street also. Pat Melroy remembers playing with Ann Browne in a tunnel in front of the Browne's Store. It had cement walls, was the width of the sidewalk above it, and had no lights, "so it was dark and scary." She did not remember a tunnel going across the street, but the story is that there was an electrical substation under Main Street between Browne's Store and the Western Auto Store. All of the tunnels were closed when the streets were reconstructed in 1987.

One day a man came into Stapleton's and stood at the tobacco counter, across the store from the soda fountain. I was allowed to cross over to that counter and sell cigarettes, so I went over and asked, "May I help you?" in my most pleasant voice. He said, "Do you have Ramseys?" I did not know what Ramseys were but, wanting to be helpful, I yelled down the length of the store, "Tommy, do we have any Ramseys?" Tommy rushed up the aisle and quietly said, "I'll take care of this." An older woman, Mildred, who worked at the fountain area with me, was trying to hold back big guffaws of laughter when I came back to that side, and she explained that Ramseys were condoms... 'rubbers' in the vernacular. I was as embarrassed as the poor guy probably was.

Another time a man came to the counter, sat down, and I asked politely, "May I help you?" Instead of hearing something like "a cup of coffee, please" or "a Coke", I heard this loud and gruff voice say, "Stand Back!" I jumped and froze for a second thinking that maybe we were being robbed. I learned then that "Stanback" was the name of an analgesic powder. I guess he had a really bad headache that day!

One day a Black man came in and ordered a Coke. I served him a Coke in a glass without a thought beyond he was probably from the tuberculosis Sanatorium, since no Blacks lived in Norton. After he left, Mildred pointedly told me to wash his glass really well and sterilize the glass rim "several times" in the sink filled with water to which Clorox had been added; normal practice was to give glass rims and silverware a quick dip in the sink to sterilize them. I assumed that the extra care was because he might have TB, but later realized that it was because he was Black.

I worked at Raney's drug store the summer of 1950, when I was sixteen. Raney's was the drug store where all the kids would go to 'hang out'. After school, or whenever there was some free time, kids would wander into Raney's just to check on who might be there. It was common to have all the big red, leather booths full of teenagers talking and having a soda or Coke together, which made it fun to work there since so many of my friends came in often. Oddly, I do not remember 'weird encounters' while working there!

This was the summer of 1950, when Norton's city leaders decided to augment the Norton baseball team with imported talent and hired several baseball players. The influx of several young athletes was of interest to many young girls in town. Kenny was the imported star pitcher and pitched game after game with no or few hits. He had a great arm, he had a 'swagger', and he was extremely 'cocky'; and, he was cute! He asked me out several times, and I thought I was hot stuff for catching his eye. However, one night, I got all dressed up and ready for our date to go to a movie, and he did not show up. As I sat at home, waiting and stewing, feeling embarrassed and rejected, Mother helped me plot what to do about it. When he called the next day, acting innocent, I told him off 'in no uncertain terms', following Mother's coaching. He was profusely sorry and said that Richard Aitken had caught him that afternoon and asked him to go on an all-night fishing trip, and he forgot all about our date! I was furious that I was so forgettable and told him to "never call me again" while, at the same time, hoping that he would. The summer ended and the baseball players left town. A 'farm team' recruited Kenny as the first step toward the big leagues, but the story told in Norton was that, unfortunately, he injured his shoulder before making it to the major leagues.

The summer between my junior and senior years in high school, when I was 17 in 1951, I worked at Moffett's. Melvin Moffet, the pharmacist and owner, was a quiet, serious man, and I tried very hard to be a good worker. This summer the influx of young men was a Geological Survey team, in town surveying something for the State of Kansas and made up of college and graduate school students. They often came into Moffet's Drug Store for their coffee break around ten in the morning, and I was there to politely ask, "May I help you?" Of course, I said yes when a couple of them asked me out. One was Harry, a geologist, and another one was a physicist, Herbie. Herbie was nice looking, but he had rather large teeth, and Dad commented, "Well, if you marry him, your kids will definitely have teeth." That was not going to happen. The Geological Survey guys were all smart and...uh...pretty 'nerdy'. However, they were some new interest for the summer.

I worked long hours. In my diary, I wrote about one Saturday when I started work at 8 AM and got off at 10 PM. I probably went home for lunch and dinner, but it was still a long day. At that time, milk came in quart-size glass bottles and, since it was not homogenized, the cream rose to the top of the bottle. Our instructions were to pour off the cream and save it to serve as coffee cream. However, I would sneak a little every now and then and make a delicious '400' drink...milk/cream and chocolate syrup.

The summer of 1952, when I turned eighteen, between high school and going to KU, I worked at the Norton Theater selling tickets. In 1948, a new movie theater was built on Main Street, two blocks east of the old Cozy Theater. My job was to sit in the box office 'cage' at the front of the theatre and sell the fifty-five cent tickets. The movies were shown twice every night, and after the start of the second showing, I could close the ticket booth and go watch the movie. This was a rather unexciting job, but the good part was that I could sit and watch all the cars go by and see who was out with whom.

The summer of 1953, between my freshman and sophomore years at KU, I was a secretary/bookkeeper at the Norton Gas Company. My job was to go over all the tickets that the meter readers brought in, enter their readings, figure up how many units the customer had used and then figure out how much to bill the customer based on a billing chart. I enjoyed this job because it was clear what I was to do and I could work as fast as I was able to get the job finished. It felt good to be able to say, "There! Done!" It felt like I had accomplished something.

I did have a varied, and educational, job career in Norton. I thought of my job switching as gaining experience and getting promotions, but maybe I just could not hold a job!

CHAPTER 26

Norton Folks

WHILE WRITING THIS BOOK, I began to realize how the whole 'village' subtly shapes a person's outlook on life. It truly is the little things that are absorbed and remembered.

I spent most of my time within the small world of my immediate family, of course, followed by my friends and classmates. Friends of Beverly and Jerry, even though a few years older, also were in my world of influencers, as were my parents' circle of close friends. Next, there were folks ten to fifteen years younger or older than my parents were; these were people they knew, but with whom they did not 'run around'. I was also aware of many other folks in Norton, and they influenced me even without personally 'knowing' them. Churches shared a different kind of stratification; people of different ages and social cliques worked together and prayed together, but many of their interactions stayed within the church arena. Peripheral relationships came from friends of friends or from service interactions, such as store clerks, repairmen, etc.

Norton, like all towns, had its cast of characters. Bankers, business owners, land owners, farmers, doctors, lawyers, teachers, barbers, ministers, pharmacists, bakers, electricians, plumbers, butchers, office workers, store clerks, city workers, repair shop workers, insurance brokers, jack-of-all-tradesmen, salesmen...all the men and women who create a 'village', the character, the ethos and spirit of community. I do not mean to imply that Norton was totally idyllic and everyone was an angel...there were some extra-marital affairs, various scandals, and wayward actions about which folks whispered "tsk-tsk". However, in spite of having the usual human frailties, most folks were hard working, honorable, and respectable. Following are some people and stories that I carry with me even today.

There were several people in town that had lived in Norton all their lives and with whom Mother had grown up and gone through school. Marjorie Milz's father had a livery stable and delivered milk from a horse drawn wagon in the early 1900s. I have the stool that he used to sit on in the wagon. Marjorie gave piano lessons to most of the children in town and played the organ at the Episcopal Church. Jerry, Beverly and I all took piano lessons from her for years. She did not marry until she was sixty-five years old when a visiting Episcopal priest, a widower who lived in the country near Phillipsburg, met Marjorie when he preached at the Norton church. She was rather nervous about being married at her age, but they had fifteen lovely years together. Marjorie relished living on the small farm, canning the vegetables from their garden and making preserves from the bounty of the many fruit trees. The Reverend also raised horses and restored many beautiful antique wagons and sleighs. After the Reverend died, Marjorie moved into the Norton Andbe Home and was one of the lucky ones able to afford a private room there.

Alice Isaac was another of Mother's closest friends from childhood. Alice and Bill had one child, Sandra, who was born two months before me. They lived a block north of our house on North Grant in a small house that had only one bedroom on the main floor. Therefore, Sandra's 'bedroom' was in the basement. The first time I spent the night with her I was surprised when, at bedtime, we went down to the basement and there was her bed. Alice and Bill were always fun and seemed very happy. He owned a furniture store in Norton. Mother said that when they were first married, Alice would clean her face at night and then apply new make-up, so when Bill awoke in the morning she would look beautiful. Perhaps Mother did, too, but she did not admit to that. A funny story that Alice told was about a man who knocked on their front door one evening, and when Bill opened the door, the man blurted out, "Do you have a G string?" Evidently, the man had a guitar and he had broken the G-string, but there was some confusion at first. Well, that was the story anyway.

Mina Johnson was Sandra Isaac's aunt and lived in a very large home on West Waverly. She had dark hair, used a lot of makeup and rouge, and generally wore a cloche hat that made her look rather mysterious. She kept to herself, but was always dressed very well when she did appear somewhere. Mother thought she was a little "touched in the head", but was always respectful of her.

Helen Fitzgerald Brantingham was a third lifelong friend of Mother's. They went to Kansas State University together, where Helen met Paul Brantingham (a Phi Delta Gamma, as was the young man to whom Mother was engaged at the time). According to mother, Helen was in love with someone from Norton, but her mother did not approve of him and forbid Helen to marry him. Helen ended up marrying Paul, to whom her mother gave her blessing. After Helen and Paul were married, Helen came to Norton alone to visit her mother and asked Mother to cover for her because she wanted to see her old boyfriend. Mother said she felt uncomfortable being complicit in this ruse, which she told me about many years after the fact. Helen and Paul lived in the Chicago area, where he worked for International Harvester and did very well financially. Mother felt that Helen became rather vain and considered herself more sophisticated than classmates who had stayed in the small town of Norton. Helen and Paul often visited her mother, Mrs. Fitzgerald, who lived across the street from the Hale house on West Waverly. When my daughter, Pamela, son, John, and I visited Norton around 1965, Mother took them over to meet Helen and Paul and show Pam and John the lovely house where Helen had lived growing up. Paul had dentures and delighted in talking to the children and then suddenly spitting out the dentures. Pamela and John jumped and screamed, of course, before thinking it was hilarious and asking him to do it again and again.

An interesting thing about these four women, who had grown up together in Norton (Mother, Alice, Marjorie, and Helen), was the friendly 'rivalry' between them through the years, as seen through my eyes. Alice was the social one belonging to many clubs and playing a lot of bridge, Marjorie taught school and piano and was the 'old maid', Helen was the one who put on 'airs' when she was in town. Mother did not enjoy clubs (she found sewing or book club meetings dull) nor attend social functions often, but when she did, she was dressed in the latest fashion and looked beautiful.

Gordon Brantley owned a furniture store in town, as well as co-owned the Scott-Brantley Funeral Home. He and his wife, Eula, were unable to have children, according to Mother. They lived down the street on the northwest corner of North Grant and West Waverly. Mother said that he always wanted to hold me on his lap when I was a baby, but I would always cry. He was always helpful to Mother and very polite, and I thought of him as almost an uncle. When Hank and I bought the house on Grandview in Merriam, Kansas in 1957, he gave us a 'pass' so we could go to a showroom in Kansas City and pick out furniture; he gave us a good price on the furniture and financed it for us. We picked out a black and white Berber area rug, a two-piece red sectional sofa, a black upholstered chair, and a walnut side table for the living room, a solid walnut round table with four chairs plus a walnut and black Formica 'hostess cart' for the dining room, and a solid walnut double bed, dresser, and chest of drawers. All the furniture was top quality and we still have the walnut bedroom suite, the hostess cart, and the side table; the walnut table and chairs were stolen from our son's garage when he was refinishing it for his home. We still fondly remember Gordon Brantley.

Ione and Sandy Jordan lived a few miles southeast of town, on Country Club road. Sandy had lost half his arm in a hunting accident years before and pinned up the long sleeve shirt over the remaining part of his arm. Every now and then, they would invite us out to their country home for homemade ice cream. Everyone had a turn at turning the crank on the wooden ice cream maker until the crank became so difficult to turn that we knew the cranking part was finished. Then towels and blankets were piled on top, and the curing of the ice cream began. After a couple of hours, the blankets came off, the metal container was lifted from the salted ice bath, and the ice cream was ready to be scooped out into bowls for the eager crowd to enjoy. Ione and Sandy, who were not able to have children, were always fun and smiling and were enjoyable to be around. I thought of them as an aunt and uncle; they were another comfort zone for me.

Dr. and Mrs. Charles Kraft moved to Norton when I was in high school. They considered themselves very cultured people, talking often about opera and the arts. She was a tall, stately woman who wore her black hair pulled back into a tight bun and held herself rather stiffly prim. She wrote poetry and he played the piano, and together they travelled to various places and presented programs, she reading her poetry while he played complimentary background music on the piano. They were considered 'different' and maybe a bit pretentious, but they were accepted into the Norton community just as everyone was…just because they lived in Norton. Carol Rhoades told me that while working at Moffet's Drug Store she overheard Dr. Kraft talking to Dr. Carl Long one day. He told Dr. Long that he and his wife were unlike people in Norton in that they ALWAYS dressed for dinner. Dr. Long looked at him and said he always dressed for dinner, too…he could not "remember ever going to the dinner table naked."

Mike Litchner was a few years younger than I was. His dad, Al, would come into Moffett's Drug Store every morning and have a cup of coffee with a dip of vanilla ice cream added to it. His dad had a small airplane and took Mike and Mrs. Litchner with him on a flight to Alaska. The shocking news came that they had crashed and Mr. and Mrs. Litchner had been killed. When the rescuers found Mike, he was hanging upside down in the plane and, although he did survive, he had lingering physical problems.

Dad told me a couple stories of encounters with other Norton 'personalities'. One story involved a paperhanger who asked Dad how he could give treatments to women and rub his hands over their bodies without getting all excited. Dad laughed and told him "after a while it's just like hanging so much wallpaper." Another gentleman commented to Dad that he and his wife's love life had become a bit stale, and he asked Dad if he had any suggestions on how to spice it up a bit. Dad, thinking he was being funny, suggested that he put a blanket, a bottle of wine, and some cheese and crackers in the trunk of his car and invite his wife to go for a drive. When they got into the country, they were to find a nice pasture to spread the blanket and have their wine and cheese; Dad told him then to make love to her in the open air. Not too long after that, the man waved down Dad and was very excited to tell him how his idea had worked out… making love in the country on a blanket had been "just splendid."

Jacqueline Broquet and her mother, Mrs. Broquet, lived in a large, elegant home on Park Avenue, just north of where the football stadium was built in the late 1940s. Mr. and Mrs. Paul Broquet had emigrated from Europe in the 1920s. There are many exotic stories of why they came to Norton, but how much is true I do not know. I just remember visiting her and seeing her and Jacqueline occasionally when I was growing up. I was visiting my parents in Norton in the 1960s, and Mrs. Broquet invited my mother, my ten-year-old daughter, Pamela, and me to her house for a tea that she was hosting. Pamela was enchanted with the grandiose European furniture and artwork and with how gracious Mrs. Broquet was.

Many people in Norton were related to each other. John Hutcherson explained the Hicks family tree:

"My mom, Leta, was a member of the Hicks clan; she married Otis Hutcherson and Joy and I appeared. Madge was the oldest and married Joe Sanderson; they had Junior, Bus, Don (Suzi Sanderson was Don's daughter therefore a 2nd cousin) and Marilyn; they ran the Silvaire. Glen Hicks married Helen Wray and their daughter was Donna. Irene married Carl Long M.D. and their offspring were Robert, James and Margaret (Peggy). Theron (TW) Hicks married Marjorie Berry and they had 4 girls Jeanne, Carla, Paula and Sue."

Ray Bower, class of 1950, explained the Bower tree:

"All the Bower families in Norton were related. My and Jay's father and mother were Hobart "Hobe" and May Bower. Dad had the Barbershop. "Skinny" Bower was Raymond and his wife, Lona. He was in the Building and Loan, she was a school teacher and over study hall. They had a son Richard "Dick" Bower. Raymond was a cousin to my dad. Janet was my cousin and her parents were Med and Laurine. Med ran the Peerless Flour Mill 'till it closed; then he was the administrator at the Norton County Hospital. Clarence "Squeak" Bower and wife Mae had the drug store (Raney's). He was the pharmacist and she just worked in the Raney's Drug Store. Med, Clarence and Hobart were brothers."

Pat Melroy, class of 1952, explained the Melroy/Browne tree:

> Pat, Bob, and Jim Melroy were cousins of Ann, John, and David L.
> Browne.   Pat traced the families to common great-grandparents.
> Mickey Melroy's mother, Hannah Browne Melroy (who started
> Melroy's Café), and 'Big Dave' (Senior) Browne's father, James
> Browne, were sister and brother.

Warren Bullock and Verle Ritter were cousins; Bonnie Underwood and Carol Rhoades and Ronnie and E.H. Allen were cousins. I am sure there were more extended families who had lived in and around Norton since the early 1900s, people who stayed where they were planted. Warren stayed where he was planted in Norton, and he served as Mayor and contributed greatly to Norton's growth and well-being through the years.

In addition to the people I have already talked about, many other people still walk through my memory when I think about Norton:

Claudia and Dwayne Bridges contributed much to Norton over the years. Dwayne was Dwight Bridges' brother (Dwight's wife, Mike, died of an infection after childbirth in 1945); Claudia had beautiful long blond hair that she wore swooped up on her head. She was elegant and very gracious.

Lee and Roy Ward, their daughter, Gloria Bee Ward Nelson, and their son, Don Ward lived in the block south of us on North Grant. Bee commented that she had walked to school with a Butler all through high school.

Pat McKinley was a year older than I was, very pretty, and a cheerleader; she became "Miss Perfect 36" in 1951. I thought that was a noble goal to strive for, but I was too thin and not curvy enough to fulfill the requirements.

Lee and Lowell Peterson joined the NCHS Bluejays in 1950 when their father opened the Norton Bowling Alley just north of the Kent Hotel on First Street. There were no automatic pinsetters at that time, so a great job for agile guys was to set those pins manually.

JoAnn Carstens, who was in my class, and her older sister, Marie, also became Bluejays around 1948.

Joyce Beatty, Joy Hutcherson, and Dorothy Harris were close friends of Beverly, and they were always laughing and having fun together. Dorothy's mother was named Rose. Her father drowned when a storm suddenly arose on the lake where a group of Norton men was fishing and the boat they were in capsized, a tragedy that was a heartbreaking shock to everyone in Norton.

Jim Maddy, Alvin Hisey (Beverly's husband), and Richard Esslinger were in Jerry's class; they visited our house many times over the years and were friends of our whole family. Whenever I visited Norton, I enjoyed running into Jimmy Maddy and Richard Esslinger and 'catching up'. Alvin's brother, Lyle, was killed when he was driving with the window down and his elbow resting on the sill when someone sideswiped him, shattering his arm. The car stopped, but the driver did not want to get blood in his car, so he left Lyle there and sent someone to help him when he got into town; it was too late by then.

Roger Dietrich was in Beverly's class. He had a Ford that many students would pile into or hop on the running boards for a ride home or to Raney's or for a picnic. He had a nice voice and sang at my wedding.

Bill Laws was in Beverly's class (they dated for a while); he broke his leg during the Oberlin-Norton football game in 1948. The game was played at a makeshift football field near the airport, because a blizzard had buried the regular football field in snow.

Donna Hicks, Esther Phillips, and Pat Adams were in Jerry's class (1947). Pat Adams' family operated the Adams' Hotel; Pat had a lovely singing voice. Donna always had a smile on her face. Esther's younger brother, Gale, was two years ahead of me.

Larry and Peggy Stull bought the house north of ours on North Grant (the Wingfield's lived there and then the Moody's). He was a coach and principal at NCHS and helped my Dad with the yardwork and a garden; the new gymnasium was named for him. I remember Peggy particularly, because she was so kind to my mother and was always so cheerful. My mother liked her so much that she gave Peggy an antique doll cradle among other things.

J. C. "Chick" Tillotson was an attorney in Norton and a Kansas State Senator. He had played the drums when he was younger and, after I sat in on the trap drums at an event, he always called me "Gene" (for the drummer, Gene Krupa). His wife, Maxine, was a gracious woman and was instrumental in converting the Tuberculosis Sanatorium to a Kansas State Hospital for the mentally challenged.

Bill Green was another attorney. He was always chewing on a stub of a cigar as he walked between his office and Stapleton's Drug Store.

Jerry Lee Horney helped Bonnie and me with a dance for a high school program. Lee Horney was my brother's boss at Horney's appliance store (mentioned earlier).

Willie Kauten was a butcher at McMahon's grocery south of the Court House. He always had a smile on his face and married Ione Jordan's sister.

Lanny Davis was a sales clerk at Browne's Clothing Store. I remember him because he was so patient helping me find shoes that I would like over the years.

George Jones was a salesperson at Hall's Clothing, which was just south of Moffet's Drug Store on State Street. It was always nice to see his smiling face, be recognized as an old friend, and chat with him when I shopped there.

The Bill Smileys and the Noah Garretts are also in my memory. When Hank, I, Pamela, and John went on a KU sponsored trip to France in 1978, I was surprised to see the Smileys and the Garretts sitting in the row behind us on the plane. That was serendipitous!

Tommy Thomason's wife, Lucille, was a vocalist and sang many soprano solos at the Methodist Church.

Clyde Wynkoop was a friend of my Aunt Ruby and worked at the post office. He delivered many letters to me at our house on North Grant.

Phil Taylor was the son of Dr. Taylor, head doctor at the Sanatorium. He was several years older than I was but the girls referred to him as 'PT Boat', because he was so handsome.

Neva Rae McCreary was the granddaughter of Neva Funk who owned the Cottage Shop. She played the piano amazingly well; I remember her playing Chopin's Fantasie Impromptu in C-sharp minor. No matter how hard I tried, I could never get my fingers to run over the keys as nimbly as Neva Rae did!

Grace Jeannine Kissell was two years younger than I was. She had a gorgeous voice and I expected her to end up singing at the Metropolitan opera house one day, but (as I understand it), she developed a heart problem that prevented her from singing professionally. She had an older sister, Martha. Their father was Judge Jean Kissell.

John Travis was in Beverly's class and gave her a lovely "Evening in Paris" cologne set for Christmas once. I was very impressed with such a nice gift in such a pretty box. John and my classmate, Sandra Isaac, were married later after John became a dentist and Sandra became a dental hygienist.

Carman Wiltrout and Phil Lesh were a few years older than I was, dated in high school, and then married. Phil had a wonderful singing voice.

Bonnie Underwood and Bill Lathrop were always the perfect couple... truly made for each other. Bonnie has kept our class communicating over the internet for years; Bill always has a witty remark to make you laugh.

Carol Rhoades and Donald Glenn found each other in junior high! Don made a career in the Air Force.

Other Norton students who found their 'true love' in Norton include: Francis Jones and Jay Bower, Carolyn Eppinger and Dillon Higgason, Joan Donovan and Roger Moffett, Wanda Persell and Neil Fisher, Marlene Harvey and Bill Wilmont, Carmen Schon and Gary Rowley, Mary Wieland and Bill Scheetz, Nancy Vancura and Bill Krehbiel, Joy Hutcherson and Don Harmonson, Marlin Bozarth and Dolores Gates, Suzie Sidman and Jim Maddy, Gladys Hazlett and Francis "Junior" Sutton, Barbara Wauffle and Joe Ballinger, Myrth Maddox and Dean Blickenstaff, Kenny Kohfeld and Mary Ann Amos, Chuck Kohfeld and Beverly Somers, Janet Bower and Richard Aitken, Roberta Wray and Jay Ryan, Ann Browne and Rex Davis, and my sister Beverly and Alvin Hisey. I am sure there are others!

I felt it would be wonderful to marry someone from Norton and have the pleasure of sharing so many Norton memories. There were a couple of guys I was 'crazy about', and a few even asked me to go steady. Maybe Mother influenced me by always saying I had plenty of time to be married and encouraging me to wait. However, I was also insecure and did not believe any man could or would 'really' love me. In addition, I did have some wanderlust and desire to 'see the world'. I just felt unready for the big "C": commitment. That was frightening.

CHAPTER 27

1952-1955: 'Cause I'm A Jay, Jay, Jay, Jay, Jayhawk

GOING TO COLLEGE WAS NOT assumed nor even talked about much when I was in high school. It was vaguely in my mind, but since I generally just 'floated' along and did not think much about the future, college was not a big issue in my mind, and the teachers did not give significant counsel about going to college. Dad never encouraged any of us to go to college. I felt he did not push us to go because of the expense plus the fact that he believed that girls would get married anyway, so there was no point in girls going to college. Since Beverly and Jerry had gone to Chillicothe Business School, and I was sure I did not want to go there, Mother and I talked about other possibilities. She wrote for information about the Barbizon School of Modeling in New York, and that, of course, sounded exciting to me: New York City! I really wanted to be a dancer on Broadway, but had no training for that, so modeling sounded like the next best thing. I had no clue nor awareness that both dreams were out of the realm of possibility: I had no dance nor modeling training and I was only five feet-four inches tall (almost anyway). I did not meet the qualifications for either career.

However, Joy Hutcherson was in Beverly's class and her brother, John, was in my class. She had received a scholarship to KU and she told Mother that I should apply for a scholarship. With her guidance, I did apply. Mother asked Beverly to help write my application letter since she had just graduated from Business College and "would know how to write a good letter". I asked two KU graduates (Bill Ryan, an attorney, and Bill Smiley, a banker) to write letters of recommendation for me. I did get a scholarship, and had my choice of either a tuition scholarship or living in a scholarship hall, Sellards Hall. The Scholarship Hall fee was $30 a month for room and board, and tuition was $180 a semester. Since it would cost more to live in a dorm or sorority, the Scholarship Hall seemed to be most cost-effective. Since I had received little financial guidance growing up, I was oblivious to the fact that this really was quite a lot of money for Dad to pay. John Hutcherson, Darrell Webber, Harlan Conkey, and Lee Breckenridge also received Hall Scholarships at KU. Ray Bower received a football scholarship to KU.

In September of 1952, Mother brought home a big cardboard box in which clothes had been shipped to the Cottage Shop, we packed up the wonderful clothes that Mother had purchased for me, and Dad drove us to Lawrence, Kansas. Sellards Hall was new that year, and it was lovely. The donors of the hall had purchased pastel blue and pink wool plaid blankets from Scotland and 'ordered' that we be served steak once a week. That was impressive! The house, three stories, plus an attic and a basement, was red brick with white shutters; a small half-circle porch with large white columns on each side led to the entrance. The basement held the dining room, kitchen, utilities with a washer and dryer, and a large recreation room. There was no TV, but there was a record player. That first semester, I discovered how beautiful Russian Easter music is while listening to someone's 33 rpm record as I studied in the recreation room.

The oversized front door of Sellards Hall opened into a large entry room. To the right of the entrance was a small reception room with a window overlooking the foyer. The person on receptionist duty sat there to greet any visitors, as well as to answer the phone. Every student was assigned a 'buzz code', based on Morse code, which the receptionist would use to direct the call. My code was dash-dash-dot. The buzzer sounded all over the house and, after a while, everyone knew everyone else's code, so we always knew who was getting a call.

The housemother's apartment was directly across from the front door, and there were a few student rooms down the hall to the right. To the left on the first floor was a large, carpeted living room furnished formally with several sofas, chairs, and tables, as well as a small grand piano. The second and third floors were student housing and bathrooms. The student rooms were set up with a central study room with desks for four girls and sleeping rooms on either side. The sleeping rooms had bunk beds and a wall of closet/drawer space. The clothes rod in the closet was about three feet wide, but I did not have many clothes so that was enough space. My roommates my first year were Joyce and Marion (Mari) and a foreign student from China. Mari was the student hall director.

One of the letters I received from KU prior to being assigned roommates that year asked if I would object to having a Black girl for a roommate. Segregation was still the norm at that time, and there were not many Black students at KU. Since I had never met nor had any personal contact with any Black person (except for the customer at Stapleton's Drug Store), it was a question I had never thought about before. Mother talked with me and we decided to respond that I would be happy to have a Black roommate. There was a Black student in Sellards Hall that year, but because she was blind, her room was on the first floor, and, since she was an upperclassman taking a different course of study, I never had the opportunity to get to know her well.

There were five bedroom 'suites' on the second and third floors, and three on the first floor. I had trouble sleeping with four girls in the room, so my junior year several of us decided to sleep in the attic where it was quiet and dark. With some help, I took the bunk bed apart and carried the mattress and bed frame up to the fourth floor attic. There were no lights in the attic, so unless the door was open from the stairwell, it was very dark. In my usual unthinking way, I never worried about critters or spiders! I would now!

Each girl in the hall had a 'chore', which generally took about an hour a day. I usually asked for, and was assigned, kitchen duty; this took about an hour before a meal plus some clean-up time after the meal. I learned to make biscuits for fifty-two girls...a very useful thing to know. My junior year, however, I chose bathroom duty, because I could do that any time and it did not take as long as kitchen duty. A bathroom on each floor had a row of toilet stalls (six, I think), a row of sinks, and two showers and one bathtub serving twenty girls.

Mother Hooper was our housemother. She planned the meals and made sure everyone was inside by 10:30 on weeknights, midnight on Friday and 1 a.m. on Saturday. Just before closing time, girls with their dates would gather on the small porch not wanting to go in until Mother Hooper opened the door and said it was time. Mother Hooper would flick the lights on and off to warn us about five minutes before the closing hour. "Say goodnight!" We were such good girls!

We had a maintenance man who took care of gathering the trash and putting it into the large trash container that sat behind the house. He was a medium stature man with very few teeth and had a habit of calling out "Bingo!" as he threw the trash into the dumpster and spat out the chewing tobacco spittle.

I did not make it to breakfast very often, but there was always cereal to eat. Lunch was usually sandwiches, some fruit and chips, and dinner was a small serving of meat (fish, hamburger, chicken, ham, or roast beef) parsley potatoes, a vegetable or salad, and a roll. Portions were 1950s size... small by today's standards. There was a meal served on Sunday at noon, for which we were supposed to dress 'nicely', and then we were on our own for Sunday evening. This meant going to one of the student 'hangouts' or to a restaurant downtown. Sunday was often date night...going to Duck's Tavern for dinner or the Stables for dinner and dancing. We were always so hungry that it is a wonder we did not scare off our dates!

When I enrolled, everyone had to go through the 'bullpen' to sign up for classes. This was in a large...very large...room, with long tables set up around the perimeter of the room. Each department (English, Chemistry, German, Geography, etc.) had a table with one or two people sitting there to register the students for the various classes their department handled. It took a long time to find the table with the class you wanted to take, stand in line to register, and then find the next class on your list. Yes, it was an ar-chaic system. Hank Evers, a senior when I was a freshman, had volunteered to be at the ROTC (Reserve Officer Training Corps) table in the bullpen to give information about the program. Clever boy that he was, he had ar-ranged a system and colluded with the people at the exit whereby he would signal that exit person whenever he saw a girl that he wanted information about. That person would ask the girl to fill out one more card, "for hometown newspapers information." I wore a gray jersey gathered skirt with a short-sleeved gray turtleneck sweater and a wide red leather belt that day, and I caught Hank's eye. He gave the signal, I filled out the extra card, and he got my name and knew where I was living.

Tea dances and open houses were designed to help students meet each other. When Sellards Hall had their open house soon after enrollment, Hank was there dressed in a sweater vest with a big Austrian eagle on it. He asked me to dance and then told me not to tell him my name...he would guess. "Miss Cook? Miss Maid? No? Miss Butler!" I laughed, of course. When I talked to Mother on the phone after the dance, she asked if I had met anyone interesting. I told her about a couple boys I had met and, when I told her about Hank, I said that he could dance and wore a really neat sweater. While we danced, Hank told me he was born on Alcatraz (that certainly could not be!), and he said he was from San Antonio. Well, I looked him up in the student directory and it said he was from Cherryvale, Kansas. He was obviously just full of tall tales! Or, so I thought. I did learn later that he was born in San Francisco at the Presidio, and he spent the first two years of his life on Alcatraz. It was a U. S. Disciplinary Barracks at the time, and his father, who was in the Army, was stationed there as a member of the Army staff.

I also met one of Hank's roommates, Bill Geyer, at the Sellards Open House dance, but I was not aware that they were roommates. Bill Geyer called me after the dance and asked me to go to dinner at Duck's Tavern. A dinner date was a new experience for me, and I remember dressing up a bit, wearing the turquoise gathered corduroy skirt, black sweater, and the black velvet wedge sandals that Mother had helped choose for my college wardrobe; I felt chic and so grown up. Bill continued to ask me out, and often at the time he was due to pick me up, I would get a phone call...dash, dash, dot, my signal for a phone call; I had to answer it, of course. The caller was always Hank, and he would keep me on the phone as long as he could while he knew that Bill was waiting downstairs in the receiving room. One night, Bill had become suspicious and asked me if I knew a

John Evers. I said no...I knew a Hank Ebbers, but not a John Evers. Hank called me every day (not just when Bill was waiting downstairs), talked for a while, and then said goodbye without asking me out on a date. Even though he could dance and had a nice sweater, I did think he was rather weird!

Dick Scott also attended the Sellards open house. William Richard Scott was in Stephenson Scholarship Hall, and he was brilliant. He thought he would become a Presbyterian minister but decided he could "do more good in the world as a sociologist." He did not smoke because he felt "adequate unto myself." That impressed me, because I definitely did not feel adequate unto myself. He wrote beautiful poetry, danced well, could play Gershwin Preludes on the piano, and even could tap dance a few steps. We dated a lot the spring semester of 1953 and even though I felt 'in love' with him, I could never bring myself to say those three words: "I love you". My family had never said those words when I was growing up, even though we loved each other. I was so insecure that I was afraid, if I admitted to someone that I loved him, he would then leave me and I would feel stupid and inadequate. Therefore, when Dick told me he loved me, as we laid on the grass in front of Sellards Hall the night before I went home for the summer, I could not express my feelings. I put my arms around him and kissed him, but those three magic words would not cross my lips. He was going to be a counselor at the Christian Camp in Estes Park that summer, and I wanted to go and be a counselor and do good things in the world, too, but Mother absolutely forbid me to go. She was afraid that I would get pregnant on a mountaintop; she might have been right. The summer was too long, and Dick's and my relationship was never the same. We were in 'different places' when September came.

I dated a pre-med student often my sophomore year. He took me with him to pick out a new car and took me home one weekend to meet his mother; he assumed we were going to be married. However, as nice a guy as he was, and as much as I liked him, my fear of commitment shouted "run". I do not remember how I told him it was over, but I am sure I did it badly and hurt him (like mother-like daughter, I guess). When Hank and I were living in Merriam around 1958, we went to a foreign movie, Ingmar Bergman's "Wild

Strawberries", at the art movie house on State Street in Kansas City. As we approached the ticket line, I saw him at the back of the line waiting to buy a ticket. My instinct was to turn around and run, but he turned just then and saw us. He and Hank had known each other at KU and there was nothing to do but say hello. So, as this rather sensual movie ran before us, I sat between them, feeling very awkward and uncomfortable. I do not remember much of the movie except a young couple lying in a field of wild strawberries making love. It seemed like a very long movie.

I dated many other guys (a football player, a Beta Theta Pi member, a guy who had an Austin-Healy convertible, and others), but none seriously. One of the 'others' was Freddie, a foreign exchange student from Austria. He had been a member of the Hitler Youth when he was in his teens; he told me he had enjoyed it because it was like being in the Boy Scouts with lots of camping, marksmanship practice, and other manly activities. He invited me to a Ball, but he insisted that we find a dance floor and practice first. He taught me how to dance the Viennese Waltz (back arched, head at the correct angle, arms just so) and the Tango. (Maybe that is why I love to watch the Argentine Tango on "Dancing with the Stars".) I also had a few dates with Pierre, a Frenchman. He asked me, as we were sitting together having a Coke at the Student Union, what brand of rubbers I thought was the best. Although I had absolutely no idea, I tried to be nonplussed by the question and told him I had heard that Ramsey's were good. Wonder where I had heard that name before?! Nothing like fake sophistication!

When I first arrived at KU in September of 1952 and saw all the classes that were available, it was like being in hog heaven. I wanted to take them all! The first semester at KU, I took an advanced analytical geometry class (I had tested out of the first required course), German, an English class, Music Harmony and Theory, and Keyboard Harmony. I found the music classes very easy and felt I knew everything about music already, so I did not see much point in continuing music the second semester. I also played the French horn in the KU concert band. At that time, girls were not allowed to march in the marching band for games, which was a good thing, because I would have found that boring and time consuming! I did join the Red Peppers, the girls cheering club, as a freshman ("everybody did", I was told), so then I had to go to the football and basketball games and cheer. However, that was not my thing! I did not enjoy going to the football games (they took up all of a Saturday afternoon) nor the basketball games. The basketball games were played in Hoch Auditorium at that time with bleachers for the students set up on the stage. Climbing up to the top of those rickety bleachers was frightening! I was not a Red Pepper my sophomore year!

One class that I loved was "Aesthetics", taught by Professor Chubb. He was the embodiment of what a professor should be. He was not very tall, skinny, dressed in 'professorial' clothing, had wild white hair and talked about ethereal principles of beauty. He invited the class to visit his home for an evening 'soiree'. His home was a two story white Victorian house that was full of mementos from his travels all over the world. He served hors d'oeuvres plus tea, made in a Russian Samovar with strawberry jam added, and served in beautiful china cups with saucers. I was enchanted.

Since I wanted to take everything and had no idea what I wanted to 'be', I took the aptitude tests offered by the counseling center. My answers indicated that I should be an engineer; the area for which I had the least aptitude was being a homemaker. No kidding!? I am just wondering, how did they test for that?! Being open to any directional help, I transferred to the Engineering Department my sophomore year and took mechanical drawing, engineering calculus, and chemistry among other courses. Mechanical drawing was monotonous; my calculus teacher was a poor (egotistical) teacher; and chemistry scared me to death. The year before, a chemistry experiment had blown up in the face of a very pretty blond girl and blinded her. Every time I walked into the lab, I just knew that something was going to explode and mutilate me. The Periodic Table seemed impossible to memorize and remembering all the chemical interactions was daunting, and, importantly in my mind, I was afraid of getting a bad grade, which would eliminate my scholarship. I took the easy way out and dropped it within a few weeks of the start of the year. After I had done so, I got my grade for the first test...a B+. I am not proud of my cowardice in not trying and working hard on a difficult subject.

I did excel at biology, however, and loved it. Thanks to Oran Burns in high school biology, I never opened a book and did so well that the professor sent a letter to my parents commending me on my academic performance. On the other hand, a letter was sent to my parents telling them that I was doing poorly...getting a D at midterm...in speech. I laughed off that letter with my usual denial of reality, tried harder, and did end up with a B in speech. One of the assignments was to pick any subject and debate it, and I used Grandpa Drummond's paper on evolution to argue against Darwin's theory. I felt I was honoring my grandfather by arguing for his beliefs, although I had not given any thought to Darwin or evolution before. By the time I completed the assignment by defending his paper, I realized that I did not agree with my grandfather's beliefs. I did learn that it is difficult and painful to give up 'inherited' views and dogmas and find your own beliefs.

I always had an outside job while at KU. The first semester of my freshman year, I worked for Dr. Kuchler, the chairman of the Geography Department. He was a short man with a limp and an accent, and smoked a very aromatic pipe. I took geography the second semester at KU and still have the atlas for that class. The world map has changed since then!

The second semester of my freshman year, as well as my sophomore and junior years, I worked in the German Language Department for Dr. J. Anthony "Toni" Burzle. He was also the head of the Fulbright Committee, so I worked as the Fulbright secretary, too. At that time, Dr. Burzle would dictate into a Dictaphone, and I would then listen with earphones and transcribe (type up) the letters and reports on the big Royal typewriter. Typewriters at that time had keys that made a clickety-clack sound as they were pressed and had a bell that dinged to tell you to hit the carriage return lever on the left side of the typewriter when you got to the end of a line. To make a copy of whatever you were typing, you used the platen to roll two pieces of paper onto the typewriter with a piece of carbon paper between them. Changing the ribbon when the ink no longer printed was also necessary. Part of my job was to file letters received and sent, copies of the transcriptions I typed up, copies of tests, etc. I had difficulty deciding whether letters should be filed under the topic or the sender or to whom they were addressed! Poor Dr. Burzle. He probably had a terrible time finding anything I filed! My job also included mimeographing tests. This entailed typing up the tests on a special purple-waxed form, with the typewriter ribbon disengaged so the metal edges of the typewriter letters could cut through the wax, making sort of a blueprint of the test. If typos were made, correction fluid was use to fill in the hole so a correct impression could be made. After getting the eight-by-fourteen inch form finished, I would separate the backing from the stencil, fill the large drum of the mimeograph machine with the rather odiferous ink, wrap the waxed stencil around the drum, and then crank the large handle of the drum to run off the test onto regular paper. The mimeograph ink had a strong, and distinct, chemical odor, and was messy!

Events at Sellards Hall included open houses, dances, parents' day, etc., the typical college activities. I was selected to represent Sellards Hall for Homecoming Queen my freshman year, but was just a Princess...again! In the spring semester, I was nominated for Military Ball Queen, but again, I was a Princess. The Hall entered a float in the Homecoming parade each year. When I was a sophomore, I thought this was silly and a waste of time and money, so I did not willingly participate and found excuses not to show up to work on the float. The die-hard fanatics duly noted this, and I was rudely awakened one morning and thrown into the shower for my lack of spirit.

Sellards Hall was located halfway down Mount Oread, the big hill that Kansas University sits on. Forty-two steps had to be climbed to reach the level of all the buildings. The running joke was that you could tell what class year a girl was by the size of her calves. There were also no elevators in any of the buildings, so every day entailed lots of stair climbing in addition to walking from building to building. There were ten minutes scheduled between classes, so if the next class was in a distant building, some running was also necessary.

I still did not know what to major in when my junior year arrived and it was necessary to declare a major. I had tried engineering and found it tedious and, other than architectural engineering, uninteresting. Medicine was of interest, but I had seen how Doctors of Osteopathy were treated and I did not want to face that discrimination; I also felt it would be an insult to my Dad if I became a Medical Doctor rather than an Osteopath. As a child, I had imagined myself being the head of a large corporation, but had never taken a business course or even been aware of any business curriculum other than Certified Public Accounting, which had a reputation for being a monotonous occupation. Since I had been working in the German Department for three semesters and did plan to take more language, I finally settled on German. I realized that this was a dead-end major, but I was still so unfocused and so indoctrinated in the mindset that women did not have 'careers' that I felt it did not matter what I majored in.

My core belief was that the only realistic future possible for ME was to get married, have children, and be a wife and homemaker. Thoughts that occasionally tempted my mind to be 'something' or to accomplish something separate from marriage were dismissed as silly pipedreams and fantasies. I played the role I felt I was expected to play, and when conflicting, out-of-character thoughts or feelings welled within me, I did not express them lest someone think I was strange, unrealistic, or uninformed. It takes a long time to act from the inside out rather than the outside in and thus become who YOU are.

PART V

Leaving Oz

Every story has an ending. But, since "all the world's a stage" and we are "the actors", sequels and spin-offs follow. Life is a series of chapters, verses, and acts. Endings become the beginnings of the rest of the journey.

CHAPTER 28

1955: Hank and Marriage

AFTER WEEKS OF PHONE CALLS without asking me for a date, Hank finally asked me to go to a Woody Herman concert in October, and we continued dating on and off throughout the fall semester of 1952. He wore khaki pants and white shirts most of the time, but, on days he had ROTC he would dress in his Army uniform; he looked quite dashing! He told me he loved me every time we went out, but I did not believe him because I knew he did not know the 'real' me. I did not feel 'adequate unto myself', and when he knew me better I was sure he would stop calling. At that time, the fall semester did not end until after the Christmas and New Year's break. Hank invited me to visit him for New Year's Eve at his parents' home in Lake Forest, a private lake near Bonner Springs, before going back to KU to finish the semester. With visions of an exciting New Year's Eve in Kansas City, Mother agreed to this, and she decided I could wear one of her sophisticated black dresses, so I would look stylish and elegant for New Year's Eve in the city. However, my idea for New Year's Eve and Hank's idea were not the same. His idea was for a quick dinner, maybe a little dancing, and then as much 'making out' as I would allow, which was not a lot!

When I arrived at the house in Lake Forest, Hank's mother was dressed in blue jeans and was bustling around the kitchen preparing a big dinner of steak, potatoes, salad, and vegetables. I was very nervous about visiting his family and could not eat much that night. Mother had given me a new pair of dark blue, silky pajamas and matching robe for this visit; I looked good, but by morning my stomach was not feeling good, which was embarrassing. I did recover with a cup of tea, some toast, and time, but I felt foolish and self-conscious for feeling ill. As nice and kind as Hank's mother was, she had a very in-command/brusque manner, and I was intimidated by her. His father, on the other hand, was charming. The first time I saw him, he was dressed in his Army uniform crouching on the floor under the tree trying to get the German tree carousel working. He was delighted when he got the carousel to work, and the tree slowly turned around and around while the music box played. I was captivated by his charm. I always teased that I fell in love with his dad first and then Hank.

Hank and I often had differences of opinions and thinking; he had a quick temper and pouted when he was upset (I learned later his dad was good at pouting, too), and we dated and broke up many times! After we had broken up one time, Hank would sit in the hall studying at the time he knew I got out of my German class so that he could sit with his head down, lower lip sticking out, and ignore me when I walked by

Hank graduated from the University of Kansas in June of 1953 and received a regular commission in the Army. Hank was raised as an Army brat and had been in the Kansas National Guard since he was fifteen, attaining every rank as an NCO. He always planned on following in his father's footsteps as an Army Officer with the goal of becoming a General.

After Hank graduated we did not see each other often, but he would reappear every now and then. Later, when he was stationed at Ft. Riley, he would call, drive to Lawrence, and we would have a few dates. Even though our relationship was on and off, there was something about Hank that always caused me to lean on him. When I was a freshman and the Red Cross was recruiting students to give blood, I volunteered and walked to Robinson Gym to donate. They examined me and said I could donate only one-half pint because I was too thin and underweight to donate a whole pint of blood. When I got up off the table, I passed out. The person I thought of to call was Hank, even though we had had only a few dates by then. I always felt I could depend on Hank and, like that old song said, he kept "coming back like a song."

I was still dating Hank on and off my junior year at KU. In the fall of 1954, he learned he was going to be sent to Germany in the advance party of Operation Gyroscope, which was the first divisional rotation between the First Division and the Tenth Division. The First Division was already in Germany and the Tenth Division was at Ft. Riley; they were to exchange places in 1955. Hank was the executive officer of the 85th Regiment in the advance party. He wanted to get married. After I got back to Lawrence from the Christmas break, we were driving in his 1953 yellow Studebaker Commander Coupe when he asked me to get something out of the glove compartment. I opened the glove box and there was a pretty, wrapped box sitting there. I asked him what it was and he said I would have to open it to see. What was inside was a diamond ring, and he asked me if I would marry him. He told me we would party every night and I could sleep until noon every day. It did sound like fun and rather exciting to go to Germany. I said yes. We were engaged and set the wedding date for June 17, 1955. Mother and I started looking at wedding dresses, and a wedding shower was planned for spring break time. About the first of April, I called Mother and told her to call off the shower because I would not marry Hank if he were the last man on earth. However, the shower was held at the Wingfield's sometime before June 17. I do remember that I was sick the day of the shower (nerves or flu?), and the pictures taken show a very wan-looking bride-to-be. Typical wedding presents at that time included ash trays, cocktail shakers, fancy candy dishes, embroidered tea towels, pretty aprons, dishes...all the things needed to be wonderful homemakers, just like our new husbands expected and like the home-making magazines portrayed.

June came and I was nervous, scared, and thinking I should not be getting married. The photo shows Jerry, me, Alvin Hisey, and Hank (holding a cigar) playing Monopoly a few nights before the wedding. Nothing like playing a game to ease any jitters or anxiety.

On June 16, the night before the wedding, Hank was stony quiet and we disagreed about some minor thing. I thought, "Well, this is not going to last. There is no way we can stay married when we argue all the time. But, it is too late now. I will have to get married tomorrow, and we will no doubt get a divorce in a year or two." (Spoiler alert: we have been married for over sixty years now.)

At 7:30 in the evening on June 17, 1955, with Reverend H. P. Woertendyke officiating, Hank and I were married at the First Methodist Church in Norton. After a reception at the Church, everyone in the wedding party was asked to stay and have pictures taken, but Hank became impatient because it was all taking so long. You might think he just wanted to whisk me away so the two of us could be alone. But, no, he had traded in his Studebaker and surprised me by driving to Norton for our wedding in a beautiful 1954 Lincoln Convertible with the Continental kit and a carriage bell. Now he was worried that, being a small town, someone would write things in soap on it and tie cans to the bumper.

Our honeymoon was driving to Biloxi, Mississippi. I had never seen the ocean, and after seeing movies with beautiful and exotic beaches, that sounded exciting and different. There were no interstate highways then, so Hank plotted a route from Norton to Biloxi on State and local roads, and it took a couple days to get there. The second night we stopped at a motel somewhere in the South. That was the first time I saw palmetto bugs. There were lights all around the outside window of our room, and they were attracted to those lights. First, I heard big thuds hitting the window and when I peeked out the door to see what was making all that racket, I was horrified to see huge, at least two-inch long, dark brown flying palmetto bugs swirling all around the lights. I quickly shut the door, but not before a few of them made it into the room. I did not sleep much that night! Dead palmetto bugs crunched under our feet as we left the next morning. One more shiver ran down my spine looking at them.

Other than in movies, I had never heard a real Southern drawl. When the waitress came to the table in the restaurant the next morning, she spoke... and I had no idea what she was saying. I could not decipher what any true Southerner said, so Hank had to translate the whole trip! By the time we got to Mississippi, the afternoon sun splattered through the big pine trees that lined both sides of the narrow road. I snuggled next to Hank with the wind blowing my long hair, wearing my new pink shorts and pink, checked sleeveless top, new sandals, and sunglasses, and feeling like a movie star. (No thought was given to any safety risks as we flew along at seventy-five mph, top down, in our new Lincoln Capri convertible with no seat belts.)

The hotel we stayed at in Biloxi was an old historic hotel (either the Broadwater Beach Hotel or the Edgewater Gulf Hotel) which sat across the street from the lapping waters of the Gulf of Mexico. I remember it as being built of dark red bricks and white trim, with a center section and slightly backset wings on each side, and a covered portico at the entrance. Large trees with the famous Spanish moss dripping from the limbs covered the grounds. It was big and luxurious to look at, just like in the movies. Our room was large, probably a suite because it had two rooms and a small kitchen. We went to local landmarks, ate at nearby restaurants, sunbathed and played in the sand and water of the Gulf, and took a boat cruise to an island where a Fort had stood in the 1800s. We did have a couple problems, however. I got sick from a shrimp po'boy (I have never had another one!), and Hank got a nasty sunburn playing in the sand on the beach. A bit of a squabble ensued when he wanted me to bandage his back. He wanted me to put salve on the sunburn and then wrap gauze diagonally across his back, around his chest, and back over the other shoulder like in pictures of wounded soldiers. The gauze did not stay in place, he was unhappy with my bandaging technique, and I told him he should have married Rosie, the nurse!

We also went to New Orleans for a night or two, strolled in Jackson Square, and went on a 'nightlife' tour, which consisted of going to several nightspots. At one club was a stripper swimming/spinning/cavorting in a giant fish bowl as she took off the few clothes she had on. At another club a rather well-endowed woman twirled her pasties up and down and all around in time with the music (I do not know how she managed to do this. I tried to imitate her but did not have the talent for it!). A third club had female impersonators singing and dancing. That was something I had never seen nor heard of. I was amazed that men could be so beautiful with makeup and wigs and, at first, I did not believe that they were really men. My education was expanding! Many years later when we lived at Lake Quivira, we went to a small blues club in Kansas City on Broadway Street and there was a stripper who did her routine to 45 rpm records. She would put a 45 rpm record on the small record player, start dancing, and take off a few things. When the record ended, she would go over, put on a new record, press play and continue stripping. It took several 45s before she was stripped! Somehow having to stop and put on another record sort of broke any spell that she might have been trying to weave!

CHAPTER 29

Fort Riley and On to Germany

HANK HAD ORDERS TO GO to Bamberg, Germany in September 1955 as part of the advance party for Operation Gyroscope. Major Berryhill was in the pre-advance party and was to come back to Fort Riley about the time we went over. Since he did not want to give up his quarters at Fort Riley, he let us sub-lease his quarters while he was gone; this worked well for him and also let a lowly Lieutenant and his bride live in Major quarters for a few months. The quarters were in a long, brick row of condominiums, with a small kitchen, living room and small dining room downstairs and two bedrooms upstairs.

The new experience of being married meant doing my husband's laundry. There was a washing machine in the quarters, but no dryer. Laundry had to be carried to the clotheslines outside the building to dry; the first time I pinned Hank's undershorts onto the line I was self-conscious and somewhat embarrassed! I giggled to myself and hoped no one was watching!

I have two other memories of that time. First, Hank wanted to have his commanding officer, Major Brogham and his wife, come for dinner, and he wanted to serve steak. I ended up embarrassing Hank when I asked every-one, including Hank, how they wanted their steak cooked. Hank thought this made it sound like we never had expensive food like steak. Of course, I had not cooked that many meals for him by that time, so I did not know how he liked his steak. Marriage is such a learning process! Wanting to be a good hostess, as pictured in "Good Housekeeping" and "Better Homes and Gardens", I set up the TV tray, which we had received for a wedding present, beside the table and put on it the electric percolator, also a wedding gift. I had never used it before, but I read the directions, filled it with water, put the coffee grounds in the basket, and had it ready to turn on at the appropriate time, so we could have after-dinner coffee with dessert. As we finished dinner, I turned on the percolator, feeling like a stylish homemaker, just like those pictures in the magazines. However, I jumped and almost fell out of my chair when it suddenly started percolating vigorously and loudly beside me. So much for sophistication!

My second memory of the quarters is being very ill there. In order to go overseas, all Army personnel were required to have certain shots and immunizations. Most children were routinely vaccinated for smallpox in grade school; I believe Beverly and Jerry had been vaccinated when the time came for Nurse Michener to vaccinate them; Miss Nora Michener was the school nurse for many years, before and after the time I was a student. However, apparently by the time I was old enough, Dad had studied more about vaccines and felt that, since there was no smallpox in Kansas, it was silly to make me get the vaccination; he refused to let Nurse Michener vaccinate me. Nevertheless, when the Army gives a command, Army wives follow orders, and since I had never had a smallpox vaccination, I had to get one. Unfortunately, the Army doctors did not say to be careful until it scabbed over, and I went swimming that afternoon. I became very ill, had a fever of over 104, and was a bit delirious. I did recover but still have a dandy scar from that!

CHAPTER 30

Goodbye to Oz

IN EARLY SEPTEMBER 1955, HANK drove me home to Norton for a visit with Mother, Dad, Beverly, and Jerry before 'deploying' to Germany. Seeing Norton in the valley below from the crest of the big hill south of Norton has always brought a sigh and that sense of 'home'. This time there was a deeply nostalgic feeling of loss, knowing that it might be a long time before I saw that view of Norton again.

Was I ready to leave Norton? Was I ready to become part of the world away from Norton? Was I ready to start living a separate life from my Norton family?

Mother, Dad, Beverly, and Jerry had guided me, shared themselves with me, surrounded me with love, and demonstrated ways to live and get along with others. The Norton schools had taught me well...the usual "readin', 'ritin', and 'rithmetic", but also teamwork, social skills, and responsibility. The Norton people had demonstrated kindness and how to persevere, as well as the cultural norms and standards for living in community.

I had learned how fleeting life can be when Alice Curry's older sister, Mona, suddenly died in grade school, when Ronnie Allen's mother died when Ronnie was in junior high, when Mike Bridges was taken by an infection that penicillin would have cured, when my Grandmother Ida suddenly died of a heart attack, when too many people I knew were killed in accidents, and when wars took too many.

I had 'played house' in my mind often after seeing all those movies and reading all those magazines. Mother had given me 'the sex talk' shortly before my wedding, and Dad had given me the book, "Sex Without Fear", the standard book of the day written for the bride (who was assumed to know nothing about sex). However, leaving the crucible of growing up meant more than sex and pretty décor, and even more than academic learning. It meant learning how to act on and share all the tenets that growing up in Norton had taught me. Time would tell if I could live a life that honored all the people of Norton who are so much a part of who I am.

On September 17, 1955, after visiting and laughing with my family for a week, Dad and Mother took me to the Rock Island depot to board the train back to Fort Riley. My heart was beating wildly when I gave each of them a last hug and boarded the train. As the Rock Island Rocket pulled away from the station, I sat by the window on the train waving to Mother and Dad until I could no longer see them. My long journey from Norton had begun. From now on, I would be only a visitor in the Land of Oz.

In Their Own Words

DOROTHY DRUMMOND AND HOWARD BUTLER TELL THEIR STORIES

TRANSCRIBED FROM JOURNALS THAT PAMELA GAVE TO HER GRANDPARENTS BUTLER TO WRITE THEIR STORIES

To Grandma, From Pam.

I do hope you write in this - and fill it! If you need another, tell me! I want to know, and especially about you. Please, write as much as you can think of and remember. Write what is in your heart and mind because you are filled with knowledge, memories, love, and wisdom...I truly want to know of it. I wish you joy in writing, and peace. I love you very much.

Take Care & Love,

Pamela Sue Evers

Dear Pamela Sue,

Thank you for the book I am writing in. I hope I can recall a few things that have happened during my lifetime. As to filling it—I would have to live forever! So, perhaps your mother can add to what I write, and later, maybe, you, and then your children?! That would make the whole book quite an authentic history, wouldn't it? Good luck to all of us.

Love, from your Grandmother Butler 1975 (Started to Write – 1960)

Dorothy Ruth Drummond Butler's Writings

Everyone seems to be writing a book, these days, or maybe "cutting a record", or perhaps painting pictures, as Grandma Moses did—but not me, I tried once to paint some violets, after being assured "anyone can do it", but gave up after my feeble efforts were a disaster.

I have decided to write a book—that is, maybe an autobiography of my life. At the moment, I can't think of a thing I ever did that would be, in any way, very interesting. Maybe my children and my Grandchildren will enjoy it tho', probably curious, thinking they might uncover some real, dark secrets I haven't told them.

Well, let's see. I was born—I must have been—I know I didn't fall off a star, and I know a stork didn't bring me—I'm afraid of birds of any kind! I was born in Downs, Kansas on October 23, 1902. I have seen the house where I was born—a tall two story house with a large covered front porch and a big red barn out back. I lived there only six weeks, so I have been told, when my father, who up to this time, had been a printer and owner of a newspaper office in Downs, Kansas, became interested in the Ministry and studied with the Deacons of the local Church. When he decided he wanted to preach the Gospel, he was ordained as a Christian Minister in Smith Center, and the first Church assigned to him was to be Pastor of a small Church in Smith Center, Kansas, a town about one hundred miles to the west of Downs.

My Mother told me that the day they loaded the large wagon with their household furniture, in all the excitement of such occasions, she had left me asleep on the bed. Some of the "helpers" came in and rolled up the mattress, with me inside, and put me on the wagon. When my frantic Mother found me, I was still asleep.

My living in Smith Center—I remember nothing, as we next moved to Norton, Kansas, a town about sixty miles to the west. While living in Smith Center, my Grandma Corfman died; she was visiting us at the time. I have always wished she could have lived so I could have known her. I think I was probably one or two years old when the family moved to Norton. I don't really know.

I haven't mentioned that there were other children before I arrived. I had a brother John, thirteen years older than I, and a sister eleven years older—her name was Ruby Rebecca. I bet I gave my parents a surprise when they knew I was on the way!

My Grandfather Corfman lived with us, too, after Grandma died. I adored him!—especially the days he would ask me to his room and give me a piece of real maple sugar that he would break off of a big "bar" that he kept in his dresser drawer in his upstairs room. Mmmm—it was good!! As it didn't happen too often, it really was a real treat.

1907: When I was five years old, we moved into a large new house that my Grandpa, who was a carpenter and cabinet maker by trade, built. It was a lovely home with twelve large rooms, with eight rooms downstairs and four upstairs. Papa had previously bought a large number of acres on the east edge of Norton and very affectionately called them "the patch". (We had lived in one of my Grandfather's houses since coming to Norton). We had a large front yard and a back yard that was on two levels and went clear down a meadow and up to the railroad tracks on the other side—a great hill for sledding in the winter time, altho' it was my brother and sister, and their friends, who got to ride on the big toboggan sled my brother made. At that time I was usually being pulled around on a very small sled, made by my Grandpa.

About this time, "Papa", as I must remember to call him and "Mamma", instead of the later mode of referring to ones parents as "Mother and Dad", because Papa never would allow me to refer to him as "Dad"!—Even when I was in my "teens" and it was the "thing" to do!

Anyhow—Papa was very attentive to his church and congregation, and Mamma was trying her best to be a good preacher's wife. It much have been very trying with Papa bringing home unexpected company after church on Sundays, and the time one of his "flock", a bustling woman in the choir, told my Mamma "Ohhh! I always did love your husband!!" And then, realizing what she had said, added in a quiet voice "and liked you!" Mamma was always a good sport tho' and after the visitor had left, Mamma and I and the hired girl had a good laugh about it all. I always had a feeling that if Mamma had had her "druthers", she would have preferred working as a dressmaker—or at the Millinery trade, which she had learned as a young girl in downtown Norton. She was the first young girl to work in a store downtown in 1882.

It was in Mrs. Kennedy's Hat Shop; and Mamma was a wonderful seamstress and dressmaker. In those days she would go and stay all day at the homes where the lady needed some new dresses made, for as many days as were needed. As I remember she received $1.00 a day, which was a lot then. This was before she was married in 1887.

I remember she kept a large box of hats, trimming, flowers, wire, straw braid, veiling and other materials to be made into hats, for those were the days when clothing and lady's hats and bonnets were all made by hand—and very lovely—with the feathers, ribbons and laces and bows under their chins. Can't you imagine?? Anyway, it was always fun to get into the big box and try on the hats, etc.

We were faithful church goers, too, and one morning I was sitting in the front row, waiting for the church services to begin—and there was Papa in his high-backed chair, sitting back of the pulpit, and at the right time, with all his dignity he stood up and walked forward to begin his sermon—I was so happy to see him!! And in my childish enthusiasm I called out good and loud, too—"Hello Pop!!" I can still hear the subdued giggles from the congregation and the stern and dignified expression on his face as he quietly looked at me and said "Hello, little girl." I was properly subdued as I sat quietly all the rest of the morning. I couldn't quite figure it out tho'. I was only happy to see him!! I imagine when he was by himself, he had a good chuckle. My Papa had a wonderful sense of humor and an infectious laugh that could be heard a block away, it would seem.

One of the things I remember must have made an impression on me—it was even before we moved to the big house on the "patch"! Papa owned a cow, which he kept there and also decided to raise pigs—prize-winning pure bred and beautiful! Everything went fine for a while. He knew he had one that would win the blue or even purple ribbons!! He worked for days to get it ready to "show" at the State Fair in Topeka, which was many miles away. It wasn't just an ordinary pig—it was a big, fat sow and, in his eyes, an object of beauty. The big day finally arrived when he was to take his pride and joy to the Fair. Everything was fine and we bid him and the pig goodbye. But pride sometimes comes before a fall, and before they could arrive at the State Fair—the sow (pig) died!! Sad was the day for Papa, and we all "felt" for him.

Mamma was also utterly disgusted with him for being so foolish and told him so, which after thinking it over, he agreed, and being Papa, he could always see the funny side, and he started to laugh and everyone joined in. I don't know if this incident had anything to do with it or not, but soon after, Papa was wanting to build Mamma a new house over at the "Patch". I have told you about it a few pages back, but want to say a little more, because it was nice! We had a large back porch, right off the kitchen, which was all screened in for the summer time with glass windows to close in the wintertime.

Whenever I think of that porch, I can see, in my mind, the hand pump, made of iron, where by pumping the handle up and down, we could have a bucket full of fresh cold water. It was about five feet high and was fastened to the floor of the porch. Beside it was a large Herrich refrigerator, which held a 100 lb. piece of ice that the ice man would carry in from his ice wagon with iron tongs. His wagon was pulled by a horse, and there were always "chips of ice" in the back, which the children in the neighborhood would come running to get—always a treat! It was fun eating around a big table on the back porch, and somehow food always tasted better out there. The fresh strawberries, of the garden, covered with cream & sugar, piled high in a large glass bowl was something to see!

Music was to be a part of our lives—not a big part but always fun. When I was very young, I remember Mamma playing on the organ, which, of course, was a "pump" organ, with two pedals that she would push with her feet, while she played chords and sang, mostly very sad ballads or love songs of her day. I remember the words of one –

"Just a package of Love Letters
Laying on the marble stand...
Just a package of Love Letters,
Written by a lover's hand."

A little different from some of the songs we hear today.

Papa played the Tuba and he played in the first cornet band that was ever in Norton, Kansas in 1885. Mamma would always shine it for him until it sparkled before every concert in the bandstand that used to be in the Court House Square. The crowd that came to hear it would sit on the grass and listen.

It was only natural that the Tuba was the first instrument that my brother, John, learned to play—I suppose since it was already in the family. I remember Mamma used to send him to his room upstairs to practice when the "oomph-oomph-oompah" used to get her down! Papa one time send him out back of the barn. Later he learned to play not only the Tuba, but nearly every other instrument as well. The violin was his love tho', and he became very good. He even attended classes in the Detroit Conservatory at one time in his life. Later, he had his own orchestra that played for many local functions and dances. Also, when the big week long shows, called stock companies, would be in town performing a different show each night on the stage in the large auditorium, it was always a thrill to me to see my brother and the other musicians emerge thru a small door to the "orchestra pit", as it was called, just below the stage, where the piano was and the instruments were all set up. I was proud of him—he always stood up to play the violin and the other musicians were seated.

Papa had bought a piano by now, especially for Ruby to learn to play. I think he had hopes of her playing hymns to accompany him on his two week revival meetings he would hold in other towns. However, I doubt if that idea appealed to Ruby. She did learn one piece quite well—some sheet music—"Stop-Stop-Stop", a rather suggestive song of the day. One day when Papa came home, unexpected, and heard her singing it, he very calmly took the music to the kitchen range, to go up in smoke! This along with some words to Ruby that I didn't understand.

I was about six years old by now, so it was time for me to learn to play the piano. I guess I kept practicing, however, I had started taking lessons on the organ before we had the piano. My music teacher used to come to the house to give me my lessons. Finally, when I could play "The Trail of the Lonesome Pine", my Papa thought I was quite an artist. Anyway, when he would perform a wedding ceremony at our house, he never failed to announce to the newly-wed couple, "Now, my little girl will play a piece on the piano for you", while Mamma and the hired girl and the happy couple would patiently (?) listen.

In the summertime everyone in our town looked forward to the Norton County Fair. It was a big event in our lives—from the youngest to the oldest—seemed like everyone in town would be there. There was the big "Floral Hall" building, where ladies of the County would show off their best hand-made quilts and embroidery work. Also jams, jellies, homemade pickles and all kinds of pies, cakes, etc. etc. etc. Then there would be prizes for the best—1st, 2nd, & 3rd, along with a blue, red, or white ribbon. It was a happy day for me when I won 2nd prize, which was 50 cents (?), for the chocolate cake I made, all by myself. In all fairness to our hired girl, she did help me a little. The same hired girl could be real cross, too, like the time my girlfriend and I made Taffy on the big old range and dribbled it all over her newly scrubbed floor. Mamma came in about that time tho', and we ran away and giggled. We thought it was so funny!

Papa always showed his prize chickens at the Fair. They were "Rhode Island Reds" as I remember, and he usually won some ribbons on them. He was always on the Fair Board, which meant we would all get free passes to the Grandstand. Marjorie Milz's (Trail) father was on the Fair Board, too, so she and I usually went to the Fair together, feeling very important, as we just walked by the man taking tickets at the gate—and condescendingly smiled at him. (Those were the days!) HA! We all watched many "sulky" races and balloon ascensions from the Grandstand, and across the race track was the stage where we saw all the entertainment—dancers, acrobats, and singers. One time we watched a man on a pony climb a high ladder to a little platform and then!!—both jumped down into a large tank of water!—while we all held our breath!

There was a bandstand next to the stage where the local band played, in uniform, while the crowd of people were being seated. I liked to go in the afternoons and watch the ladies and men, too, sitting in the Grandstand, most of them with a large palm leaf fan in their hands, keeping themselves nice and cool. People dressed up in those days, hats, gloves, purses, and fans waving—quite a sight to see! We were all at the races.

About this time in my life were the days of the first movies—a long time before the "talkies" as we call them today. Since one couldn't hear the action or the voices, you could follow the story by reading the sub titles that were flashed on the screen and by trying to read the actors "lips"—like deaf people learn to do. However, it wasn't really all silent because there was always a piano player trying to play suitable music for the action on the screen, slowly and quietly for the sad scenes and loud and furious for the Cowboys and Wild Indians as they went chasing each other over the plains—all the while shooting their shotguns and arrows, while riding their horses at a furious speed!! Oh! It was exciting!—believe me! We could hardly wait a whole week for the next installment! Some serials would go on for six weeks! And the suspense was terrific! All of this action for only 10 cents a ticket. I remember the titles of two of the shows. "The Million Dollar Mystery" and "The Perils of Pauline"—I had a copy of sheet music about her! "Poor Pauline—I pity poor Pauline", etc.

I could never quite make up my mind whether I wanted to be a Cowgirl or an Indian Princess. At times I would be Pocahontas or "Minnie Ha Ha"—all dressed up in Mamma's fringed, red tablecloth, wrapped tightly around me, and my hair in long, tightly braided pigtails—a band around my head and, of course, a tall feather stuck in it. Some days I would be a Cowgirl riding a broomstick for a horse. I'll always remember the time I took all of the fringe off of Mamma's new dark green window blinds and sewed it around the bottom of my Cowgirl skirt! Oh! My life was happy and exciting in those days.

I'll tell you about my "play house" now—because I remember it well. It was about six feet wide and 8 feet long. A "rippled" red tin roof and the sides were covered with wide meshed chicken wire, which in the summer was completely covered with blue morning glories—some on the inside of the roof, too. I loved it!! And I spent many happy hours playing "house"—sometimes by myself (and dolls) or, now and then, a neighbor girl and her dolls would come for a visit. Looking back on those carefree days, I must have had a wonderful childhood, and "spoiled"—no doubt about it.

Mother always made my clothes, as most mothers did in those days. She dressed me in dresses with ruffles and styles of the day—usually worn with long pink or blue or white stockings—some of them with lace effect or else the common ribbon. These in the summertime, worn with black patent or white canvas slippers with buckles or laces, and on top of my head was usually a large hair ribbon bow to hold back a couple of long curls, which she curled (brushed) over her finger. I remember tho' in the winter time, as I grew older the long underwear, long wool (silk & wool) stockings, panty waists to hold them up, and high button shoes! Even "leggings" on snowy days—buttoned to the knees! up the side—and how much fun it was on a cold winter morning to get out of bed and dash out to the living room and dress by the big base burner, where I had left my clothes the night before. I feel sorry that my children and Grandchildren never saw a big base burner with its gold and red flames shining and flickering thru the glass. It was beautiful!

And on Christmas Eve, we would sit around the base burner, making stockings out of green and red net, to be filled with Christmas candy and hung on the tree, by a little yarn drawstring run thru the top of the bag. There was one for everyone in the family, and also on the tree—a large white linen handkerchief, pinned at the center, for every man in our home. We would do this on Christmas Eve, before Santa arrived. Along with the strings of popcorn and cranberries, tinsel and ornaments—and, oh yes, in those days before the electric lights for the tree, there were tiny tin candle holders clamped to the branches—each with its own tiny red or green candle. Our tree was a large one, and always stood in the bay window in our living room.

There are so many things I could remember and write down, but I must stop somewhere and leave these wonderful years of childhood and start to grow up. I'll hurry over the Grade School years, with the usual things as all children have—roller skates, playing jacks, hopscotch, home-made kites, etc. etc. etc. Of course, there were a few boyfriends along the way. I remember graduating from the 8th Grade and the dress my Mother made for me to wear, with yards of ruffles and narrow lace sewn on the edge—all by hand. I remember, too, the silk full-length underskirt that my brother's "new wife" made to wear under the dress. You know her—your Aunt Anna Drummond.

August 5th, 1975: I found this again today, among other "things" I have saved thru the years. Small reminders of the past, but very dear to me. Now I am seventy years of age—and time goes by.

I'll just skip the high school years—the good times, the "blue" times, the "never forget" times. The day I bobbed my hair—which I had been cutting a little every day, until it was short enuf, that Mother asked me "What is the matter with your hair?"; I bet she knew all the time. Most of the girls in high school were doing the same. It was the Vernon and Irene Castle years—which was the dance team of that year, and she was the first to Bob her hair. We all wanted to look like her!! I can't think of any very serious romances in high school—just a few to keep life interesting. Anyway, most of us survived, with only a few bruises or heartaches.

The next thing was College! Where would I go? Mamma wanted me to go to Lindsburg, Ks to become a piano and music teacher; a girls school in Missouri?—that didn't sound good to me! Then, as now, there was K.U. at Lawrence or K State at Manhattan. It ended up being Kansas State Agricultural College, which is what K State was called then. Papa and Mamma and I drove down in our new "Studebaker", found me a room, and there I was—living with a girl I had never known and didn't like from the first time I met her. Then one day I was asked to join a Sorority, Phi Omega Pi—which all members were daughters of Masons. I said no and offered some kind of an excuse. I don't know why I did—it was a good group of girls—I just didn't know much about Sororities. Later, I did pledge one—Alpha Delta Pi. About the same time the Delta Zetas gave me a bid, I had just accepted the ADPi. So—I was a Sorority girl.

We were all "Flappers" in those years—the "Roaring Twenties". I think the reason we were called Flappers is: We wore large, men's, 3 buckle overshoes, with the buckles left dangling and the overshoe flapping along with every step! We also wore bright yellow oiled slickers (coats) when it rained, which were autographed all over by our friends. We wore rolled hose, below our knees, with skirts that barely covered them, but a little later, the skirts had to be well above our knees (which we had rouged), and we wore long silk hose and 3" high heels when we dressed up, and on the campus thick crepe soles and leather tops—about like the girls today (1976).

Beauty spots were the thing, too. We would buy them in small boxes, little cut out stars, circles, half-moons—all cut out of court plaster—to place on the most becoming place on our faces. We used liquid mascara then, which one night I spilled down the front of a red satin (pillow case) dress, just before my date rang the doorbell! Oh, boy—what a mess! We did make it to the dance tho'.

Songs — 1920-23 "Last Night on the Back Porch", "Marehita", "Yes, We Have No Bananas", "Collegiate", "Red Hot Mamma", "Sittin' on the Inside Looking at the Outside", "Margie" & "Barney Google", "Charleston", "Do-do-do", "I Wanta Be Loved By You".

1923 — Oh, yes! I forgot to mention the dance that everyone was doing!—the "Charleston"! I'm sure you know what I mean? I loved it—as we all did—and it's still around. The clothes we wore then seemed to be specially styled—short and fringed, with rows of fringe that would shiver and shake, as we danced. Short, of course, and usually made of satin or silk crepe or georgette. Add a pair of black satin 3 inch heel shoes with rhinestone buckles, and you can imagine your Grandmother in 1923-24. Of course, there were other dances like the "Camel Walk", the "Flea Hop", "Ballin' the Jack", and the "Castle Walk", but nothing could compare with the good old Charleston!! Wheeee!!

There were no student cars on the Campus then. Our dates would have to hire a taxi to take us dancing. The boys in the 20s were called Sheiks and tried to look like Rudolph Valentino—the Greatest Sheik of them all—a Movie Star!! They used some beauty aid to make their hair sleek, shiny, and greasy! But as I remember College days, it was just fun. If you know the popular song, "Collegiate", you know exactly how it was. No red hot flannels—no garters—never, never hurry or never, never worry! And, oh yes—we did study because we had to, and the usual dates—a couple of quite serious Romances—even to getting "pinned". But, "parting is such sweet sorrow", and at the end of the year, he went home to Southeast Kansas, and I went home to Northwest Kansas.

After a couple of months dating the local Norton boys, I met a young, good looking doctor, who had just recently started practicing his profession as a D. O.—Doctor of Osteopathy—in Norton. He kept asking me for dates. I told him I was engaged, showed him the Fraternity pin, and told him my boyfriend lived in Burlington, Kansas and he was coming out to see me at Christmas time (1925). When he (Bill) did visit, he brought me a beautiful diamond ring, and before that he had sent a dozen red roses and also a Christmas gift. Bill and I had dated steady at college for a year. He graduated and I didn't go back to college. We wrote to each other every day and a special delivery on Sundays. He wanted to be married at least in nine months, but I kept putting it off. So he went back to Burlington, where he worked in his uncle's printing office. Absence makes the heart grow fonder? I kept dating Howard, and Bill found a home town girl. One day I sent the engagement ring back without one word of explanation. (I'm sorry I was so rude.) He wrote a short letter to me saying it would never have ended that way if we could have seen each other more often. People didn't drive far in those days and phones weren't very far advanced. So ended a College Romance!

Howard and I dated almost steady from the first date, and two months later, he asked me to marry him. I wasn't ready to get married, but we continued dating and, about a year and a half later, we were married. He had office rooms down town, and there was a connecting apartment, which we turned into our "Blue Heaven"—as the song says—and everything was wonderful. We were in Love! "Our" Songs: "5 foot 2 Eyes of Blue", "Who", "Sleepytime Gal", "Yes, Sir, That's My Baby". Three children arrived in the next seven years—a boy first. We were so proud of ourselves. We named him Jerry. Our Song? "Sonny Boy". A girl two years later, our little Beverly, and our song was "Tea for Two"—a boy for you and a girl for me. We were busy and we were happy. Three more years and another little dark haired girl with a little black curl on top of her head arrived—Marlyn Sue. Now, life was really complete—"Mighty Like a Rose" and "Sleep Little Baby of Mine".

The following years were the ones referred to now as the "Dirty 30s" or the Depression Years. But we never "suffered" in any way that I can recall. In 1934, the dust storms were terrific. The first one I remember was one evening, we just sat down to eat. Alice and Bill Isaac were our guests and we were going to the movies later. All of a sudden, the wind hit. It was in the summer and the doors were open. The white tablecloth was covered with dust until it was gray. The doors slammed shut!! And then, the wind stopped and we went on to the movies. Before the first show was over, it hit again. We could hear it from inside. Everyone was frightened! It was flashed on the screen for everyone to stay seated, that we couldn't see to drive home. Of course, many tried it and some made it. Alice and I were panicky because we had left our children with baby sitters. Marlyn was sleeping in her large willow baby buggy, and when we arrived home, the girl had been thoughtful enuf to cover the whole buggy with a wet sheet. She was O.K., as were Beverly and Jerry. We hung wet sheets at all windows for a long time, and also sand bags on the window sills.

Our babies grew up, fell in love, married. It was strange and a little empty to be alone again. The house seemed larger than it had been. The basement room where they used to sing and dance with their friends to an old record player, play checkers till midnight—clickety-click—as the game progressed, was quiet. And, so did our lives change. They were on their own and in their own homes. Grandchildren—ten, in fact—the first a boy, Richard Alvin, followed by Gregory Allen, Pamela Sue and next Laura Lei, Patricia, and Lila Laurine, John Howard, Mike, and another girl Lisa and a boy Aaron.

They have been our pride and joy...

We are blessed...

We are thankful...

We Love them All...

It's been a good life.

Grand Mother Butler   XO

(Notes on a small piece of paper in book: Side Curtains, Rainy days, Like today we were dragging Main, Squirrel cage, Rabbits, Orange Long H. cats, Down Incubators, Cyclone cave)

To Grandpa,

I do hope you write in this, I know really very little about you. You know so much, of medicine, of college, of taking care of a family, of how you were raised, and of life in general. Please write, because there is so much I can gain from your heart and mind. Know that I love you very much and write with that knowledge. Take care.

Much Love,

Pamela Sue Evers

Dr. Howard Gustav Butler's Writings

Well I really don't know where to start so maybe the best thing to do is to start when I was born. I was born believe it or not many years ago. In fact it happened some time during the day or nite of Dec. 2, 1901. I really don't remember too much about that event. The people who were kind enuf to give me a home were known as Elmer and Ida Butler. There had been several other children who had come to live at their house before I arrived. The oldest was a boy named Henry. Then another boy and he was called Ralph. Then a girl and she was called Edna. Then I arrived. Then later another girl arrived and she was called Blanche. The home was a farm a short distance from an inland town called Barada in Richardson County in south east Nebraska. Close around were many uncles and aunts from both sides of the family. From the time that I can remember, my growing up was the same for all. Eating & sleeping, working and playing, going to school, having whooping cough, chicken pox and measles seemed to be part of growing up. No D.P.T. shots those days. Doing chores was a part of living. Picking up bushel baskets of cobs for the pig pen, chopping and carrying wood, milking cows and feeding calves, feeding chickens and gathering eggs. We had lots of fruit trees of all kinds. Cherry, apricot, peach, crabapples and a large apple orchard. Canned meat, cured meat, smoked meat and fried down meat stored in jars of lard. Apple cider by the barrel. Mother was a wonderful cook and we had lots of good things to eat always.

Then in the spring of 1911 we moved from Richardson County out west to Thayer County on to a farm one and a half miles north of Hebron Nebraska. Of course the farm house was very similar to the one back east. The farm back east had been hilly while the farm land at Hebron was quite flat. Made it easier to farm. My growing up was about the same as it had been back east. But as I was growing up my jobs increased. Besides helping with milking, separating, feeding calves, pigs, & chickens and what all, I was to help in the farming. So besides getting up early and doing a day's work it seemed doing chores, then we would go to field and do a day's work farming, then in evening doing that same day's work doing chores, and finally get some supper. I had decided by then I was not going to be a farmer. During the summer or farming season, besides doing the chores morning and nite, it was getting horses harnessed and ready for field. My earlier jobs were riding a mower long hours a day. Then riding a hay raker to rake it into winnows. Then riding a buck and bucking hay to stacker and stacking it. Then ride a cultivator and plow corn. Then cut small grain and then shuck it. Then more hay to make. Then lay by corn. Then plow stubble. Then pitch bundles to thrash machine. Then more hay to make. Finally it was time to go to school again so only chores morning and nite and then school all day except Saturday when we had to shuck corn.

Finally I got thru 8th grade and then on to high school. But the days were the same as before. I did enjoy high school more. I played some football and basketball and we had a Boy Scout baseball team and as I was left handed I did the pitching. Even later I did some pitching for the grown up town team. I had a pretty good curve ball and had good control. By the time I graduated from high school my two older brothers had left home and were on their own and Dad realized I was not going to stay on the farm so he sold the farm and we moved into town in Hebron. During the summer of 1920 since we weren't on the farm anymore I went to Stockton Kansas to help my brother-in-law, Les Lindals and sister Edna, in harvest working in a header barge. There I hurt my left arm and shoulder and finally had to go back home. I went to an M.D. for it. He x-rayed it and said no bones broke so gave me some pain pills. But it still hurt & I couldn't use it so I went mostly thru my mother's insistence to Dr. Baincroft, who was an osteopath. It took several treatments, but he & Osteopathy brought me right out of it so by the time he had me well again I had decided to go to Kirksville, Mo and study Osteopathy. So that's how I came to be what I am and what I have been for 52 & ½ years as of now.

My four years of College was pretty much college routine. Get up, go to class all morning. Then do lab work in afternoon and then do a little studying and then at times quite a bit of playing around. Sometimes with the boys and sometimes with the girls. Never did get serious with one but my senior year did date a girl by name of Pearl pretty steady, but left Kirksville in June '24 after I graduated without taking her along. She was a good sport and a wonderful dancer but didn't think I wanted to sleep with her yet. I did join a fraternity. Some things I liked about frat life and some I didn't, but it was good training. It taught you to give a little and take a little to get along with 36 brothers living under one roof. I didn't play any sports there except intramural. Our frat played some basketball which I wasn't good at and baseball which I took turns pitching in. My mother & sister Blanche came to Kirksville for my graduation and my folks gave me a 17 jewel Elgin watch which I still have. After I graduated Mother, Blanche, & I took train for home. Later I took Nebraska State Board and somehow passed it & got my license. On July 17 1924 I opened an office in Nelson, Nebraska to start practice. No one can realize how disappointed I was when I opened my door that morning and didn't see a line of people a block long waiting to get in to my office. I had been told by Doctors who had been out several years how people lined up to see them. I know now they were damn liars. I really never did set the world on fire at Nelson.

I was young and had a brand new Ford Model T coupe and I still liked the girls, so I spent too much time taking them for rides. I did do some practice and gained some experience. However in Fall of 1925 I had a brother Ralph & family living at Norton, Kansas and a Dr. Brown who was practicing in Norton wanted to sell his practice and asked Ralph if he thought I'd be interested. Ralph wrote me and I was interested, so I drove to Norton, saw Dr. Brown, and we finally made a deal, & I bought his practice and took possession Dec. 1 1925 and have been here ever since.

First several months here I roomed at Ralph & Ann's house. I also had a new Atwater Kent battery radio. Radio was still pretty new then. Ralph & Ann had friends called Roy & Ruby Dean. They were at Ralph & Ann's one evening soon after I came & we were listening to an orchestra playing on the radio & Ruby said her sister Dorothy would love that music. I said take my car & go get her. They did and that's how I met a gal by name of Dorothy Drummond.

Well, that was the beginning of the end. I kept calling her for a date and she always said yes. Well, I finally asked her if she would marry me and she said yes. So we got married. Well things went along pretty good and in about 2 years a baby boy came to our house. I wanted to give him a name they couldn't make a nick name out of so we called him Jerry Milton. And he still is called Jerry. Well he grew and grew and finally a couple years later a baby girl came to our house. Dorothy decided to call her Beverly Jean. Well she grew and grew and about three years later another baby girl came to our house. So as each had to have a name we called her Marlyn Sue. And she also grew and grew. Well they all grew and grew and finally they all went to school. They all seemed to get the idea and so they all finally graduated from the eighth grade and then went on to high school from which they all finally graduated. In the meantime Mom & I kept on keeping house and taking care of the brats. At the same time I kept kinda busy seeing people about their ills, aches & pains.

Jerry after high school went to work in the Burlington Depot as helper. He decided he liked it so went to Chillicothe Mo to take telegraphy. Then he went to work for Burlington in Nebraska and then about that time the Army said they wanted him so he went to Fort Sill, then to Germany for two years. Before the Army he traveled and play with the Jack Everett Orchestra for almost a year. Then he was in the Army and went to Germany where he was in Special Service most of the time. After he got back from Germany he went to work for the Rock Island Railroad. He was in Cedar Rapids Iowa then Kansas City Kan and to Goodland Kan where he still is with railroad. At Goodland he met a girl by name of Lena Weiss. Well, one thing led to another and finally they got married. Well in time a girl came to their house and they called her Laura Lei. Then another girl and they called her Lila Laurine. Then another girl and they called her Lisa Lynn. Then a boy and they called him Aaron Howard. Well they all still live in Goodland and are all fine and doing real well.

Well Beverly after she got out of high school decided she wanted to be a secretary. So she went to Chillicothe and took a secretarial course. After she got thru there she came back and became Secretary to the principal of the high school. Well about that time Alvin Hisey who had been in Air Force in Alaska for three years came back home. Beverly & Alvin had had some dates in high school and they started doing it again. Well as you'd expect they ended up getting married. They moved to Oberlin where Al operated a Western Auto Store for several years. While there they had a boy they named Richard which turned out to be Rick. Then a couple years later another boy they named Gregory. Then they moved to Kimball Nebr on to a large ranch where they did real well. Later another boy came and they named him Michael. Still later a girl arrived at their home and they named her Patricia Ann. That turned out to be Tricia. Well they kept on with the ranch life but now they have a nice home in town. Rick & Gregg still work with their dad on the ranch. Mike just out of high school and hasn't decided yet which way he will go. Tricia is still in high school but doing fine. Rick got married to a gal named Becky Joe and they had a girl they named Shellie Ann. That didn't turn out so good so they are divorced. Beverly in the meantime bought a dress shop. She still operates it and does very well in her store. So things at Kimball are as always...everyone busy all the time.

Well this girl Marlyn made good grades and on graduation from high school got a scholarship to K.U. Well among the many people she met at K.U. was a guy by name of Hank Evers. Hank was in advanced R.O.T.C. and was planning on making the Army a career as his dad had done. After he graduated he went to Fort Benning to take officer training school. Then he was transferred back to Fort Riley. Well he & Marlyn kinda renewed their friendship or something like that and anyway in June 1955 they got married. Lived at Fort Riley for a couple months then transferred with the Army to Germany for three years. While they were in Germany a little girl came to their house and they called her Pamela Sue. Well Hank decided he didn't want to make Army a career so they all came back and settled in K.C. where Hank worked for Proctor & Gamble. Then a boy came to their house and they named him John Howard. John after his dad, granddad and great granddad and Howard after me. Then later they all moved to California where Hank worked for Hunts. Then Hank went to work for Arthur Young & Co and was moved back to Kansas City. They had a nice home out at Lake Quivira. Then Pam graduated from high school. About that time Hank was transferred by Arthur Young to the Chicago office. So they moved to Chicago and Pam enrolled at Kansas State that same fall and now in a little over a week from now she will graduate from K State. John is still in high school so don't know where he will go to College. So that brings kids and grandkids pretty well up to date.

In the meantime this gal called Dorothy and I have kept living on in this ole house on the prairie. In the meantime however the gal Dorothy who you best know as Grandma has had a lot of problems with her health. So we don't know at this date if we will be able to go to Manhattan and see Pam graduate or not but we sure do want too. So what the future holds for all these people I have written about I do not know, but it has been a good life and I'm glad I had a part in living it. Goodbye till the next chapter which you will have to write.

Made in the USA
Lexington, KY
26 December 2018